ISANDLWANA
TO
ULUNDI

ISANDLWANA TO ULUNDI

THE ANGLO-ZULU WAR OF 1879

CHRIS SCHOEMAN

AMBERLEY

First published 2021

Amberley Publishing
The Hill, Stroud
Gloucestershire, GL5 4EP

www.amberley-books.com

Copyright © Chris Schoeman, 2021

The right of Chris Schoeman to be identified
as the Author of this work has been asserted
in accordance with the Copyright, Designs and
Patents Act 1988.

ISBN 978 1 4456 9930 1 (hardback)
ISBN 978 1 4456 9931 8 (ebook)

British Library Cataloguing in Publication Data.
A catalogue record for this book is available
from the British Library.

1 2 3 4 5 6 7 8 9 10

Typesetting by SJmagic DESIGN SERVICES, India.
Printed in the UK.

CONTENTS

INTRODUCTION

With the centenary of the Anglo-Zulu War of 1879, there was understandably renewed interest in South Africa, the United Kingdom, Commonwealth countries and the USA in the epic event, and numerous publications on the topic saw the light. While the initial stream of literature has since subsided, from time to time there are still books or articles in journals being published on the war. This of course was also the case some twenty years ago, on the centenary of the Anglo-Boer War (1899–1902), and still books and articles on this conflict appear regularly.

Years ago, looking around at the Fort Laramie national historic site in Wyoming, I met a US National Parks preservation officer who asked me about the Anglo-Zulu War – and who had a good old laugh about his own pronunciation of 'Gingindlovu'. As a South African, I found his interest in, and his knowledge of, the war quite remarkable, and over time have discovered that the Zulu War fan club is quite substantial. This same interest, of course, moved another American to write a popular book that in 1966 made Zulu history up to the end of the Anglo-Zulu War so vividly accessible to a fascinated readership around the world. Written like a great adventure tale, Donald Morris' *Washing of the Spears* remains a most thorough work speaking of years of research, while since then authors such as Ian Knight and John Laband – two of the most prolific writers on the subject – have become very familiar to students of Anglo-Zulu War literature.

Why has so much been written about this war, and why have so many read the avaiable literature? Simply because it has grabbed the public's imagination – as it did during the war and afterwards – when British and colonial newspapers brought the drama, emotion and brutality of the battlefields into civilian lounges around the world. Fought in 1879 by the British against the Zulus of Cetshwayo, the Anglo-Zulu War was notable for several particularly bloody battles, as well as for being a landmark in the timeline of colonialism in the colony of Natal, with the war signalling the end of an independent Zulu nation. The battles varied from embarrassing failures to successes, from the disaster at Isandlwana to the final conquest of the Zulu nation at Ulundi. On 22 January 1879, the Zulus inflicted the worse defeat in colonial history on the British, when 20,000 to 25,000 Zulus armed mainly with spears overran a British force of 1,500 well-armed men at Isandlwana. Later the same day, on the other hand, a much smaller British force of only around 120 men heroically stood their ground at Rorke's Drift against 4,000 Zulus and beat them off. That day, no fewer than eleven Victoria Crosses were earned – the largest number ever awarded for one day's fighting.

With regard to literary sources, apart from the numerous general works on the subject, there were the valuable memoirs of some of those characters who played a significant role in the war, such as Sir Bartle Frere, the British commander Lord Chelmsford, Colonel A. W. Durnford, Colonel Henry Harford, Horace Smith-Dorrien and Colonel Walter Dunne, as well as Charles Norris-Newman, who accompanied Lord Chelmsford's expeditionary force into Zululand as a special correspondent. Fortunately, there was also an abundance of letters from soldiers from the front, written to their loved ones at home and published in the newspapers of the time, and also contained in, amongst others, Frank Emery's *The Red Soldiers*. These writings convey the ferocity of battles, the hardships suffered while garrisoned, and interesting observations of their stay in a harsh, unforgiving African country. The British Newspaper Archive (britishnewspaperarchive.co.uk), which at the time of writing had some 36 million pages digitised, was a fascinating and extremely valuable source of information on the events and personalities of the Zulu War. Other sources of great worth were the articles relating to the Anglo-Zulu War that were published in journals, especially the

Military History Journal, as well as others such the *Journal of the Society for Army Historical Research* and *Natalia.*

In compiling this book, I tried to give as complete a picture as possible of the war within the page restraints. The story of Zululand is also the story of Natal, of the colonisation of the land, the British scheme of federation and Zulu-Transvaal Boers disputes, and therefore the background to the conflict is set in the early chapters. I have looked at the military capacities of both the British and the Zulus, the makeup of the imperial and colonial forces and aspects such as the presence of firearms in the Zulu kingdom, British (over)confidence before the first shots were fired, the ammunition controversy following the catastrophe at Isandlwana, the British deployment of military squares that stood them in good stead in the later battles, and the tragic death of Imperial Prince Napoleon Eugene at the start of the second invasion of Zululand.

Starting with the battles of Inyezane, Isandlwana and Rorke's Drift, the British suffered serious setbacks in spite of the heroics of the latter, and the first invasion was a failure. The next two months were used to regroup and build a fresh invading force, when the British government rushed seven regiments of reinforcements to Natal, but disturbingly for the British, they suffered further setbacks at the battles of Intombe and Hlobane, before their victory at the battle of Khambula started to turn the tide. In the meantime, victory at Gingindlovu and the relief of the besieged garrison at Eshowe had further helped their cause. With the second invasion of Zululand, the might of the Zulus was finally broken at the decisive battle of Ulundi.

War is always about death and caring for wounded soldiers and thus I have covered the medical arrangements during the war, at a stage in British history when military nursing was still in its infancy; and in conclusion, the capture of Cetshwayo and the final years of his life that included a stay in London to further his cause for reinstatement, and where he became something of a celebrity before his return to his homeland in Natal.

I

THE ZULU KINGDOM

The region that is known as Zululand is situated on the south-east coast of Africa between the Drakensberg Mountains and the Indian Ocean. It is a landscape of rolling emerald hills, waving grassland and lush forests that drop from the inland heights to the subtropical coastal strip, and is intersected by several river systems running through deep and wide gorges.

Twenty years after the Zulu War, a young Winston Churchill described Natal as a region 'of possibility ... wide tracts of fertile soil watered by abundant rains ... the delicious climate stimulates the vigour of the European. The highway of the sea awaits the produce of his labour. All Nature smiles, and here at last is a land where white men may rule and prosper. As yet only the indolent Kaffir enjoys its bounty, and, according to the antiquated philosophy of Liberalism, it is to such that it should for ever belong.'[1]

The countryside used to teem with game – antelope, wildebeest, elephant and lion – until decimated by nineteenth-century hunters, black and white alike. In addition, it was covered abundantly with grasses that made it some of the best cattle country in South Africa. Cattle played an important role as a source of a food and hides, and also as a sign of status.

The racial group to which the Zulu belong, the Nguni, moved into the area during the seventeenth century in search of new pastures for their cattle. Here they spread across the countryside settling in clan groups. According to oral tradition, a man named

Zulu settled on the southern bank of the White Mfolozi River in around 1670. Zulu means 'the heavens', and the name amaZulu, which his followers took on, 'the people of the heavens'.

The Zulus lived in a series of village homesteads that were basically family units, and each village consisted of a number of dome-shaped huts built in a circle around a central cattle enclosure, surrounded by a stockade. The Zulus were polygamous and a man might have as many wives as his wealth would allow him. He would therefore live at the top of the homestead with the wives and children of the senior house to the right, those of the subordinate house to the left, and any dependents at the bottom. Daily activities for the men consisted of tending the cattle and doing the heavier tasks around the homestead, while the women cultivated cereal crops and performed all household duties.[2]

The men were armed with spears, known as *umkhonto*, and small oval shields made of cowhide. Spears had different functions: the broad-bladed spear, *isiphapha*, was used for hunting game; the *isijula*, on the other hand, was used for fighting in warfare. These spears were forged by blacksmiths, who were a respected and highly important guild, in which the secrets of their trade were jealously guarded and handed down from father to son. Their services were much sought-after, for only they could supply the weapons of war and the implements such as the hoes with which to cultivate their gardens. They were skilled in smelting brass and forging it into prized ornaments. There was also the large-headed knobkerrie (*i(li)Wisa*), which was in general use in both civilian and military life as a weapon for both throwing and striking, though Zulu warriors normally used it only for striking. Knobkerries were always made of some hard wood, and varied considerably in size and form.

With regard to dress, a man would wear an *umncedo*, a sheath of plaited grass and leaves, but it was also customary to wear a loin covering over it, consisting of a thin strip of hide around the hips, with soft dressed cow skin low on the buttocks (*ibheshu*) and strips of fur (*umutsha*) at the front. The fur was mostly obtained from the civet, genet and green monkey, while sheepskin and antelope were also used. Chiefs were the only ones allowed to wear a cloak of leopard skin, with leopard's claws as a necklace; they often also carried sticks with carved wooden heads as staffs of office. Married women's clothing consisted of a large pleated leather skirt, while unmarried girls wore a fringe of brown strings low on their hips, or a small leather skirt. The women wore their hair in a distinctive fashion, with a small circular patch teased out, covered with red ochre, and the head shaved around it. Once the European traders had arrived towards the middle of the nineteenth century, ornamental beads became very common amongst both men and women. Both sexes pierced their ears and wore large plugs of ivory, bone or clay in the lobes.[3]

The Rise of Shaka
Warfare in Zululand was fairly infrequent but by the late eighteenth century the country was becoming congested, and disputes over grazing rights became more common. At this stage the Zulus were a minor clan living between the Ndwandwe of King Zwide in the north and the Mthethwa of King Dingiswayo in the south-east. Around 1786, the Zulu chief Senzangakhona had a son with a maiden called Nandi of the eLangeni clan, which she named Shaka. Resented and driven away by the Zulu chief, Nandi and her son ended up amongst the Mthethwa, where Shaka grew up and joined its army.

Youths of about seventeen were banded together into guilds (*amabutho*) for the ceremonies attendant upon the onset of manhood, and Dingiswayo used these age groups as a basis for military units. Shaka deviated from the customary style of warfare at the time, preferring to charge down upon the enemy and engaging in hand-to-hand fighting. He exchanged the light throwing spears for broad-bladed spears for close combat. He called these spears *iklwa*, the sound it was said to produce when withdrawn from a deep body thrust.

Shaka soon established a reputation as a fearless warrior, and when the Zulu chief Senzangakhona died in 1816, Dingiswayo nominated Shaka as his preferred successor to the Zulu throne. Shaka organised all the available fighting men into four regiments, armed with the broad-bladed *iklwa* and new large shields, the *isihlangu*, which covered the warrior from shoulder to ankle. They also adopted a new attack formation: the 'beast's horns'. One body, the 'chest' rushed the enemy in a frontal assault, while flanking groups, the 'horns', rushed out to surround them;

a fourth group, the 'loins', was kept in reserve. It was highly effective against neighbouring clans and signalled the beginning of 'the crushing', a period of ruthless conquest known as Mfecane. Mention of this formation will be made later in this book where battles are discussed.[4]

Feeling threatened by the new Zulu leader, allied to the Mthethwa, King Zwide of the Ndwandwe in 1818 decided to move against Shaka. However, at the battle of Gqoki Hill in April 1818, Shaka's army of some 4,000 warriors, and outnumbered at least two to one, defeated Zwide's men. In the aftermath of the victory, Shaka added more clans to his group, then absorbed Dingiswayo's former empire after the latter was killed in a campaign against Zwide's Ndwandwe.

The following year, Shaka smashed the Ndwandwe, and Zwide and part of his clan fled to the Eastern Transvaal. The largest obstacle to his power now removed, Shaka embarked on a series of campaigns against strong groups in the Drakensberg foothills and south of the Tugela River between 1819 and 1824. Many were wiped out, others driven over the mountains into the interior or southwards, while some ended up as refugees amongst the Mpondo and Xhosa tribes on the borders of the British Cape Colony. By 1824, Shaka had expanded his army to some 15,000, of whom the vast majority were unmarried. The latter phenomenon gave Shaka better control over his military resources, for the longer he could prolong bachelorhood the more he could maintain his force at full strength.[5]

To the Zulu warrior, it was regarded 'beautiful' to die for the king, and more often than not, death without glory would be the alternative, and thus men were prepared to die anyway. In order to retain his warriors in this state of indifference to death, Shaka frowned on the care and caution that resulted from marriage, and therefore marriage without his special permission was simply prohibited. Permission for marriage would normally only be granted to a regiment as a whole, and only after it had served sufficiently long and well. By that time the average age of the prospective grooms would be between thirty-five and forty years.

Shaka also paid close attention to the training of the individual. A warrior had to be strong and agile, capable of enduring any amount of hardship. The cow-hide sandals that were normally worn as protection against the many thorns and stony terrain were seen as impeding the speed and sure-footedness of his warriors in wartime. His men had to learn to march barefoot; to test whether the soles of their feet were properly hardened, they had to dance on thorn-covered ground at times.

He favoured the development of individual reponsibility in the people that he appointed to lead regiments and their sub-units. The commander of each regiment and section of a regiment was regarded as its embodiment, and had to take all the blame if it suffered a setback. His warriors knew well that, irrespective of the size of the force they had to oppose, they had either to conquer or die. His men were taught to be utterly ruthless towards any enemy and, unlike Dingiswayo, who took prisoners and released them on ransom, Shaka taught his men to fight to annihilate; not only armed enemies, but every one connected with them, including their women and children. On his command they would kill anyone who had incurred his displeasure or who was considered to be no longer of any use to the Zulu cause. From time to time, therefore, all infirm or aged persons would be despatched and these exterminations would be carried out without hesitation, even if the doomed individual was a close relative.

His army's outstanding feature was the iron discipline that prevailed, which became almost a way of life. One of the basics of his upbringing that would turn a Zulu youngster into a natural soldier was his complete submission to the authority of his elders. He would be enrolled in his age-grade (*iNtanga*) and his section leader would control his every move, and eventually this absolute authority would be exercised by the king, whether directly or through his military commanders.

When his armies returned from battle, the king would call his soldiers together and hold a review in one of the garrison kraals or the principal royal kraal. The commander-in-chief had to report there, where award or punishment could be decided on, and if fortunate a regiment might be rewarded by permission to marry. A warrior would then advance from being a 'boy' (even though the person might be forty years old) to the estate of a married man with the right to wear the head-ring (*isiCoco*). Officers would also point out those who had disgraced themselves in action, and the unfortunate soldiers were unceremoniously dragged out of the ranks and at once killed by impalement, or by the more 'merciful' way of being clubbed to death with a knobkerrie, or by having their necks twisted and broken.

The Zulus were most susceptible to superstitions and fear of the mysterious or unknown, and like everybody else Shaka and his successors believed in the effect of rituals and 'medicines', and in their immensely powerful psychological effect on his warriors in conditioning them for victory. This belief in invincibility through supernatural means and protection, in conjunction with their discipline, worked wonders for the Zulus when they faced their enemies on about equal terms. Of course, it had disastrous results when they charged an enemy armed with firearms – like the British soldier of 1879 – in the belief that their shields were impenetrable. Normal practices of 'doctoring' basically involved three aspects: the doctoring and protection of the individual, the doctoring or strengthening of the army, and the cleansing ceremonies after the battle. The warrior would first visit his home to solicit the protection of his ancestral spirits and to fortify himself with certain charms.

The Zulu army would only go to war after having been specially strengthened by the king's doctors (*iziNyanga*), which took a few days. It involved, inter alia, the sprinkling of the troops with liquids containing substances supposedly having magical properties, and the ritual bare-handed killing of a bull. The most potent of all these medicines was considered to be human flesh, and in the war of 1879, for instance, a white man, O. E. Neal, was killed by the Zulus and parts of his body used for 'doctoring' the Zulu army. When returning from battle, it was equally important to undergo the cleansing ceremonies.

Among the *iziNyanga*, one class of 'doctor' specialised in the medicinal use of plants and the treatment of sickness and wounds. In wartime he would accompany the army and deal with wounds and injuries, but only to his own people in the light of Shaka's instruction to take no prisoners. They would therefore kill a severely wounded opponent on the spot; any wounded man who could get away in spite of his injuries would thus do so as soon as he was able. In the case of the wounded who managed to get away, the wounds caused by assegais would be flesh wounds and would usually heal after treatment, but severely wounded men, even their own, had their skulls crushed by knobkerrie.

The Zulu Organisation

Shaka's evolution of a formation of four separate groups when going on attack during battle – the chest, horns and loins – has been referred to earlier. Each of these four tactical units could be composed of numerous subdivisions. The only organisation of males that existed among the Nguni tribes of that time were age sets or circumcision guilds (*iNtanga*), each of which consisted of about fifty men of the same age and organised on a district basis. When Shaka assumed the chieftainship over his own tribe, he drafted his eldest groups into the amaWombe regiment; the next group he named uDubinhlangu and the younger men were called umGamule. The pattern was thus set and was expanded to absorb the ever-increasing flow of recruits. The original size of an iNtanga was increased to approach one hundred men rather than fifty, and to form a company (*i(li)viyo*) under a captain who had from one to three junior officers, depending on the size or nature of the company. Among the functions of these junior officers was the daily distribution of meat to their men and the supervision of the manufacture, storage and handing out of shields. There was no limit to the number of companies in a regiment, which had its own distinctive name and uniform, and consisted of from one to two thousand men. Each regiment had its own commander (*inDuna*) with a second-in-command and two wing officers.

Serving in the king's army was obligatory for every young man, and only the unfit and diviners were exempt. As a regiment grew older, one or more younger regiments were affiliated to it so that the younger warriors could draw on the experience of their elders and also keep up the name and prestige of the kraal. In this manner three, four, or five regiments could be formed into one corps, such as the Undi Corps during the reign of Cetshwayo. The corps consisted of 9,900 men in the age groups twenty-four, twenty-eight, and forty-three to forty-five years. With the advent of what amounted to a standing army it became necessary to establish military kraals (*i(li)Khanda*), which became the headquarters or garrisons where the various regiments were accommodated. The establishment operated on a full-time basis but its individual members were given home leave for months at a time.

Of these military kraals Captain Allen Gardiner[6] wrote: 'The whole kingdom may be considered as a camp, and every male

belongs to one or other of the following orders: – "Umpakati",
veterans; "Izimpohlo" and "Insizwa", younger soldiers; "Amabutu"
lads who have not served in war. The two former are distinguished by
rings on their heads; the others do not shave their hair. Throughout
the country there are "Ekanda", or barrack-towns, in which a
number of each class are formed into a regiment, from six hundred
to a thousand strong, and where they are obliged to assemble during
the half year ... In the whole country there are said to be sixteen
large "ekandas" and several of a smaller size, and it is supposed
that they can bring fifty thousand men into the field.' The kraal was
under the supervision of the regimental or corps commander who
was responsible for order, discipline and general administration.

The men garrisoned at a military kraal had to be kept occupied.
Bryant stated: 'While ease and freedom were abundant, stern
discipline continuously reigned, but it was wholly a moral force, the
young men being thrown entirely on their honour, without standing
regulations and with little supervision ... They were there for the
sole purpose of fulfilling the king's behests. They acted as the state
army, the state police, the state labour gang. They fought the clan's
battles, made raids when state funds were low. They slew convicted
and even suspected malefactors and confiscated their property in
the king's name; they built and repaired the king's kraal, cultivated
his fields, and manufactured his war-shields, for all of which they
received no rations, no wages, not one word of thanks.'[7]

In Wartime

The organisation to which a warrior belonged while garrisoned
at one of the military kraals was retained on campaign, but the
commandant of a military kraal was not necessarily a commander
in the field. In addition to the regimental commanders there was
also a recognised commander-in-chief of the army, who was
assisted by staff. Periods of war were to the men the natural and
desirable state, as the risks to life and property in peacetime were
no less than in wartime. But times of war had the added advantage
of booty like cattle and women, opportunities for personal
distinction, and, as mentioned before, collectively the permission
for a regiment to marry.

War campaigning generally occurred in winter after the crops
had been harvested. To mobilise his army, the king sent messengers

to the commanders in charge at the different military kraals to order all warriors to proceed to the royal kraal. The movements of the regiments were so swift that the concentration of the whole Zulu army at the royal kraal could be effected within two to five days; regiments within a distance of some fifteen miles from the royal kraal could even congregate within twenty-four hours. Each regiment camped by itself, some distance apart, to prevent quarrels, as rivalry between regiments was so keen that faction fights were not uncommon. Regimental pride was so high that individual soldiers would identify themselves by their regiment in preference to their own clan name. Their esprit de corps had to be sustained by a sense of security, provided by the strengthening rituals referred to earlier.[8]

Provisions

While living at the military kraals, the warriors refrained from eating sour milk and lived on foods that would give them strength, such as meat, cooked mealies and beer. When at the royal kraal, meat and beer were supplied by the king. At the other military establishments, meat was supplied to a lesser extent from the royal herds and the warriors had to rely on supplies from home. They also had to supply their own uniforms and weapons, assegais and knobkerries. The shields, however, were generally manufactured at the military kraals from the hides of cattle slaughtered there and thus belonged to the kingdom, and were only issued on mobilisation and had to be returned at the end of the campaign.

During wartime the provision of supplies was in the short term by carriers and in the long term by capture. Youngsters between the ages of ten or twelve to eighteen years served as baggage carriers (*u(lu)Dibi*). They were attached to the regiments which, on reaching military age, they would eventually join. They normally marched at the rear and either to the right or left flank of the main body at a distance of a 1–3 miles. These youths carried mats, cooking pots, and mealies, and some spare rolled-up shields. They also acted as drovers of small herds of cattle, which could serve as food for the army, but were used mainly as guide animals to lead captured cattle back to the home kraals. Once the supplies they had been carrying were depleted, they returned home and from then onwards the warriors had to look after themselves by commandeering food at the various kraals on the way or by plundering food stores in enemy territory. On prolonged forays Shaka's armies had to endure extreme hardship when unable to obtain food supplies in the enemy's land.[9]

Intelligence

Shaka was well organised in terms of military intelligence and security, with a spy system keeping him advised on circumstances within Zululand and which provided him with all the necessary military intelligence before and during a campaign, as was the case with Cetshwayo during the Anglo-Zulu War in 1879. His spies would go out and determine the terrain, the locations of the enemy, their strengths and strongholds, as well as the hiding places of corn and cattle should they need to supplement their own supplies. The Zulu warriors also employed passwords and signs in order to distinguish between friend and enemy when on the march at night or when encamped. Most of the time, Shaka kept the object of a campaign and the routes to be followed a secret until it was time to set out, thereby preventing any treasonous advanced communication with the enemy.

Going into battle, Shaka's leading strategy was to encircle the enemy and force them into combat at close quarters. Immediately preceding an engagement his impi were rapidly drawn up in a semicircular formation and briefed by the warrior in overall command on the positions to be taken up by the various regiments. As mentioned before, their classical battle formation represented the head of a steer, and consisted of four formations. The chest (*isifuba*), composed of veteran regiments, formed the centre and faced the enemy fairly squarely. A large reserve force was positioned a short distance behind them. The elderly warriors composing it were directed to turn their backs on the battle scene so that they were unable to watch and become either discouraged or too elated at the outcomes of battle. Two horn-like formations (*u(lu)Pondo, izim-*) on either flank were composed of the younger, swifter regiments. The commanding officer and his staff took up a position on high ground to watch the progress of battle, and further directions were sent on by runners.[10]

The Zulu army would go into battle in stages: the chest (the veterans) would advance towards the enemy, halt, and feign a withdrawal to draw the enemy and cause them to break ranks. The veterans would then suddenly change onto attack, throwing the dislocated enemy into confusion. With the enemy having thrown its assegais, they would then be at the mercy of the Zulu *iklwa* (short assegai). The two horn formations would deploy in a flanking movement. Either both horns would remain hiding and take the enemy by surprise or one horn would move openly and cause a distraction while the other horn would move undetected under cover to spring a surprise attack. Obviously, these manoeuvres required training and timing. Sixty years later under Cetshwayo's reign a timing breakdown at the British camp at Khambula ended in disaster, but more about that later.[11]

Shaka's Successors
Dingane (1795–1840)
Following Shaka's assassination in September 1828 after at least two previous attempts, his brother Dingane took power and continued his work, expanding his army by creating new regiments and strengthening existing ones. His campaigns against neighbouring tribes were not at the same vast scale as those of Shaka, but he was the first Zulu monarch to engage in armed conflict with Europeans, though only towards the end of his reign.

On one of their visits to Dingane, in 1830, the Port Natal settlers arrived at his kraal on horseback for the first time. Dingane, who had never seen a horse before, was overwhelmed by the sight. He proclaimed that it would be impossible for native warriors to make a stand against mounted troops, and the Zulus did subsequently find against the Boers that their stabbing assegai was of almost no use against these mobile mounted men. As a consequence, they increasingly turned to their original throwing spear.[12]

After the murder of Piet Retief and his companions on the orders of Dingane at his royal kraal in February 1838,[13] Zulu impis attacked the Voortrekker camps and aided by the element of surprise scored initial successes. But when the Boers were well prepared for an attack and fighting from a laager, the Zulu courage or 'doctoring' would not be sufficient to beat them, as at Veglaer[14] near Estcourt, for instance. Then, at the Battle of Blood River on 16 December 1838, the futility of the Zulu fighting methods in the face of the Boers' firearms was spectactularly exposed. A Voortrekker commando of 464 men under their leader Andries Pretorius fought from a wagon laager against an estimated 10,000 to 15,000 Zulus on the bank of the Ncome River in Natal, which left 3,000 warriors dead on the battlefield or floating on the Ncome that was turned into a river of blood – hence the name.[15]

Mpande (1798–1872)

After his massive defeat at Blood River and the destruction of his royal kraal, Gingindlovu, Dingane fled to the northernmost corner of Zululand. This led to the rise of a half-brother of Shaka, Mpande, who all along had been regarded as politically incompetent and harmless. Mpande had refused to follow Dingane into hiding and fled across the Tugela River into Natal where he sought the Boers' protection, and the number of his followers increased steadily; at the same time, those of Dingane decreased. Then there came a stage where Mpande felt strong enough to challenge Dingane to the Zulu throne, and supported by a Boer commando, his army crossed the Tugela to take on Dingane. At the Battle of Magongo in February 1840, Dingane was defeated and he had to flee again to seek refuge in the tribal lands of the Nyawos, but here he was captured and killed.

Upon his death, Mpande was proclaimed king of the Zulus, probably more so by the Voortrekker government of the Republic of Natalia than by the Zulu nation. During Mpande's reign, he maintained good relations with the Boers and then with the British government, which later succeeded them in Natal. Left in peace, the Zulus could restore the losses suffered in the years before and in the aftermath of Dingane's death. While regimental discipline was relaxed during Mpande's reign in the absence of war, it was still maintained. During all this time, only a single military campaign was undertaken, against the Swazi.[16]

Cetshwayo (1826–82)

In a kingdom like the Zulu, sooner or later the period of peace and inactivity had to come to an end. For some time, Mpande had had his hands full to keep the peace between two of his sons, Cetshwayo and Mbulazi, who both aspired to succeed him to the Zulu throne. Both sons were mustering support and were building up their personal armies, and to avoid a clash between the two, Mpande separated them territorially, sending Mbulazi to a kraal on the Mfoba Hills where he was to live with his mother and his followers, the iziGqoza. To Cetshwayo he allocated the old Mthethwa kraal, eMangweni, where he was to reside with his mother, Ngqumbazi, and his uSuthu followers.

However, a military clash had always been inevitable and on 2 December 1856, the two factions fought each other at Ndondakusuka, with three white men siding with Mbulazi's men, but leaving as soon as they saw that Mbulazi was facing defeat. One of these whites was John Dunn,[17] the settler and hunter who later gained influence and power with Cetshwayo when the latter was Zulu king. Cetshwayo's army of 20,000 destroyed Mbulazi's 7,000 men, together with 3,000 women and children who formed part of this faction; so 10,000 iziGqoza members, including their leader Mbulazi, died in battle or drowned while trying to cross the flooded Tugela River into Natal where they were hoping to find refuge. Hereafter, Cetshwayo was acknowledged as the successor to the Zulu throne by both his own people and the Natal government. Cetshwayo acted as regent because of Mpande's incapacity to rule until Mpande died, aged seventy-four, in 1872. In 1873, Cetshwayo was crowned king of the Zulus during an official ceremony by Theophilus Shepstone, then Secretary for Native Affairs.

Under Cetshwayo the Zulu military system was fully restored until it consisted of some twenty-six regiments, the Zulu king having gathered the old regiments and forming new ones and establishing numerous military kraals. On the eve of the Zulu War, with a population of over half a million people, Cetshwayo could call on almost 50,000 swift-footed warriors. Like Shaka and his father Mpande before him, he had hoped to avoid conflict with the white forces, but the mere existence of his huge army spelt trouble for him.[18]

During and after Shaka's reign whole clans had fled Zululand and shortly before the Zulu War a whole section of the Gobamakhosi regiment had sought refuge in Natal. These at the time so-called 'Natal Natives' were unsympathetic towards the Zulu regime, notwithstanding the fact that many of them were actually of Zulu origin, and many were openly hostile and thirsting for revenge for injustices and hardships suffered under a Zulu king. Therefore they voluntarily supported the whites to break Cetshwayo's army, which made it possible for the Natal government to recruit nearly 7,000 'Natal Natives' within weeks to serve in the Natal Native Contingent (NNC) against Cetshwayo.

2

FIREARMS IN ZULULAND

The earliest references to the Zulus' reaction to firearms go back to the 1820s, when Shaka's warriors harboured a fear of them, but not necessarily related to the missiles the rifles discharged, but to the scary noise and the smoke they emitted during firing. The Zulu kings Shaka and Dingane both showed an interest in firearms. The conventional Zulu tactic during battle was to use their basic weapon of attack, the short stabbing spear, combined with the hide shield. Their aim, as mentioned, would be to encircle the enemy; when they advanced, flanking movements, known as 'the horns', would be employed to do this while the main body of warriors, known as 'the chest', led the charge. The formation was very flexible and could be adapted as circumstances and conditions required. These warriors were very mobile and skilled at using the cover of bushes, rocks, dongas or other means of concealment. During campaigns they travelled lightly, taking small quantities of necessities and depending more on plundering for their support.

It was only during the late 1860s that significant numbers of firearms made their appearance in Zululand. Vast quantities of weapons became obsolete when between 1867 and 1875 nearly all the European countries armed themselves with metallic cartridge breech loaders, and traders in Africa made good profits by selling antiquated weapons to African tribes. Obsolete weapons from Europe probably made up the bulk of the firearms that were imported into southern Africa during this period. Between 1872 and 1877, 60,000 firearms were illegally imported into Natal, of which two-thirds were re-exported, half to Delagoa Bay. It is likely that with this distribution of firearms in southern Africa, the Zulus were reluctant to fall behind other tribes. To increase the strength of the faction supporting his claim to the Zulu throne, Cetshwayo needed firearms, and on his kingdom's north-western border the threat of Boer encroachment was also increasing. In his decision to import firearms, he was encouraged by the well-known trader John Dunn. This not only brought good profits to Dunn, but also increased his status in Zululand.

Delagoa Bay was the main source of most of Cetswayo's weapons, although others came into Zululand from Natal and the Transvaal. In the case of John Dunn, merchants in Natal arranged for the dispatch of firearms to Delagoa Bay, where Dunn collected them, traded them for cattle in Zululand, and then drove the cattle across the Tugela River to be sold in Natal. Between 1875 and 1877, an average of 20,000 rifles with percussion caps, 500 breech loaders and 10,000 barrels of gunpowder passed through Delagoa Bay, of which three-quarters went to Zululand. The official estimate provided during the war of 1879 of firearms in possession of the Zulus, however, was only 8,000, which seems a small figure compared to the above.

To train his warriors in the use of firearms, Cetshwayo employed deserters from the British army and the services of Sotho gunsmiths to maintain them. The Zulus' biggest problems were judging distances and making the necessary adjustments to the sights of the rifles. The Zulus may have realised that the rifles they had bought were outdated and difficult to maintain, for they had not adapted their battle strategy in a way that may have enabled them to use them more effectively in battle. An intelligence report issued to all British officers at the start of the invasion of Zululand stated that the Zulu 'methods of marching, attack formation, etc., remain the same as before the introduction of firearms among them'. The commander of the British forces, Lord Chelmsford, based his strategy on the assumption that the Zulus would attack them in their traditional manner. He ruled out a war of manoeuvre as the columns were slowed down to a crawl by the long wagon trains supporting the soldiers. It would therefore be essential for them to entice the Zulus into a position where they would be exposed to concentrated rifle and artillery fire.

In all their major battles with Chelmsford's forces, the Zulus employed conventional tactics, the warriors approaching the enemy and the horns beginning their flanking movements with the chest trying to reach a position from which it would charge. Consequently, win or lose, the Zulus suffered heavy losses. In the case of Isandlwana, the British frontline was too extended to maintain a concentrated fire, and when the supply of ammunition from the wagons was interrupted, a section of the frontline broke. This enabled the Zulu to break cover and reach the lines, wiping out about 900 of the 950 whites in the camp and about 500 African levies. The Zulus themselves, however, probably suffered just as great a loss. Later, at the battle of Khambula, their losses were even higher. While the Zulus had made use of firearms throughout the campaign, their employment always remained subordinate to that of the assegai. Zulu fire on the enemy was seldom very successful due to poor aiming. From positions of good cover, they inflicted more damage. At Rorke's Drift, Khambula and Ulundi small groups of men provided covering fire for the attacking warriors. Although their fire was generally inaccurate, snipers at Rorke's Drift were responsible for most of the British casualties. At Isandlwana, the Zulus captured some 1,000 Martini Henry rifles and 500,000 rounds of ammunition, which may account for greater effectiveness of the Zulu fire in the later part of the campaign. An officer wrote that they had 'suffered considerably ... at least 70 killed and wounded principally by Martini Henry bullets' at Khambula.[1] And when the square formation came under fire at Ulundi, the British suffered seventy-nine casualties, but compared to those of the Zulus, who suffered losses of thousands killed, the imperial butcher's bill was cheap.

Firearms to the Zulus were secondary armament, only to be used before they closed with the enemy; they failed to evolve tactics by which they could be used to their best advantage. The quality of the firearms they possessed would have played a role in the ineffectual firing, and in the lack of confidence in these weapons. However, if the musket or rifle had not been subordinated to traditional tactics, they could have been used to greater advantage.

There is evidence that Cetshwayo tried to avoid charges on strongly defended positions as they cost so many casualties, but a lack of discipline hampered his attempts. At Isandlwana, for instance, the camp was attacked on impulse when the British scouts stumbled on the Zulu army when it was resting in the valley. At Khambula, the Zulus attacked the camp without waiting for the flanking horns, against the express orders of Cetshwayo. At the time, Cornelius Vijn recalled:

> When the King heard of the lost battle, he was exceedingly angry, and asked: 'Who had given the word for his people to be allowed to fight against the Whites who had already entrenched themselves, since even in the open field one White man was nearly as good as 10 Zulu? ... for the King's plan had always been, whenever the Whites entrenched themselves, to make his army pass them, in order to bring the Whites into the open field, or else surround them from a distance, and make them die of hunger. But his people had not the patience for all this; and, each time they fought, they must go and rest again for two or three months before beginning another fight.[2]

It has to be said that shortage of food and fear for their unprotected families and property at home drove the Zulus into making precipitated attacks, following which they would disperse to their homes. From the Zulu commanders' view, therefore, it was very difficult to initiate new tactics in terms of the use of their firearms or plan a coherent and prolonged strategy.

The Battle of Ulundi is generally seen as the one that finally convinced Cetswayo's Zulus of the superiority of the white man's arms and which destroyed the military system that Shaka had founded sixty years before. Ulundi provided the token military victory that Britain required in Zululand. It was easier and less costly to elevate Ulundi to the status of a crushing military victory and abandon plans to subjugate the Zulu nation than to create the force of mobile fighting units that would have been required to conquer the Zulus completely. The Zulus had been under arms for six months, many had lost their food supply and cattle, so they needed peace as well.

The Ninth Frontier War 1877–78
The Ninth and final Frontier War involved several powers, the Cape Colony government and its Fengu allies, the British Empire, and

the Xhosa tribes, the Gcaleka and Ngqika. At the time, the British government sought to increase control in southern Africa by uniting all the states of the region into a confederation under the overall rule of the British Empire, the same policy that was successfully applied to Canada. This confederation scheme required the remaining independent black states to be annexed. Like the Zulu War later, a frontier war was an ideal opportunity for such a conquest.

The Fengu had quickly adapted to the changes coming to southern Africa by taking to urban trade, while in contrast, the Gcaleka in the independent Gcalekaland had suffered greatly from the effects of war, alcoholism and the so-called Xhosa Suicide of 1857.[3] They bitterly resented the material success of the Fengu. A great drought had started in 1875 in Gcalekaland and had spread to other parts of the Transkei and the Cape Colony-controlled Ciskei, and by 1877 had become the most severe drought ever recorded. Ethnic tensions began to boil over in September 1877 at a wedding celebration after some Gcaleka harassed the attending Fengu, and later in the same day, Gcaleka attacked a Cape Colony police outpost predominantly manned by Fengu.[4]

The attack on the police force at the outpost was seen by the Cape Colony government as tribal violence, to be left for local police to solve. However, the Cape Governor, Sir Bartle Frere, used the incident as a pretext for the British conquest of the independent Gcalekaland. He summoned Sarhili,[5] the paramount chief of Gcalekaland, but the latter declined the invitation, fearing arrest and coercion. Frere then wrote to him, declaring him deposed and at war with Britain.[6]

Sarhili mobilised his armies to move them to the frontier; at the same time, the Cape government extracted a promise from Britain that imperial troops would on no account cross the frontier. When a Gcaleka force of 8,000 attacked a Cape police outpost near the frontier at Ibeka, a fierce battle followed in which the Gcaleka were dispersed, but soon several other outposts along the frontier also came under attack. The Cape Colony's local paramilitary mounted commandos under Chief Magistrate Charles Griffith,[7] a former commander of the Frontier Armed and Mounted Police, swiftly engaged and defeated an army of Gcaleka warriors armed with rifles. Advancing into Gcalekaland, they formed three fast-moving columns, dispersing the Gcaleka and pursuing them right through

Gcalekaland until reaching (neutral) Bomvanaland. With the war finished in three weeks, the Cape government recalled their commandos, who then disbanded. [8]

In the meantime, Governor Frere had established a 'war-council' at King William's Town to direct the war with himself and his Lieutenant General Sir Arthur Cunynghame[9] representing Britain and two Cape ministers, John X. Merriman and Charles Brownlee, representing the Cape. There was trouble from the outset, as Frere refused Gcaleka appeals and worked towards full British occupation of Gcalekaland for white settlement and Carnarvon's envisaged confederation. The Cape government, however, was opposed to its local commandos being brought under British imperial command in what they saw as a local conflict. They also regarded the slow-moving British troop columns unsuitable for frontier warfare. A large bone of contention was Frere's idea that the Cape government also pay for the British imperial troops. While the Cape government was satisfied to fund and employ its own forces, it was against British troops operating in the Cape Colony, let alone funding them as well.[10]

The conflict entered a second stage when Frere ordered the disarmament of all black peoples of the Cape, resulting in confusion and anger amongst the black soldiers and furious protest from the Cape government. As militia deserted and protest increased, Cunynghame overreacted by unilaterally deploying the imperial troops to throw a thin circle around British Kaffraria. The Cape government then demanded that Cunynghame be sacked, the disarmament policy be abandoned and the Cape government be allowed to deploy its own forces. But Frere replied by bringing in imperial troops to enforce the disarmament, upon which his troops invaded Gcalekaland again to annex and occupy it for purposes of white settlement.[11]

Copying the Cape's Gcalekaland campaign, the British divided into three columns, but the slow-moving troops were unable to engage the swiftly-moving Gcaleka, who had now regrouped and were able to slip past them into the Cape Colony. Here they were joined by chief Sandile,[12] who had stirred his Ngqika nation into rebellion, and these two combined Xhosa forces caused havoc in destroying Fengu and other frontier settlements, disrupting supply lines. As the British retreated, outposts had to be evacuated.

The Cape Prime Minister Molteno now left for the frontier in person, where he confronted Frere and demanded the free command of the Cape's indigenous forces to contain the conflict. Frere then appealed the the British Colonial Office to formally dissolve the Cape government and to assume direct imperial control over the entire country. While increasing numbers of Xhosa warriors now poured across the frontier and towns and farms went up in flames, many of the British troops still remained idle in Gcalekaland. Fortunately for Frere, he could still deploy the frontier militia and Fengu regiments of the (former) Cape government, and the Gcaleka were finally defeated on 13 January 1878 near Nyumaxa. They were assisted by the imperial troops, but the latter were exhausted, short of rations and barely held off a subsequent attack on 7 February at Kentani with substantial help from the Fengu and the local Frontier Light Horse militia. Although the Gcaleka finally pulled out of the conflict, Sandile's Ngqika rebels carried on fighting, eluding the imperial troops and vanishing into the Amatola Mountains.[13]

In the meantime, Sir Arthur Cunynghame had been replaced by Lieutenant-General Frederic Thesiger.[14] His British troops entered the mountain ranges in March 1878 to chase out Sandile's men, but their slow-moving columns were eluded and outmanoeuvred and repeatedly ambushed. Inexperienced in this environment with stretched supply lines and experiencing sickness and other hardships, they went through a difficult period, but once they had adopted the strategy recommended by the locals from the beginning, they had success. They divided the operational territory into eleven military provinces with a mounted garrison stationed in each. If a rebel group was encountered it was chased until it entered the next military province, where the next garrison would take over the pursuit. The valley exits from the range were also fortified. Under this strategy the rebels quickly splintered and began to surrender. Sandile himself fled into the Fish River Valley where he was killed by Mfengu troops.[15]

The last frontier war had continued for a year and signalled the end for the last independent Xhosa state, Gcalekaland, afterwards administered as a British territory. Sir Bartle Frere next applied the same tactics to invade the independent Zulu kingdom the following year, where the slow-moving troop columns featured once more at Isandlwana.

3

ON THE BRINK OF WAR: THE ULTIMATUM

The Boer-Zulu Border Dispute

The Boer Republic of Transvaal had been established to give the Afrikaners their own land away from British interference, but some of them had remained within the Natal borders, settling in the remote north-west, around Blood River. Being cattle owners, they were attracted to the grassy uplands to the east in Zululand. At that time, Mpande was king of the Zulus and they sought his permission to use the area for their cattle. Prepared to maintain good relations with the Boers, he allowed them to move in, but there were no clearly defined boundaries and the Boers slowly edged their way further into Zulu territory.

When Cetshwayo became Zulu king, he wanted the Boers out of his country, and consequently the area, stretching from Rorke's Drift in the south to the Transvaal border in the north, became disputed territory. The Boers claimed that Mpande had given them the land but Cetshwayo argued that it was merely a loan. At first, the British supported the Zulus in the argument, but when the Transvaal was annexed in 1877, they felt that it would be better to placate the potentially hostile Boer population by supporting their claim.

Apart from the fact that the border dispute between the Boers and Zulus needed to be settled, Sir Bartle Frere had his reasons for provoking the Zulus into war. He believed that a show of military might would demonstrate what would happen if the Boers or natives opposed it, and a victory would increase confidence in the British administration. He saw the Zulus as a threat to Natal's national security and spread the idea that the Zulu king was planning to invade Natal and kill off the population. Another motivation was that the government needed black people to work in the diamond fields.[1]

The Boundary Commission 1878

The Lieutenant-Governor of Natal, Sir Henry Bulwer, was not as keen as Frere on the idea of provoking a war with the Zulus. He believed that should it fail, Natal would be overrun by a Zulu army and all would be lost, and even if a British invasion was successful it would ruin race relations for many years to come. He therefore proposed that a commission be set up to take evidence from the Boers and the Zulus and then decide who was at fault in their dispute. Frere approved of this proposal because he was confident that it would provide confirmation of his views. The Commission set up to resolve the border dispute consisted of three members: Lieutenant-Colonel Anthony Durnford, Royal Engineers (who was later killed at Isandlwana); John Wesley Shepstone, brother of Sir Theophilus, and M. H. Gallway, Attorney-General of Natal. The Commission convened at Rorke's Drift in March 1878 and listened to the claims from both parties.

The Boers were represented by Henrique Shepstone, another brother of Sir Theophilus, who was Secretary of Native Affairs in the Transvaal; also Gert Rudolph, the Landdrost of Utrecht, and Petrus Lefras Uys, a prominent farmer in the disputed area. The Zulus were represented by Chief Sihayo whose tribe lived near Rorke's Drift, and two of Cetshwayo's officials, Gebula and Mundula. But the king also sent a loyal servant named Sintwangu, to provide a confidential report on the proceedings for the king's ears only.

The Commission was careful to appear as impartial as possible, the process lasting a month. They scrutinised a large amount of evidence, with much of the Boer evidence suspect, and the final outcome was that the Commission found in favour of the Zulus. The Commission stipulated, however, that some of the more predominently Boer-populated areas should be allowed to remain in Boer possession.[2] While this was good news for the Zulus, Frere was not at all pleased with the verdict. So when another excuse for war presented itself, Frere seized the opportunity.

When Chief Sihayo of the Qungebe, a supporter of Cetshwayo, was away in Ulundi, his sons discovered that two of his wives had absconded and were in Natal. One of them was staying in the homestead of Mswagele, a border policeman. Thereupon Sihayo's three sons, along with his brother and a force of thirty armed and mounted men and a large following of foot soldiers, crossed the Buffalo River at Rorke's Drift into Natal in broad daylight on 28 July 1878. Having caught the wife, they dragged her back into Zululand, knocked her teeth out and either clubbed or strangled her to death. The following day, the second wife met the same fate.[3] These murders shocked the colonists in Natal, and vindicated Frere's warnings about the barbarity of the Zulus. It also brought Bulwer round to Frere's way of thinking.

In January 1879, Sir Michael Hicks Beach[4] wrote to Bartle Frere:

I may observe that the communications which had previously been received from you had not entirely prepared them (Her Majesty's Government) 'for the course which you have deemed it necessary to take. The representations made by Lord Chelmsford and yourself last autumn as to the urgent need of strengthening Her Majesty's forces in South Africa were based upon the imminent danger of an invasion of Natal by the Zulus, and the inadequate means at that time at your disposal for meeting it. In order to afford protection to the lives and property of the colonists, the reinforcements asked for were supplied, and, in informing you of the decision of Her Majesty's Government, I took the opportunity of impressing upon you the importance of using every effort to avoid war. But the terms which you have dictated to the Zulu king, however necessary to relieve the colony in future from an impending and increasing danger, are evidently such as he may not improbably refuse, even at the risk of war; and I regret that the necessity for immediate action should have appeared to you so imperative as to preclude you from incurring the delay which would have been involved in consulting Her Majesty's Government upon a subject of so much importance as the terms which Cetywayo should be required to accept before those terms were actually presented to the Zulu king.[5]

Hicks Beach had earlier confessed his helplessness with regard to Frere's actions in a note to the Prime Minister: 'I have impressed this [non-aggressive] view upon Sir B. Frere, both officially and privately, to the best of my power. But I cannot really control him without a telegraph (I don't know that I could with one), I feel it is as likely as not that he is at war with the Zulus at the present moment.'[6]

The Ultimatum to Cetshwayo

Rather than publish the Boundary Commission's findings immediately, Sir Bartle Frere decided to sit on the report to give himself time to think about how he was going to present this to the Zulus without losing face. So he came up with an ultimatum that he intended to put to the Zulus alongside the findings of the Commission, and it constituted a blatant provocation that could only have one outcome. Frere imposed the following conditions on Cetshwayo:

1. The surrender of Sihayo's three sons and his brother, to be tried in the courts in Natal.
2. The payment of a fine of 500 head of cattle for the above offence and for failure to comply.
3. The payment of a fine of 100 head of cattle for the offence of intimidation of Messrs Smith and Deighton during a surveying exercise on the Tugela River.[7]
4. The surrender of the Swazi Chief Umbilini[8] and others to be tried in Transvaal courts.
5. The observance of promises made by Cetshwayo at his coronation.
6. That the Zulu army be disbanded and the men allowed to go home.
7. That the Zulu military system be discontinued and other military regulations be adopted, to be decided upon after consultation with the Great Council and British representatives.

8. That every man, when he comes to man's estate, be free to marry.
9. All missionaries and their converts, who until 1877 lived in Zululand, shall be allowed to return and reoccupy their stations.
10. All such missionaries shall be allowed to teach, and any Zulu, if he chooses, shall be free to listen to the teachings.
11. A British agent shall be allowed to reside in Zululand who will see that the above provisions are carried out.
12. All disputes in which a missionary or European is concerned shall be heard by the King in public, and in the presence of the Resident.
13. No sentence of expulsion from Zululand shall be carried out until it has been approved by the Resident.[9]

On 11 December 1878, representatives of Sir Bartle Frere met a Zulu delegation led by King Cetshwayo on the Natal bank of the Tugela River, just below the British camp, Fort Pearson. An awning was set up under a large Natal fig tree, which was to become known as the Ultimatum Tree.[10] Frere allowed Cetshwayo twenty days from 11 December to comply with his conditions. On the 18th, Cetshwayo sent word that he would try to send the cattle and the wanted men, but that the river was in flood and that it may take longer. He never really had any intention of disbanding his army, and was hoping that there would be some negotiation if he appeared to be trying to comply. Frere granted a concession until 11 January 1879. On 10 January, having still not heard from Cetshwayo, the British troops were poised on the border, and the following day crossed into Zululand.[11]

4

BRITISH CONFIDENCE

In the build-up to the Zulu War, the overriding attitude amongst most of the British was characterised by overconfidence and even arrogance, from the lowest to the highest rank, from the private to the general. The commander of the British forces designated to lead the Zululand campaign, Lord Chelmsford, wrote to Theophilus Shepstone in July 1878 giving his views on the British prospect of war with the Zulus: 'Half measures do not answer with natives. They must be thoroughly crushed to make them believe in our superiority; and if I am called upon to conduct operations against them, I shall strive to be in a position to show them how hopelessly inferior they are to us in fighting power, altho' numerically stronger.'[1]

Even a veteran like Sir Garnet Wolseley, with experience of the African continent and who later was to command the British forces in the closing stages against the Zulus, displayed a sense of racial superiority towards the African: 'It must never be forgotten by our soldiers that providence has implanted in the heart of every native of Africa a superstitious awe and dread of the white man that prevents the negro from daring to face us in combat. A steady advance or charge, no matter how partial, if made with determination, always means the retreat of the enemy ... they will not stand against the advance of white men.[2]

Just two days before the catastrophe at Isandlwana, private George Pettit wrote to his mother on 20 January, echoing the overconfidence and sense of superiority of his commanders: 'The

General [Lord Chelmsford] says it will not last long, for all the petty chiefs are giving in; they are coming in daily, which will soon make old Cetshwayo squeak ... we shall have no difficulty in finding out Cetshwayo and breaking up all his tribes.'³ Another private, Owen Ellis of the 1st/24th Regiment, wrote that 'The farmers who live in the surrounding country say that the Zulus will only be tempted to fight the Europeans once and that they will afterwards fly away for their lives, because they have not the weapons which we have.'⁴

This optimism was shared by the British press, the *Pall Mall Gazette* commenting that 'If the worst that is possible happens to us in Natal, we shall in the end succeed in beating a savage chief whom we never ought to have allowed to beat us.'⁵

Captain George Vaughan Wardell of the 'H' Company, 1/24th Regiment, was attached to the Centre Column and along with his comrades was waiting for the invasion along the border of Natal and Zululand at Rorke's Drift. The day before the invasion, on 10 January 1879, Wardell wrote a letter to his parents about their final preparations for the advance across the Buffalo River into Zululand, as well as their prospects against the Zulu enemy. Like most others, he was understandably optimistic about the forthcoming campaign. Considering the professionalism and training of the British soldier, and the British victory over the Xhosa on the Eastern Frontier the previous year, they were expecting that it would be relatively easy to conquer the Zulus with their assegais, rawhide shields, knobkerries and antiquated muskets and rifles. The technological gulf was made even wider by the British breech-loading Martini-Henry:

I must write a few lines before bidding adieu to Natal, as very early tomorrow morning we commence crossing the Buffalo, into Zululand to bring that great and sable potentate Cetchwayo (sic) to his bearings. Our column is now all ready prepared for advancing, and we are only waiting the finishing strokes to be put to the pontoons that carry us across the river. It is not very wide, but has a good clear of water, and is pretty rapid. We are encamped alone 800 yards from the river. Just behind us are the 2/24th. Our column also consists of one battery field Royal Artillery, about 500 horsemen, and a native contingent about 2,000-strong comprised of Natal Zulus with European officers ... all in all we have for South Africa a tidy little army in the field.

I do not think we shall meet with much opposition at first or even afterwards. I don't fancy that after the first brush they will care about facing us in the open country. I only hope that it will not be a long business, for I am getting pretty really tired of this kind of life, and have had enough of it of late to last me for a long time to come. We have had some pretty trying time of it as far as weather is concerned since we landed in Natal. Soldiering at home in a barracks, with a roof over your head, is pleasant enough ... The life we lead is very far different ... I can assure you all is no child's play. We have now said good bye to a civilised life.[6]

In a letter of 6 November 1878, Wardell nevertheless acknowledged that the Zulus would offer a far more difficult challenge than that posed by the Xhosas the year before: 'Zulus are far more powerful and better armed than the last.' Apparently, the only British concern was that the Zulus would refuse to confront them in a pitched battle and thereby deny the possibility of a decisive victory. He expected the three columns would reach 'the king's great kraal' at Ulundi, and 'astonish their heroes before very long ... I don't want to see any poor devils bowled over but I am curious to see our field battery open fire on them in mass. I think it will open their eyes.'

Wardell ended his letter with: 'If all is well I will send you a line again.'[7] But this turned out to be the last letter that he wrote. On 20 January, the Centre Column departed from Rorke's Drift and established their new camp at the base of Isandlwana Hill, and two days later Wardell became one of the many British victims of the Isandlwana massacre.

On the other hand, a note of caution was struck by some of the soldiers. Before the campaign had begun, Corporal H. Brown wrote to his wife on 29 December to tell her: 'I don't think that we shall finish this war so soon and easy as the other [referring to the 9th Frontier War the year before], for they are a better lot of men and more of them and they have got rifles the same as we have.'[8] Private John Thomas also remarked that 'they will have to remember that the Zulus have got Martini-Henry rifles as well as we.'[9]

And with the humiliating defeat of the British at Isandlwana, their perceived superiority was confounded. The same realisation dawned on the British forces the next day at Rorke's Drift and later at Eshowe. Following these events, they were obliged to reappraise the preconceptions they had carried into the campaign that the Zulu were inferior to them battlewise.

At the besieged mission station of Eshowe, Colour Sergeant J. W. Burnett admitted in a letter to a friend on 24 January – the last mail to leave Eshowe before Pearson's column was cut off – that they had all along been wrong about their enemy's ability: 'The Zulus stood for about four hours, our people firing shells, rockets, Martinis, and the Gatling guns,' he wrote, 'I never thought niggers would make such a stand. They came on with an utter disregard of danger ... I tell you what it is: our "school" at Chatham, over one hot whisky, used to laugh about these niggers, but I assure you that fighting with them is terribly earnest work, and not child's play.'[10]

A veteran of the 2/24th Regiment, Sergeant W. Morley, wrote to a fellow soldier stationed in Britain: '...they were like lions and not afraid of death. As soon as one man fell, another took his place, and those that think the niggers in Zululand will not fight, are sadly deceived.'[11] Private Joseph Morgan, another soldier of the 24th Regiment, wrote in a letter to his parents on 1 February: 'It was a fearful sight to see 600 British soldiers lying dead on the plain, killed by savages ... Before the war the General sent home for more troops, but was told he had enough, and now they find out their mistake, that the Zulus are a stronger and more powerful race of people than they thought.'[12]

The well-known Zulu War historian John Laband, however, does ask the question whether the Zulu's military reputation had been entirely deserved. 'The stunning and unexpected success of the Zulu army over the British at the battle of Isandlwana on 22 January 1879 forced the invading British drastically to reassess Zulu military capability and brought Zulu military prowess dramatically to the attention of the British public,' he says. 'The death of the ill-fated Prince Imperial of France in Zululand on 1 June 1879 while out on patrol further cemented internationally the reputation the Zulu already enjoyed in southern Africa as a warrior people who were a constant threat to the security of their neighbours. More than that, it ensured that their reputation has survived to this day as the quintessential warrior race. So often a commonly held perception turns out to be essentially a myth created (whether unconsciously or by design) and nurtured until it is accepted as fact.'[13]

He asks whether assumptions about the war readiness of Zulu fighting men has been sufficiently questioned. Has the effectiveness of the Zulu army been blown out of proportion? 'The subsequent Zulu defeat in the Anglo-Zulu War once the British had adjusted their tactics appropriately to make proper use of their overwhelming fire-power in all-round defensive positions like laagers and infantry squares, was consequently cried up as a hazardous and laudable achievement by British arms over a truly formidable foe,' he writes. 'Disastrous Zulu defeats such as at Khambula on 29 March 1879 and Gingindlovu on 2 April 1879 were not therefore presented as Zulu strategic and tactical failures so much as noteworthy British successes against heavy odds.'[14]

He points out that this is the position that has endured in much of the literature of the Anglo-Zulu War, 'for where would the drama be if the war was really nothing but a predictable British military promenade through Zululand, punctuated by a few careless lapses that gave the Zulu some unexpected and undeserved victories?'[15] There is more about this issue later.

Apart from the press reaction to the news of Isandlwana, the British public was as affected by the battle as they had been by no other colonial campaign since the Indian Mutiny. Details of the disaster and slaughter of the British soldiers, reports of disembowelment and mutilation, led to the public's imagination seizing onto the Zulus as the quintessential savage enemy, and with feelings of both fear and respect, the people wanted to learn more and more about the nation.

In the wake of Isandlwana, press reporting of the Zulu campaign and the Zulu people in general reached fever pitch. It only subsided once the war was over after the rout of the Zulus at Ulundi and public attention was diverted to the ongoing campaign in Afghanistan and the upcoming general election. This fascination was fed by lecture tours by Otto Witt, the Swedish missionary whose station was based at Rorke's Drift and who had witnessed the drama of 22 January after Isandlwana, and by the display in municipal theatres that summer of a troupe of Zulu warriors who were claimed to have been present at the battle.[16] The Zulu 'atrocities' committed at Isandlwana were considered symptomatic of the Zulu's savagery and brutality and as confirmation of 'the African's position at the bottom of the hierarchy of races'.[17]

Understandably, it revived fears of torture and cannibalism among the settlers of Natal and the British and irregular soldiers serving in Zululand and was seen by many of the British as confirmation of 'the natural cruelty to which the African was believed to be prey, and for which they were to be justly punished', and calls for revenge grew among the troops and the public at home. It is worthwhile to note that the aftermath of Inyezane, which took place before Isandlwana, saw relatively gentle treatment of Zulu wounded and surrendering prisoners, while after the battle of Khambula there had been a markedly different attitude towards them.[18]

5

THE IMPERIAL AND COLONIAL FORCES

Before going into the operations and developments of the war, it is useful to look at the various regiments of the imperial forces and the colonial forces that took part in the Zululand campaign. For this purpose a brief summary of their origins and development is provided.

With regard to the imperial forces, the 24th Foot Regiment has inevitably received most attention in Zulu War literature, having been so strongly associated with the most widely known battles of the campaign, namely Isandlwana and Rorke's Drift. The infantry regiments that advanced into Zululand in January 1879 were the 3rd Foot, 13th Foot, 24th Foot, 90th Foot and 99th Foot. After the massacre at Isandlwana, the 21st Foot, 57th Foot, 58th Foot, 60th Rifles, 88th Foot, 91st Foot and 94th Foot were sent out as reinforcements. At the outbreak of hostilities, the 80th Foot was already present in Natal but being held in reserve, they were not part of the initial invasion. A mounted infantry unit did serve at Isandlwana later, while the regiment served at the Battle of Ulundi in early July 1879.

In addition, units of the Royal Artillery, the Royal Engineers and a Naval Brigade also participated in the initial advance, while after Isandlwana, cavalry units of the 1st King's Dragoon Guards and 17th Lancers and further detachments of the Royal Artillery and Royal Engineers, a further Naval Brigade, and units of the

Army Service Corps and Army Hospital Corps were added to the British forces.

The colonial units are grouped under the columns as they advanced into Zululand, for instance under Pearson's column, Colonel Glyn's column, Colonel Sir Evelyn Wood's column, Durnford's reserve column, and Colonel Rowlands' Fifth Reserve Column. Colonial units that were not part of the invading columns but raised subsequently will also be included, The imperial regiments will be dealt with according to their seniority within the establishment of the regular army.

The regiments of colonial mounted volunteers that were involved in the campaign were the Natal Hussars, the Durban Mounted Rifles, the Stanger Mounted Rifles, the Victoria Mounted Rifles, the Natal Light Horse, the Natal Carbineers, the Natal Mounted Police, the Newcastle Mounted Rifles, the Buffalo Border Guard, the Frontier Light Horse, the Cape Mounted Rifles (Colonial), Baker's Light Horse, the Natal Volunteer Guides, Lonsdale's Mounted Rifles and the Border Horse. The irregular mounted units were Schutte's Corps, Ferreira's Horse, the Kaffrarian Vanguard, Piet Uys's Commando, Raaff's Horse and Eckersley's Contingent. Native units can be categorised separately as they were imperial creations as opposed to colonial, yet remain associated with Natal. They therefore differ from, for instance, Eckersley's Contingent, which was composed of Transvaal natives and raised by an individual.

There were also a number of regiments such as the Isipingo Mounted Rifles, the Pietermaritzburg City Guard, the Pietermaritzburg Rifles and the Durban Rifles, but that were not actively engaged in the campaign within Zululand to destroy Cetshwayo's Zulu force, and so they have been excluded here.

Colonial Units
General
In the colony of Natal the system of Commando service was unpopular, even though it could be legally applied, but it was nevertheless rarely enforced. Irregular units like Raaff's Horse, Schutte's Corps, Ferreira's Horse and Eckersley's Contingent were raised in either the Transvaal or the Cape Colony, where the Commando system had been entrenched for many years. In Natal,

however, it had no identical counterparts as the settlers preferred the organised and mounted units modelled upon the British Yeomanry. What the Natal volunteer regiments had in common with the Cape and Transvaal commando, however, was the fact that the officers were elected by the regiment, and secondly that all men found their own uniforms, horses and saddlery. The mounted corps were organised on lines which can be described as a combination of the characteristics of the British Yeomanry and the Commando system.[1]

In Natal, the settlers, finding themselves amongst masses of natives, were opposed to the Cape's system of employing non-European levies. The Natal Native Contingent was raised by the General Officer Commanding for the Zululand campaign, Lord Chelmsford, who requested permission from the Governor of Natal, Sir Henry Bulwer, to raise the NNC. Bulwer vetoed the project, fearing a backlash from the settlers should he dare arm so many of the Natal natives. However, Sir Henry eventually consented as the Colonial Secretary, Sir Michael Hicks Beach, refused to send more imperial reinforcements and the NNC had become essential. The commander of the 1st Regiment of the NNC, Colonel A.W. Durnford, had originally proposed the incorporation of Natal natives into the Natal Mounted Police, but he met with fierce opposition from the Natal colonists. Colonel Durnford also initiated the founding of the Natal Native Pioneers and the Natal Native Horse.[2]

Pearson's Column (the right column)
Natal Hussars (1866–87)
The original name of the regiment was the Greytown Mounted Rifles, which came into being for the protection of the districts of Greytown, York and Noodsberg in the Natal Midlands. In 1866 the Natal Hussars was raised by a Major Eastwood in the same area and in 1869 the two units amalgamated under the designation of the Natal Hussars. In December, its forty troopers joined the 1st Division, No. 1 Column, and fought at Nyezane. On 28 January, it returned from Fort Eshowe to Natal with the other mounted men of No. 1 Column. Until the corps was mustered out in July, it served by patrolling the border along the lines of communication between Fort Pearson, Stanger and Ntunjambili (Kranskop) in

Colonial Defensive Districts VI and VII and participating in cross-border raids.[3]

Durban Mounted Rifles (1873/5–88)
The unit was raised on 8 November 1873 with a strength of thirty-six, though C. T. Hurst gives the date as being 1875, when it had two troops of around fifty.[4] At the time of the invasion of Zululand, when becoming part of Pearson's column, it numbered sixty-four under Captain Shepstone. The DMR featured in the action at Inyezane, but upon news of Isandlwana were summarily sent back to Natal where they occupied defensive posts on the Natal side of the Tugela River, patrolling and guarding the frontier against possible Zulu raids.

Alexandra Mounted Rifles (1865–88)
The regiment was founded in 1865, raised on the south coast of Natal, and was the parent corps of the Natal Mounted Rifles. The regiment's first commanding officer was Major Dunbar Moodie; its strength varied from between 70 to 130 and was organized in three troops. When he crowned Cetshwayo in 1873, Sir Theophilus Shepstone took a small force with him that included a detachment of the AMR. They saw service at Inyezane, and after being withdrawn from Zululand, sent men to the Natal Volunteer Guides and patrolled the Natal border along the lines of communication between Fort Pearson, Stanger and Ntunjambili in Colonial Defensive Districts VI and VII and participated in cross-border raids. They were commanded by Captain Arbuthnot in Pearson's Column.

Stanger Mounted Rifles (1875–87)
The unit had a strength of two troops of twenty men each, and was led by Captain Friend Addison. It mobilised in December 1878 and joined No. 1 Column at Fort Pearson, leaving a few men behind at the Stanger laager for defense duties. It fought at Nyezane and on 28 January returned from Fort Eshowe to Natal with the other mounted men of No. 1 Column. Until the corps of around fifty men was mustered out in July, it continued to serve by patrolling the border along the lines of communication between Fort Pearson, Stanger and Ntunjambili (Kranskop) in

Colonial Defensive Districts VI and VII. In March, nearly half its men volunteered for active service in the Natal Volunteer Guides.

Victoria Mounted Rifles (1862–88)
The regiment was originally a troop of the Royal Durban Rangers founded in 1861 and a year later became a separate unit. In 1875, part of the regiment was formed into the Stanger Mounted Rifles. From its original strength of around sixty, they rose to 250 in 1888. As was the case with the Alexandra Mounted Rifles, a detachment of the VMR formed part of the small force sent into Zululand for Cetshwayo's coronation. The VMR was commanded by Captain Charles Saner in the column. It was mobilised in December 1878 and joined No. 1 Column at Fort Pearson. It advanced into Zululand with the column and fought at Nyezane and on 28 January returned from Fort Eshowe to Natal with the other mounted forces of the column. Until the corps of fifty men was mustered out in July, it served by patrolling the border along the lines of communication. Major Percy Henry Stanley Barrow (1848–86) of the 19th Hussars was placed in overall command of all the above mounted units.

Natal Native Contingent (1879)
The NNC was commanded by European officers and NCOs, and the men carried native arms, with 10 per cent armed with rifles. After Isandlwana, the original three regiments, totalling seven battalions, were reduced to five battalions, with many of the NCOs transferring to Lonsdale's Horse. In some of the battalions a few men were mounted and proved useful as scouts. There was general consensus that the fighting value of the force was extremely low, especially after events at Isandlwana. The officer commanding the unit in Pearson's Column was Major Shapland Graves. Notable personalities who served in the regiment were Corporal Schiess, 3rd Regiment, who won a Victoria Cross medal at Rorke's Drift, and (later) Major General Sir Henry Lukin., who commanded the South African Brigade in France in the First World War.

Natal Native Pioneers (1879)
The overall strength of the NNP was 273 and they were organised in three companies, one with each of Chelmsford's three invading

columns. The unit was responsible for the repair of roads and tracks and while in Pearson's Column was commanded by Captain J. K. E. Beddoes.[5]

Glyn's Column (the central column)
Natal Carbineers (1855–)
They were known for three weeks as the Pietermaritzburg Irregular Horse after being raised on 15 January 1855 and gazetted on 13 March of the same year. In 1861 the regiment numbered eighty-five men, and although the original unit was recruited in Pietermaritzburg, troops were soon established in Richmond, Karkloof, Estcourt, Ladysmith, Newcastle and Dundee. The Natal Carbineers campaigned against the San (Bushmen) in the 1850s and l860s, and in 1873 against the Zulu rebel Langalibalele when they suffered casualties. At the Battle of Isandlwana they lost two officers and nineteen men of other ranks. The seventy Carbineers joined No. 3 Column at Helpmekaar in December 1878 and advanced with it into Zululand, taking part in the skirmish at kwaSogekle on 12 January. The corps retired with No. 3 Column to Helpmekaar and spent the rest of the war on the Natal border. It took part in the patrol of 21 May to begin the burial of the dead at Isandlwana and mustered out in July 1879.

Natal Mounted Police (1874–1913)
The NMP represented the only permanent force in Natal. Initially it had very little support from the colonial authorities and their commanding officer, Major John Dartnell, had great difficulty in obtaining arms and equipment for his men. The NMP, consisting of twenty-five men under sub-inspector Phillips, made up Sir Theophilus Shepstone's sole escort when he annexed the Transvaal in 1877.[6] On 2 November 1878, on the eve of the Anglo-Zulu War, they were put under military command and took up position at Helpmekaar, where Glyn's Column was assembling. A detachment remained stationed at Harding in Colonial Defensive District No. IV to help the Ixopo Mounted Rifles defend the southern border of Natal, and another small detachment remained at Fort Durnford, the NMP's headquarters. The majority of the NMP crossed into Zululand with No. 3 Column, taking part in the skirmish at kwaSogekle on 12 January, while twenty-six were

killed at Isandlwana. Three members of the NMP took part in the defense of Rorke's Drift. The NMP retired with No. 3 Column to Natal, where a detachment remained at Rorke's Drift while the rest took up position at Helpmekaar. In June, the NMP received recruits from England and Natal. In July, a detachment escorted General Sir Garnet Joseph Wolseley from Rorke's Drift to the Mahlabathini Plain. One section then joined Clarke's Column in the hunt for King Cetshwayo kaMpande, while another joined Baker Russell's Column. In September, all the NMP returned to peacetime duties. The regiment's title was changed to the Natal Police in 1894.

Newcastle Mounted Rifles (1876–79)

Founded and raised in Northern Natal in 1876, the regiment served in the Zulu War with a strength of sixteen men. They were present at the Isandlwana battlefield and lost seven men. During the course of the Zulu war it was merged with the Natal Carbineers. In December 1878, they joined No. 3 Column at Helpmekaar with thirty-six troopers. Most advanced with the column into Zululand, but a few remained in Natal patrolling the border. Those still with No. 3 Column took part in the skirmish at kwaSogekle. Half the corps was absent with Major John George Dartnell's reconnaissance in force when the remainder left behind in the camp at Isandlwana suffered heavy casualties. They retired with No. 3 Column to Natal, where it garrisoned Fort Pine between February and July 1879. It spent the rest of the war engaged in patrol work, cross-border raids, escort duty and dispatch riding. It took part in the patrol of 21 May that began the burial of the dead at Isandlwana.

Buffalo Border Guard (1873–80)

The Guard was raised on 2 October 1873 and was a small unit of around thirty men. They were disbanded in 1880. In Glyn's Column they were led by Captain Robson, and at the massacre of Isandlwana only three of its members escaped alive from the Zulus. The corps of forty troopers joined No. 3 Column at Helpmekaar in December 1878 and the majority advanced with the column, though a few men remained in Natal patrolling the border. The corps took part in the skirmish at kwaSogekle on

12 January. Two-thirds of the corps were absent with Major Dartnell's reconnaissance in force when the remainder left in the camp at Isandlwana suffered heavy casualties in the Zulu attack. The corps then retired with the column to Natal, where it was also garrisoned at Fort Pine between February and July 1879.

All the above units were commanded by Major John George Dartnell of the Natal Mounted Police. This column of Colonel Glyn also included the 3rd Regiment, Natal Native Contingent, under the command of Major William Black of the 24th, who had replaced its previous commander, Commandant Rupert La Trobe Lonsdale, and a unit of the Natal Native Pioneers, under the command of Captain J. Nolan.[7]

Wood's Column (the left column)
Frontier Light Horse (1877–79)
Its personnel were paid, equipped and maintained by the imperial government, but it was raised within Cape Colony by Lt F. Carrington of the 2nd/24th Regiment at King Williamstown in 1877. The command soon passed to (then) Major Redvers Buller. During September and October 1878 the regiment saw service against the Pedi of Sekukuni, and in November returned to Natal. Its strength in the Zulu War was 216. On 28 March, 1879, the FLH, which acted as a rearguard during the withdrawal from the Hlobane Mountain, lost almost 20 per cent of the 156 of all ranks engaged. The regiment's commanding officer in the column, Captain Robert Barton of the Coldstream Guards, was killed at Hlobane, and was succeeded by Captain Cecil D'Arcy. Two squadrons participated in the White Mfolozi reconnaissance in force and fought at Ulundi. After the breakup of Wood's Flying Column in late July, they joined Baker Russell's Column and were disbanded in September.

Border Horse (1879)
This regiment was raised and commanded by Lt Col Frederick Augustus Weatherley (1830–79), an ex-imperial officer in the Transvaal, for the Zulu War. The regiment, sixty-nine strong, lost its commanding officer (along with his fourteen-year-old son Rupert) and thirty-eight of all ranks killed, and one wounded, at Hlobane. It served under Major Dennison at Khambula the next day, but shortly afterward they left the camp for Pretoria and disbanded.

Baker's Light Horse (1877–78, 1879, 1880–82)

Major Francis James Baker, who commanded the unit, raised it three times, the first time being in the Eastern Province for the Ninth Frontier War. Disbanded at the close of hostilities, it was once more raised at Port Elizabeth in 1879 for the Zulu War, with a strength of 240, and served at Hlobane and Ulundi. They wore yellow or brown corduroy uniforms and the customary wideawake hat. It was disbanded again in August 1879, and Baker again raised his regiment in Natal on 2 October 1880, with a strength of approximately 200, and served in the Griqualand East area throughout the Basutoland rebellion. It was retained after the end of hostilities in April 1881, and it was proposed that the regiment be retained as the Cape Cavalry, but it was rejected and the regiment disbanded.

Ferreira's Horse (1877–81)

During the first occupation of the Transvaal, Colonel Ignatius Ferreira, CMG, raised three irregular mounted corps at Pretoria, of which the first saw action against Sekukuni in June 1878. The second corps, numbering 115 men, served in Wood's Column and also took part in the capture of Sekukuni's Mountain in 1879. The third corps was known as the Transvaal Horse, had a strength of 300, and included two 9-pounder field guns. It saw action later in Leribe in Northern Basutoland until it was disbanded in August 1881.

Uys's Commando (1879)

In the Official of the Zulu War (1879) this unit is referred to as the Burgher Force. Its commanding officer, Commandant Piet Uys, was killed at Hlobane Mountain. The strength of the commando was 45, and all members were unpaid relatives of Uys, and they proved very effective in scouting and raiding. Uys was a son of the Voortrekker leader Petrus Lafras Uys Sr. The Uys family acquired farms in the Republic of Natalia, but after the British annexation of Natal, Piet Uys was among those who in 1847 settled in what became the Utrecht District. On the eve of the war, Brevet Colonel Henry Evelyn Wood tried to raise a burgher force from the Boers of the district, but most remained resentful of the British annexation of the Transvaal in 1877. Only Uys, his family and associates came forward, motivated by the vulnerability of his border farms and his desire to acquire land in the disputed territory. They formed part of Buller's force raiding Hlobane Mountain on 28 March 1879. During the rout, Uys was killed at the bottom of Devil's Pass and his men abandoned the British camp at Khambula before the Zulu assault the following day.

All the colonial units in Wood's Column were commanded by Lt Col Redvers Buller.[8]

Durnford's Reserve Column

This column consisted of the 1st Regiment, Natal Native Contingent, five troops of Natal Native Horse, Sikali's Horse, which consisted of C, D and E Companies of the lst/3rd NNC, drawn from Sikali's Reserve and mounted, and a rocket battery.

Natal Native Horse (1879, 1888, 1899–1902, 1906)
The NNH was regimented in 1879, and formed from five separate groups of natives living in Natal. The men volunteered for service, father to son, from 1866 to 1906, serving as scouts on their own ponies and occasionally as transport men. They were first employed in 1866 against raiding San (Bushmen). Colonel Durnford took five troops with him to Isandlwana, where they fought their way out of the encircling Zulus and covered the far bank of the Buffalo River to cover the flight of the survivors. They claimed that they wished to take Durnford with them, but he refused, preferring to fight to the death. Contemporary accounts speak well of the NNH, especially their contribution at Hlobane and Khambula, and in reconnaissance work before the final battle at Ulundi. The groups thatsaw most service during the Zululand campaign were Hlubi's Batlokwa from near Rorke's Drift, a Basuto tribe who never owed allegiance to the Basutoland paramount chief; and Christian Swazis and Zulus from the Edendale and Driefontein Missions. Other groups were the Amangwane from Northern Natal, who had a bitter feud with the Zulu kings, and Chief Jantji's men of south-west Natal. The Edendale Contingent had John Zulu at their head and Sergeant Simeon Khambula as senior NCO in their ranks. After Isandlwana, with the officers killed, Sgt Simeon Khambula found himself in command of the survivors, and later fought with Major Redvers Buller at the Battle of Hlobane Mountain on 28 March.[9]

Rowland's Reserve Column
The Fifth Reserve column was commanded by Colonel H. Rowlands and was initially stationed at Luneberg. In addition to the Cape Mounted Rifles (Colonial), Schutte's Corps and Eckersley's Contingent, it also comprised originally the Border Horse and Ferreira's Horse. These latter units were later transferred to Buller's Command and are dealt with under Wood's Column.

Schutte's Corps (1879)
The corps consisted of Transvaal volunteers raised for the Zulu War. The commanding officer was Captain Schutte.

Eckersley's Contingent (1879)
The unit comprised Transvaal natives raised by Mr John Eckersley, RM, for service in the Zulu War and against Sekukuni, and had 207 members.

Cape Mounted Rifles (1855–1913)
Not to be confused with the regiment raised by the imperial authorities in 1806 with the same name, this colonial regiment was raised in 1855 with the designation of the Frontier Armed and Mounted Police. Its name was changed to the Cape Mounted Rifles in 1878. The FAMP had an original strength of seventeen officers and 500 other ranks, and until the disbanding of the imperial CMR carried out police duties in the Eastern Province of the Cape Colony. After 1870 it was increasingly deployed for military duty, especially in areas where there were native disturbances. When the new title was adopted in 1878, the name of the older imperial regiment was deliberately chosen. Colonel Hans G. Moore commanded the regiment between 1878 and January 1879, who was succeeded by Colonel Z. S. Bayly between January 1879 and 1892.[10]

Colonial Units Raised After Isandlwana
Natal Volunteer Guides (1879)
It was commanded by Captain Richard Addison[11] of the Stanger Mounted Rifles and was formed from various contingents of the colonial mounted volunteers (i.e., the Durban Mounted Rifles, Stanger Mounted Rifles, Alexandra Mounted Rifles and Victoria Mounted Rifles). They served at Gingindlovu and in early July withdrew to the Natal border, and were mustered out by the end of the month.

Lonsdale's Mounted Rifles (1879)

Also known as Lonsdale's Horse, they were raised by Commandant Rupert La Trobe Lonsdale, who had commanded Mfengu levies during the 9th Cape Frontier War, and were formed from the European NCOs of the Natal Native Contingent after Isandlwana. They numbered 236, divided into eight troops, and also served at Gingindlovu. During the first stage of the war, Lonsdale was given command of the 3rd Regiment, Natal Native Contingent. In the reorganisation of forces after Isandlwana, Lord Chelmsford ordered him to the Cape to recruit a unit of mounted irregulars. He raised four troops, three of which joined the 1st Division, South African Field Force, and advanced with them to Port Durnford. On the breakup of the 1st Division in late July, two troops joined Clarke's Column and one joined Baker Russell's Column. The latter took part in the final operations against the Kubheka in the Ntombe Caves on 5 and 8 September. The unit mustered out in September.

John Dunn's Scouts (1879)

The well-known Natal trader John Dunn was of English descent and became known as the 'White Chief of Zululand'. 150 members of this native unit served at Gingindlovu.

Natal Light Horse (1879)

The unit was raised from a troop of the Frontier Light Horse in March 1879, numbering 138 men. They were commanded by Captain W. Whalley and they served at Ulundi. Whalley took the field in May 1879 when they joined Wood's Flying Column. A troop took part in the skirmish at Zungeni and in the White Mfolozi reconnaissance, and both troops fought at Ulundi. After Ulundi, detachments garrisoned Fort Evelyn and Fort Albert until the withdrawal of the British troops from Zululand. Some elements might have joined the Frontier Light Horse when that unit was attached to Baker Russell's Column.

Raaff's Horse (1879)

Also known as Raaff's Transvaal Rangers, they were raised by Commandant Pieter Raaff (later CMG) with a strength of 138, and enlisted both European and coloured staff. The unit recruited large numbers from the Kimberley mines. It served in the attack upon Hlobane and Khambula and also at Ulundi.

One should also note the existence of a regiment that, although raised at the outset of the Zulu War, did not advance into Zululand with the invading columns. This was the Kaffrarian Vanguard, which was formed by Commandant Frederick Schermbrücker[12] in the Eastern Cape. At the outset of hostilities he collected together forty-two of his German neighbours, equipped them as infantry and named them the Kaffrarian Vanguard before taking them to Natal. Chelmsford sent them to guard their German compatriots in the Luneburg area and, after Isandlwana, had them mounted. They also served in the attack upon Hlobane. Not to be confused with the Kaffrarian Rifles raised in 1883.[13]

Imperial Regiments
General
The imperial regiments which were part of the advancing columns were:

Pearson's Column: the 2nd Battalion of the 3rd Regiment of Foot (the 'Buffs'), six companies of the 99th Regiment, and detachments of Royal Artillery and Royal Engineers.

Glyn's Column: seven companies of the 1st Battalion, 24th Regiment and 2nd Battalion of the 24th, a detachment of Royal Artillery, and a company of Royal Engineers, supported by the Natal Native Pioneers.

Evelyn Wood's column: the 90th Regiment, 1st Battalion of the 13th Regiment, and a detachment of Royal Artillery. Also attached to Pearson's Column was the Royal Navy in the form of a contingent of 174 sailors and forty-two Marines from HMS *Active* under Commander H. J. F. Campbell, RN.

The 1878 Army List names 109 regiments of Foot, which since their raising had been designated by number. Most of the numbered regiments bear a territorial title or county association. Apart from these Regiments of Foot, the infantries comprised the Foot Guards and the Rifle Brigade. The order of seniority is based upon the order of precedence in the Army List, which is as follows with regard to those regiments participating in the Zulu War: the Guards Cavalry, the Cavalry, the Royal Regiment of Artillery, the Corps of Royal Engineers, the Regiments of the Line, the Commissariat and Transport Department, the Ordnance Store Department, the Medical Department and the Royal Marine forces.

1st King's Dragoon Guards (1685–1959)

They were raised mainly in London during the Monmouth rebellion in 1685; between 1685 and 1714 its designation was the Queen's (or 2nd) Regiment of Horse and between 1716 and 1959 the 1st King's Dragoon Guards. The regiment gained much distinction at Waterloo and subsequently served in the Crimean War, Indian Mutiny, China and India, returning to England in 1866. A detachment under Major Richard J. C. Marter captured Cetshwavo after Ulundi.

17th Lancers (Duke of Cambridge's Own) (1759–1922)

Founded in 1759, its designation was the 18th Light Dragoons; between 1763 and 1766 the 17th Light Dragoons; between 1766 and 1769 the 3rd Light Dragoons; between 1769 and 1822 the 17th Light Dragoons; between 1822 and 1876 the 17th Lancers; and between 1876 and 1922 the 17th Lancers (Duke of Cambridge's Own). They served in the Crimea, taking part in the famous Charge of the Light Brigade. They later served in India (1858–65) before returning home. The regiment was based at Hounslow and Hampton Court when it received orders to proceed to Natal, where it served at Ulundi in the second invasion of Zululand, playing a key part in the mounted pursuit of the Zulus. They were commanded by Colonel Drury Curzon Drury-Lowe and made up half of the Cavalry Brigade attached to the 2nd Division, South African Field Force. A detachment was based at Fort Marshall to protect the line forward. The regiment was part of the patrol to Isandlwana in May 1879 to bury the British dead. A squadron also saw action in the skirmish at Zungeni, and two squadrons participated in Brigadier-General Evelyn Wood's raid on the emaKhosini Valley.

Royal Regiment of Artillery (1722–)

To be distinguished from the Royal Horse Artillery, founded in 1793. Prior to its raising, a train of artillery had to be authorised by royal warrant, which led to much delay, so on 26 May 1716, two companies of artillery were created by King George I at Woolwich. On 1 April, 1722, these two companies were grouped together with the companies at Gibraltar and Minorca to form the Royal Regiment of Artillery. In 1855 the RA, together with the Royal Engineers, came under the Commander-in-Chief and the War Office like the rest of the Army. Four years later, the RA companies ceased to be organised into battalions, and were brigaded instead; they were also then referred to as batteries instead of companies, which were divided into field batteries and garrison batteries.

Corps of Royal Engineers (1716–)

With the introduction of cannon a Board of Ordnance was established in the early fifteenth century to administer all matters relating to the king's fortifications, arsenals and other military equipment. The military engineers, surveyors and artillerymen required were retained on the Board's permanent establishment. Ordnance trains, officered by 'military gentlemen' of the Board of Ordnance and consisting of engineer tradesmen and gunners, were raised for specific campaigns and disbanded when no longer required. In 1716, the Artillery and Engineers were constituted as separate establishments. In 1722 the Soldier Artificer Company was formed at Gibraltar for the construction of fortifications, and this was the first unit of permanent engineer soldiers in the British Army. It was commanded by officers of the Corps of Engineers, which in 1787 was granted a Royal title. In the same year a corps of Royal Military Artificers was formed for the construction of seaward defences at home and overseas as a precaution against a French invasion, and officers for this corps were supplied by the Royal Engineers. Ten years later the Gibraltar soldier artificers were incorporated into the Corps of Royal Military Artificers. The title of Royal Military Artificers was changed to that of Royal Sappers and Miners in 1812 to denote the changing role of the military engineers during the Peninsula War. In 1856, the latter was absorbed into the Corps of the Royal Engineers, ending the long-standing anomaly whereby officers and soldiers of the engineering arm of the British Army were members of two distinct corps.

2nd Battalion, 3rd (East Kent, The Buffs) Regiment of Foot (1665–1961)

The regiment traces its origin back to a 'Holland' regiment in 1572, under the command of a Captain Thomas Morgan, and was not absorbed into the English establishment until 1665. It was one of those sent to the Netherlands by Elizabeth 1 to assist the Dutch Protestants in their rebellion against Spanish control. Between 1665 and 1689, it was known as the Holland Regiment; between 1689 and 1708 as Prince George of Denmark's Regiment; between 1708 and 1751 as The Buffs; between 1751 and 1782 as the 3rd (or The Buffs) Regiment of Foot; and between 1782 and 1881 as the 3rd (East Kent, The Buffs) Regiment of Foot. The designation 'Buffs' appears to have originated from the colour of parts of the uniform or equipment. They took part in all the major British campaigns and its first Victoria Crosses were gained in the Crimean War. A 2nd Battalion was added in 1858, having previously served in the Ionian Islands and the West Indies. Towards the end of 1878, the HQ and five companies of the Buffs were ordered to concentrate at Thring's Post, near the mouth of the Tugela River. Early in November 1878, three more companies arrived from Mauritius, which constructed the earthwork on the right bank of the river that became known as Fort Pearson. The regiment served at the Battle of Inyezane, and two companies of the 3rd were present at the Battle of Gingindlovu. They had been detached from Pearson's Column for convoy duties, thereby escaping being besieged at Eshowe like their comrades. The regiment formed part of Major-General Henry Hope Crealock's 1st Division in the second invasion of Zululand.

1st Battalion, 13th (1st Somersetshire) (Prince Albert's Light Infantry) Regiment (1685–1959)

The regiment was formed in 1685, and until 1688 was designated Colonel The Earl of Huntingdon's Regiment of Foot. Then between 1688 and 1751 its title changed with the colonel's name; thereafter until 1782 it was known as the 13th Regiment of Foot; from 1782 to 1822 the 13th (1st Somersetshire) Regiment of Foot; from 1822 to 1842 the 13th (1st Somersetshire Light Infantry) Regiment; and between 1842 and 1881 as the 13th (1st Somersetshire) (Prince Albert's Light Infantry) Regiment. The regiment played a major part in the Battle of Culloden (1746). It was converted to Light Infantry in 1822, and in 1838 attained lasting fame during the 1st Afghan War for its defence of Jellalabad. They were granted a 'Royal' title (i.e. 'Prince Albert's Light Infantry'). The 13th served in the Crimean War and in the Cape Colony in 1856/57 during the Eastern Frontier disturbances. They then served in India, Gibraltar and Malta, and in South Africa in the Sekukuni campaign. During the Zululand campaign, the regiment was involved in the defence of Khambula and afterwards served at Ulundi.

2nd Battalion, 21st (Royal Scots Fusiliers) Regiment of Foot (1678–1959)

Raised in 1678, the regiment was issued with fusils (light muskets) instead of muskets, hence its title. Between 1678 and 1686 its designation was Colonel The Earl of Mars Regiment of Foot and between 1686 and 1707 the title changed with the colonel's name. Between 1707 and 1712 its official designation was the Scots Fusiliers Regiment of Foot; between 1712 and 1751 the Royal North British Fusiliers Regiment of Foot; between 1751 and 1877 the 21st (Royal North British) Fusiliers Regiment of Foot; and between 1877 and 1881 as the 21st (Royal Scots Fusiliers) Regiment of Foot. They had been involved in most major engagements of the British Army. The 2nd Battalion was sent from their Curragh camp in February 1879 to Natal, where they served at the Battle of Ulundi.[14]

24th (2nd Warwickshire) Regiment of Foot (1689–1969) (later South Wales Borderers)

The regiment was founded in 1689 and until 1751 was known as Colonel Sir Edward Dering's Regiment of Foot. Later, the title changed with the colonel's name. From 1751 to 1782 the regiment was known as the 24th Regiment of Foot, changing to the 24th (2nd Warwickshire) Regiment of Foot between 1782 and 1881. Interestingly, Monick[15] points out that this regiment, which found itself trapped at the battles of Isandlwana and Rorke's Drift, had been characterised throughout its history by perpetual ill luck.

No Regiment of the Line could surpass them for reliability, and their reputation for steadiness and bravery go back through Alexandria (1801) and Malplaquet (1709) to Blenheim (1704). On the other hand, however, the 24th had been a consistently ill-fated regiment.[16] In this regard, the advance into Zululand in January 1879 marked almost exactly the thirtieth anniversary of Chillianwallah (13 January 1849), when the British were completely beaten by the Sikhs.[17] Ironically, just two days before the advance, the officers of both battalions had dined together at Helpmekaar. Captain William Degacher, second-in-command of the 1st Battalion, proposed the toast, 'That we may not get into such a mess again, and better luck next time'. Alas, twenty-one of the officers present were to die in action within the forthnight, including Captain Degacher.

The 1st Battalion had been in South Africa since 1874, and had served against the Gcalekas and Ngqika of the Transkei in 1877. Sir Arthur Cunynghame, who was GOC at the Cape, used a small force of approximately fifty mounted infantrymen of the lst/24th Foot, the 88th Foot and a Naval Brigade, under Captain Wright, from HMS *Active* and *Florence*. On 9 March 1878, the 2nd/24th arrived in South Africa from England, and the two battalions of the regiment for the first time served in the same country and under the same command.

57th (West Middlesex) Regiment of Foot (1741–1881)
It was raised in 1741, with the title of the 57th Regiment of Foot, and was subsequently renumbered the 46th in 1748. Between 1755 and 1757 it returned to its original renumbering. Between 1757 and 1782 it was known as the 57th Regiment of Foot, and between 1782 and 1881 as the 57th (West Middlesex) Regiment of Foot. The regiment served in the Peninsula War, the Crimean War, the Indian Mutiny, in New Zealand (1861–86), and in Ceylon until February 1879, when it was ordered to South Africa. The 57th served at Gingindlovu, and formed part of Crealock's 1st Division during the second invasion of Zululand.

58th (Rutlandshire) Regiment of Foot (1740–1881)
Between its raising in 1740 and 1748 the regiment was successively designated the 58th Regiment of Foot, the 47th, and later the

1st Battalion Loyal North Lancashire, In 1756–57 it reverted to its original numbering of the 58th, but was renumbered the 56th. Between 1755 and 1757 it was the 60th Regiment of Foot, renumbered to the 58th. Between 1757 and 1782 it was known as the 58th Regiment of Foot, and between 1782 and 1881 as the 58th (Rutlandshire) Regiment of Foot. It was one of the five regiments that manned Gibraltar during the siege of the island from 1779 to 1783. Earlier, it had also fought under General Wolfe at Quebec in 1759, and performed distinguished service at Alexandria in 1801. Between 1864 and 1874 the regiment was stationed in Bengal and by 1879 at Dover, when it was ordered to proceed to Natal. The regiment served at Ulundi in early July 1879.

3rd Battalion, 60th or The King's Royal Rifle Corps (1755–1958)
There was another unit, the 60th Regiment of Foot (1741–48), with the same name but which has no connection with this regiment. It was founded in 1755, and until 1756 was known as the 62nd (Royal American) Regiment of Foot. Between 1756 and 1824 it was redesignated the 60th (Royal American) Regiment of Foot. In 1824 its title changed to the 60th (Duke of York's Rifle Corps), between 1824 and 1830 it was known as the 60th or the Duke of York's Own Rifle Corps, and between 1830 and 1881 it was known as the 60th or The King's Royal Rifle Corps. The regiment is quite distinct from other Line Regiments, in so far as it was raised to deal exclusively with the problem of guerilla warfare. It was raised in America and was recruited mainly from American colonists. Its first colonel was the Earl of London, who was then Officer Commanding of the English forces in America. The regiment's first active service was against the French in Canada who, with their Native American allies, were disputing British rule in North America. This conflict formed part of the Seven Years War (1756–63), which was also fought in Europe and India. In keeping with the circumstances of 'bush' warfare, the 60th Foot adopted light, inconspicuous clothing and equipment as opposed to the standard red coats of the British Line Infantry. During the Zulu War, its uniform of rifle green distinguished it from that of other infantry regiments. It took every possible step to ensure rapid movement combined with a high level of marksmanship. In 1759, the regiment

played a leading role in the capture of Quebec. During the Peninsula War, it performed outstanding service in scouting, skirmishing and convoy duties. The regiment's service record includes the Crimean War and the Indian Mutiny in 1857, when they particularly distinguished themselves at the Siege of Delhi. The 3rd Battalion was raised in Dublin in 1855 and embarked for India in August 1857, serving in India, Burma and Aden until 1871. It was stationed at Colchester when it was ordered to Natal in February 1879. The 60th served at Gingindlovu and formed part of Crealock's 1st Division during the second invasion of Zululand.

80th (Staffordshire Volunteers) Regiment of Foot (1793–1881)

Prior to the appearance of the Staffordshire Volunteers in 1793, two previous regiments numbered the 80th were raised and subsequently disbanded. Between 1793 and 1881 it was known as the 80th (Staffordshire Volunteers) Regiment of Foot. The regiment was represented at Isandlwana by the presence of one mounted infantry detachment. One of the survivors of the massacre was Private Samuel Wassal, who earned the Victoria Cross. Like the 24th Regiment, it had also had its fair share of ill luck through its long history. On three occasions the regiment was shipwrecked in troopships, at one time losing all its records and mess silver. Further, the regiment had been involved in the action at Myer's Drift, 5 miles beyond Luneberg, where the road crossed the Intombi River. Here at Myer's Drift, on 12 March 1879, a company of the 80th Regiment under Captain D. B. Moriarty, sent out to escort a convoy, was attacked by a strong force of Zulus and lost sixty-two men of all ranks, in addition to fifteen natives, two wagoners and the civilian surgeon, Cobbins. The 80th had served in South Africa in 1856 on the Eastern Frontier and subsequently in India and Ceylon, and returned to England from India in 1866. Between 1872 and 1877 it served in the Malacca Straits and China. In 1877 it proceeded to South Africa once again and served in the Sekukuni campaign. At the outbreak of the war in 1879 it was attached to the Reserve column of Colonel Rowlands, and was stationed at Luneberg, whence the main supply route between the Transvaal and Natal started. The regiment served at Ulundi in early July 1879.

88th (Connaught Rangers) Regiment of Foot (1793–1881)
Two previous regiments numbered the 88th were raised and disbanded prior to the raising of the Connaught Rangers. Between its raising in 1793 and 1881 the regiment was designated the 88th (Connaught Rangers) Regiment of Foot. The regiment's record of service was characterised by daring and its nickname of 'The Devil's Own' was conferred upon it by General Picton during the Peninsula War in response to the 88th's utter contempt for danger. The Duke of Wellington said of the regiment, 'I don't know what effect they will have upon the enemy, but, by God, they terrify me.' In 1810, at Bussaco, the regiment defeated a force five times its own strength. They served in the Crimean War and in India until 1870, then also in the Frontier War of 1877–788 in the Transkei. At the outbreak of the Zulu War the regiment was widely dispersed with its headquarters at King Williamstown, one company at St Helena (from where it sailed to South Africa on the HMS *Shah*), and three companies at Mauritius. After Isandlwana, the HQ and one company transferred to Pietermaritzburg, whilst the three companies marched to Fort Tenedos, where they acted as a reserve until after the relief of Eshowe. Three companies remained at Mauritius. The 88th served in Crealock's 1st Division during the second invasion of Zululand.

90th Perthshire Light Infantry (1794–1881)
Raised in 1794, the titles of the regiment have been the 90th Perthshire Volunteers between 1794 and 1815, and between 1815 and 1881 the 90th Perthshire Light Infantry. Its first colonel was Thomas Graham, Laird of Balgowan. During the Peninsula War, at Barrosa in 1811, Colonel Graham and the 90th Foot were abandoned by the Spanish, but nevertheless fought on and eventually defeated a vastly superior French force. It served with distinction during the Crimean War and during the Indian Mutiny, remaining in India until 1869. The regiment had previously served in South Africa in the Frontier War of 1846–47, and again on the Eastern Frontier in 1878, before being included in Colonel Evelyn Wood's column. The 90th served at Khambula and Ulundi.

91st (Princess Louise's Argyllshire) Highlanders (1794–1881)
The regiment was raised in 1794, and was preceded by three regiments also ranked as the 91st, which had all been disbanded

before the appearance of this one. Between 1794 and 1798 it was designated as the 91st (Argyllshire Highlanders) Regiment of Foot, and between 1809 and 1821 its designation was simply the 91st Regiment of Foot. During this period its distinctive title was probably discarded for the same reason that the Highland dress was abandoned at the same time – i.e. both were considered to be an impediment to recruiting. Between 1821 and 1864 it was known as the 91st (Argyllshire) Regiment of Foot; between 1864 and 1872 as the 91st (Argyllshire) Highlanders; and between 1872 and 1881 as the 91st (Princess Louise's (Argyllshire) Highlanders. In 1802 the regiment raised a 2nd Battalion in Scotland, but this was disbanded in 1816. The regiment had a the close association with South Africa. They had served in the Frontier War of 1846–47, and the wars of 1851–53, after which the senior battalion returned home. A smaller 2nd Battalion, which had been formed at the Cape, remained in the colony until 1856, when it was sent home and absorbed into the senior battalion. Its namesake regiment of 1794–96 had actually been raised in the Cape. Before the Zulu War, it had served in India until 1869 and was stationed at Aldershot when it received orders to proceed to South Africa. The 91st served at Gingindlovu and Ulundi.[18]

94th Regiment of Foot (1823-1881)
Between 1823 and 1881 the regiment was known as the 94th Regiment of Foot. Four previous regiments had been allocated the number 94 as their designation. The 94th served in Gibraltar and Malta from 1828 to 1834, and then for fifteen years continuously in India. In fact, a major portion of their operational career appears to be associated with the sub-continent. The regiment was back in England in 1854, but returned to Karachi in 1857 and served at Peshawar, on the North West Frontier, and in central India until 1868. During the Zulu War, it served at Ulundi in early July.

99th (The Duke of Edinburgh's) Regiment of Foot (1805–81)
The regiment was founded in 1824 as the 99th (Lanarkshire) Regiment of Foot, which remained its title between 1824 and 1874. Then, between 1874 and 1881 it was known as the 99th (The Duke of Edinburgh's) Regiment of Foot. They served in New Zealand from 1845 to 1847, and in China and Japan in the 1860s.

Thereafter they served in the Cape and Natal until its return home in 1869. It was still stationed at Chatham when, in November 1878, it received orders to sail for South Africa. During the Zulu War, the 99th served at Gingindlovu and Inyezane.

Naval Brigade (including the Royal Marines)

Naval Brigades had been engaged with the Army in various campaigns during the latter half of the nineteenth century, including the Indian Mutiny, the 1860 China War, the Abyssinian expedition of 1868, and the Ashanti War of 1873–74. During the course of the Zulu War, contingents from the HMS *Active, Shah, Tenedos* and *Boadicea* assisted the land forces at Inyezane, Khambula and Gingindlovu. With reference to the Royal Marines, founded in 1755, from 1664 a number of Line Regiments had served as marines for various periods, and a number of regiments were raised especially as Marines during the late seventeenth and first half of the eighteenth century. The present Corps of Royal Marines was raised by the Board of the Admiralty in 1755. In 1859 the RM were converted to a Light Corps, comprising separate divisions of Royal Marine Light Infantry and Royal Marine Artillery. The RMLI and RMA amalgamated as a single corps in 1923. In 1870 the abolition of the Woolwich division reduced the number of RMLI companies to three.

Commissariat and Transport Department and Army Service Corps (1875–)

The unit was formed in 1875 when the Control Department and the Army Service Corps were disbanded. The Commissariat and Transport Department were succeeded by the Commissariat and Transport Staff and Army Service Corps (1880–81), and the Commissariat and Transport Corps (1881–88). The department's personnel were closely involved in the Zulu campaign of 1879. One corporal and two privates of the unit were among the casualties of Isandlwana, whilst Acting Assistant Commissary James L. Dalton was awarded the Victoria Cross after his conduct at Rorke's Drift. Assistant Commissary W. A. Dunne and Acting Storekeeper W. A. Byrne were also present, together with three other ranks. In the final drive on Ulundi, General Crealock's Division included fifty personnel, General Newdigate's sixty, and General Wood's Flying Column, nine personnel from the department, which was therefore represented at Ulundi.

Ordnance Store Department (1875–)
This was the second department formed from the old Control
Department. There was a close relationship between the
Commissariat and Transport Department and Ordnance Store
Department. Both had formed components of the Control
Department. Prior to absorption into the Control Department, the
Ordnance Store Department's duties had been performed by the
Military Store Department and the Military Store Staff Corps. In
1877 the four companies performing Ordnance Store duties were
separated from the Supply and Iransport Companies and styled the
Ordnance Store Branch of the Army Service Corps.[19]

Army Medical Staff (or Army Medical Department) (1873–98)
The Army Medical Staff owes its existence as an independent
department to a royal warrant of 1873, which abolished the
appointment of regimental medical officers, subject to certain
conditions and reservations. A member of the Army Medical Staff,
Surgeon Major Reynolds, gained the Victoria Cross at Rorke's
Drift. Various works refer to Surgeon Major Reynolds as being a
member of the Army Hospital Corps, but there was a fundamental
distinction between the Army Medical Staff and the Army Hospital
Corps. Both were amalgamated into the Royal Army Medical
Corps in 1898. The citation to his Victoria Cross refers to his
being a member of the Army Medical Staff. During the Anglo-Zulu
War, Surgeon-General John Woolfryes broke his limited personnel
into small detachments with each column in the first invasion, and
personnel were present at all engagements, and then at Gingindlovu
with the Eshowe Relief Column. During the second invasion of
the war, they were attached to specific units and were present
at Ulundi. Personnel, assisted by a number of volunteer civilian
doctors, were in charge of the convalescent station at Pinetown, the
base hospitals in Durban, Pietermaritzburg, Ladysmith, Newcastle
and Utrecht, the hospital at Fort Pearson, and the field hospitals
with the forces operating in Zululand.[20]

Army Hospital Corps (1855–98)
The Medical Staff Corps was formed in 1855 and consisted of the
non-commissioned ranks of the Army's medical services. In 1857
this designation was changed to the Army Hospital Corps. In 1873,

when medical care in the British Army was brought under control of the Army Medical Department, the Army Hospital Corps was to provide trained orderlies. During the Anglo-Zulu War, when there was a serious lack of medical personnel even when reinforcements were brought in after Isandlwana, small detachments of orderlies were assigned to base hospitals and attached in the first invasion of the war to the various columns, and in the second invasion to particular units. They were consequently present at all the major engagements of the campaign. During the Anglo-Zulu War, the corps was armed with Martini-Henry rifles.[21]

Note: The Bearer Corps

During the Anglo-Zulu War, there were not enough orderlies in the Army Hospital Corps to adequately staff the base and field hospitals. Thus, African auxiliaries were recruited during the second invasion of the Anglo-Zulu War to help bring in the wounded to field hospitals and to the convalescent facilities in Natal. The wounded were transported in hammocks slung between poles that two bearers supported on their shoulders. These bearers were present at the Battle of Ulundi in early July.

Final Notes on the Imperial Regiments

It is interesting to note the large number of regiments that had previous experience of serving in South Africa at the time of the Zulu War in 1879, namely the 13th, 24th, 80th, 90th and 99th Regiments. This suggests not only that South Africa was the source of recurring military crises, but also that colonial defence continued to be inadequate to meet these crises throughout the nineteenth century. The reasons for such a reluctance by the South African colonists, especially in Natal where the system of commando service had been unpopular, to organise regular forces on a large scale were dealt with in the section on the colonial units on pages 42-3.

Another point is that the British Army that served in the Zulu War campaign of 1879 was a fledgeling and still imperfect version of the force that was to serve in the First World War (1914–18) and Second World War (1939–1945). The outstanding anomalies that separate the British Army of 1914 to 1945 from the Victorian army of the Zulu War had been removed during the course of the

1870s. The purchase of commissions had been abolished by the Regulation of the Forces Act (1871), which had also centralised control of the militia and volunteers, removing them from the former authority of the Lords-Lieutenant of the counties. So the Regular Army had finally been absorbed into one military system. Similarly, the War Office Act had subordinated the Commander-in-Chief to the Secretary of State for War, as the latter's principal military adviser – as in the case of Lord Chelmsford having been subordinated to Sir Garnet Wolseley.[22]

6

WAITING FOR WAR

In various military posts around Natal, soldiers were waiting for things to happen. One way of passing the time was to write letters to their loved ones at home, and it is from these letters that we have been able to learn about their observations of the country, especially Natal, their recollections of battles, their fears and frustrations. Sergeant John Lines of the 2/24th, a long-service soldier, was stationed at Pietermaritzburg by October 1878 and even then was very worried about the British prospects ahead: 'The Zulus have about 40 thousands of a standing army, and we have only about 6 thousand Europeans and 9 thousand volunteers (mostly Natal native levies), so I think we shall lose a good many, for they are too strong for us. And these Kaffirs are a very barbarous lot; if they catch a man wounded they cut him open and take out his heart and eat it. Africa is a very heathen place, much more so than England. You can get land for about 4 shillings an acre, and some of it good land.'[1]

A young subaltern of the 90th Light Infantry, Robert Black Fell, was enjoying his first posting overseas. The plentiful wildlife appealed to his sporting instinct as he marched up country, carrying the regimental colour, from Pietermaritzburg in the early days of November 1878. 'The buck we have seen since landing are hartebeest near Sundays River and on the Buffalo flats, also reebok, oribi, duiker, and some wildebeest. The hartebeest is a splendid animal, the reebok is the commonest, they utter a bark like a dog. The reebok were hard to find, but have pretty horns.

The only herd of wildebeest we saw are curious looking beggars, on seeing us they went off flourishing their heels and tails and cutting wonderful capers. The buck do give a jump when the rifle bullet comes under ... Utrecht [where Fell's march ended] has a laager for the Boers in case of a Zulu war, a few houses and a big store and a court-house. There is a vlei close by and a stream comes down from the Burghers' Pass, which is thickly covered with thorn trees. There is an infernal duststorm blowing now, it is an awful place for sand storms, and seems to be always blowing a gale. The sandflies are in such swarms that one can hardly see two feet in front of you ... The Boers say there are still occasional lions on the veldt between here and the Pongola bush. I made friends with a Boer called Uys living at Uys Kop, and he took me out guinea-fowl shooting but also shot reebok.'[2]

On New Year's Day 1879, Fell was stationed at Van Rooyen's Farm and getting ready to take part in Chelmsford's Zululand campaign. 'An old hunter named Rathbone and the Dutch leader Piet Uys, who has joined us with his clan, told us all about the Zulus. This little farm is in a comfortable position and has a very good orchard, garden, and an avenue of eucalyptus trees. The old Boer owner is a famous hunter, of course we eat what we want as he has trekked with his family too, gone into laager to avoid the Zulus ... We have been having the most terrific thunderstorms lately. At Balters Spruit the other day tents were struck, the lightning running down the tent-poles, splitting the rifles, fusing cartridges, destroying pouches and belts, and knocking men over. None of them were killed by it.'[3]

Returning to Bemba's Kop from a raid down the Buffalo Valley, Fell wrote: 'We revenged our troubles in a way by taking 8,000 head of cattle besides sheep and goats from the scattered kraals around. It is simply marvellous what herds these kraals possess. I was on day picquet by one of them, the Zulus seemed friendly and gave me some milk. They were fine looking people ... Zululand as far as we have seen it is destitute of wood and undulating, some of the hills pretty high, and covered with luxuriant grass on which our cattle and horses fatten splendidly.'[4]

Private Owen Ellis was a veteran of the 1st Battalion, 24th Regiment, and son of Mr. Thomas Ellis of Caernarvon. On 31 December 1878, he wrote from the military post at Helpmekaar to his family in North Wales. The name was derived from the Afrikaans 'help each other', from transport riders having had to assist each other in making a road over a nearby hill. Apart from being clearly awed by the regular thunder and lightning of the countryside, and a very heavy hailstorm over the area, he also reported on military developments at the post.

In this spot, Helpmekaar, the days are as fine as those of summer, but we meet every night with heavy rains, accompanied by thunder and lightning, which continue until six o'clock in the morning. On 12th December there fell a heavy shower of hailstones which were as large as your fists, making it dangerous for anyone to be out at the time. One of them, weighed by the bandmaster, was three ounces in weight. I saw a hen that had been killed by the shower. There is very good cattle pasture here, far better than what is on the other side, viz. Transkei, and this is beneficial to the farmers...The second battalion of the 24th Regiment arrived here about 4 o'clock on Sunday afternoon. They came from Grey Town [Greytown, Natal] and the first battalion welcomed them by treating them to tea and bread and meat. There are also here three companies of the Cape mounted police and many volunteers ... King Cetywayo has a brother who is a great chief of the Zulus. This chief resides about ten miles from this place and he has about 2,000 Zulus under his command. He has proclaimed against his brother and has allied with the British Government to fight against him. The Government has supplied his fighting men with Martini rifles and ammunition. If Cetywayo does not come to terms, we will demand his lands, kill his people as they come across our path and burn all his kraals. The Zulu chief claims the title of King and this is his reason for making war against his brother, Cetywayo. The chief is acquainted with every hole and corner in the country and he will remain with the English army unless a reply from the King is received by the appointed day. The farmers who live in the surrounding country say that the Zulus will only be tempted to fight the Europeans once and that they will afterwards fly away for their lives, because they have not the weapons which we have ...

Two thousand Zulus have now arrived here. They are those that intend fighting against King Cetywayo. They were met by the band of the 1st Battalion of the 24th Regiment and were played into camp. The leader of the Zulus, King Cetywayo's brother, appears to be a very stalwart fellow. We had a splendid sight of the two thousand Zulus marching; they have now encamped above us on a little hill.[5]

His 2/24th comrade, George Morris, while waiting for Chelmsford's Third Column to assemble for the invasion, wrote to his mother at Pontypool. 'I never seen such lightning in my life as in this country. I wish I was a civilian here for some time. I could soon save a lot of money as wages are very good here, and provisions not very dear. I suppose by the time or before you receive this we shall be on active operations against the Zulus, and they are very numerous and well armed, but God protect the right. There are lots of wild animals around here, deer, tigers [leopards], jackals and poisonous snakes; the mosquitoes are a regular nuisance.'[6] Morris would be one of the casualties of the Battle of Isandlwana.

Two weeks later, Private Ellis again wrote to his to his family from Rorke's Drift where they had been posted in the meantime, having already crossed the Buffalo River a few days earlier:

Since the time I sent you my last letter I have removed about ten miles inland viz., to the border of Zululand. We are about to march from this place at an early date in order to proceed through and occupy the country of the Zulus, inasmuch as King Cetywayo did not submit to the terms demanded by the British Government. It is now too late for him as we have crossed the Buffalo River by means of pontoons. Rorke's Drift is the name by which the place where we crossed is known. Sooner the better we march through Cetywayo's country, as we have about one hundred miles to travel from this locality to the place where the King resides, viz., the 'Grand Kraals'. After arriving there, the Queen's flag will be hoisted and King Cetywayo will be made into atoms if captured by us and unless he has escaped like Kreli[7]. Several English magistrates have come with us in order to be appointed to magisterial offices in Zululand and to administer the English law in that country. This war will be over in two months' time and then we shall all be hurrying towards England.

We are about to capture all the cattle belonging to the Zulus and also to burn their kraals; and if they dare to face us with the intention of fighting, well, woe be to them! As in Transkei formerly they shall be killed as they come across us. We intend starting nine days hence from Rorke's Drift for the "Grand Kraals" where King Cetywayo resides ... The order of march is as follows: – Firstly, there is Cetywayo's brother with 2,000 of his fighting men well armed with rifles and ammunition; secondly, 500 mounted men with rifles; thirdly, a battery belonging to the artillery with six 6-pounders; fourthly, 500 Cape Mounted Police; fifthly, 1 – 24th Regiment; and sixthly, 2 – 24th Regiment. All much at a distance from each other as you see the militia do in companies. There is another column about to start simultaneously within about seventy miles of this place, so as to meet together. This column which starts from a place called Utrecht, consisting of the 80th and the 3rd Buffs Regiments. Another column comprising the 90th and 13th Regiments depart from a place called Stanzer [Stanger]; therefore, you will observe that all the troops will meet each other at the Grand Kraals. General Thesiger [Lord Chelmsford] is with us and he has remained with us since the time we left Pietermaritzburg.

All our clothes or kits have been sent down to Durban ... We have only enough clothes to change, viz. two shirts, two pairs of stockings, two pairs of trousers, etc. Our best clothes have been packed on board the ship at Durban. There are only seventeen days' rations for every man; so I think that we shall not be a long time doing our work. I know that we shall arrive at the Grand Kraals in about a week's time ... We have already captured 1,300 head of animals, comprising cattle, horses and goats ... The bands of the first and second battalions of the 24th Regiment have been sent to Durban, where they will await our return to proceed on board the ship, whenever that will take place.

I am happy to tell you that all the boys and myself are in excellent health.[8]

He wrote again four days later on 19 January. It had transpired that roadmaking across the marshy Bashee Valley had to be done before the advance could continue, but as the work had progressed well, Lord Chelmsford could order the advance by the next day. The letter read:

I send you this letter in order that you may understand that we are shifting from Rorke's Drift at 6 a.m. tomorrow morning, the 20th of January for the Grand Kraals of King Cetywayo and perhaps it will take us a week or nine days to reach that place. All the regiments, viz. nine regiments besides the Artillery, the Cavalry and the Cape Mounted Police will meet each other at the Grand Kraals and occupy the country and appoint English magistrates to administer the law unless Cetywayo will submit to the terms now laid before him. Not a single word has yet been received from him but it is said that he is willing to conform to every demand except one and that is giving up his arms. The English Government will therefore do with him as was done with Kreli and Sandili in Transkei ...

We had a sermon on the field this morning. The 1-24th Regiment, the 2-24th Regiment, the Artillery, the Cape Mounted Police and the Cavalry had formed themselves into a square, with the chaplain, General Thesiger [Lord Chelmsford] and all the staff officers in the centre, the drum constituting the pulpit ...

After this war is over we shall not be barely a fortnight before reaching Cape Town ... It is said that we shall embark at Durban and take up the wives in passing ... If they would only finish with this row so that I might go to some town where I could see something besides grass land! I should like to go to Cape Town rather than Durban because there are fine barracks at that place and a large town too in which one may see something; but, never mind, we shall not be long before going to Cape Town or Durban and if I have time to write a line or two before embarking, I will send to let you know a

little about the history of the journey, how I came through it
and other minor matters ...

P.S. Perhaps I shall be for a long time after this without
writing; therefore, don't be uneasy about a letter. I will send
as early as possible. Good afternoon.[9]

This turned out to be Private Ellis's final letter. The *North Wales
Express* of 7 March 1879 carried an editorial note stating that
'The official list of the officers and privates of the ill-fated 24th
Regiment who were killed at the battle of Isandula [Isandlwana],
Zululand, was published yesterday. Among the names which
include those of many Welshmen we find that of Private Owen
Ellis ... The deceased soldier with several other young men from
this town, joined the 24th Regiment about five years ago.'[10]

As one of Evelyn Wood's staff, Captain Edward Woodgate was
an experienced officer (who had relatives in the colony) who had
direct responsibilities for bringing the Fourth Column, based at
Utrecht, into a state of readiness for war. He therefore looked
closely at the local resources of transport, fodder and roads, as
well as building up the intelligence system of spies and advisers.
Natal suffered serious droughts in the late 1870s, and Woodgate's
observations were useful in assessing their effects. The summer and
winter of 1878 were very dry, so when Woodgate rode up-country
in September that year, he found little grazing along the last 40 miles
of road before Ladysmith, where 'all the country is dried up. People
are all anxiously looking out for rain, which ought to commence
this month'. But the rains did not come, and the ground remained
'as dry as a piece of toast and as hard as a turnpike road'. There
was a little rain that fell on 11 October but this had little effect, and
for the next five weeks the grass showed no signs of flourishing.
Only by 27 November at Utrecht could Woodgate say that the
drought had broken: 'I don't think it has reached Natal yet, but the
country is beginning to look less brown than it was; when the sun
is shining on the hills, it is just possible to distinguish a very slight
greenish tinge.'[11] The shortage of fodder for oxen, horses and mules
certainly contributed to the slowness of the British preparation for
the war along the Zulu borders. The drought years also heightened
the competition for grazing by Boer and Zulu in these disputed
lands, which was a prime cause of the war.

Woodgate also visited the townships of Natal and his observations are revealing. Ladysmith had originated in 1850 when a trickle of settlers reached the Klip River farmlands, and Woodgate coomented: 'It would be called a village in England and consists of about 25 houses of one kind or another. It has been going some 20 years, consequently the timber is pretty well grown, but the town itself progresses slowly.' When he went to buy wagons and oxen at Wesselstroom, he found 'two small hotels, about the size of fifth-rate pot-houses in England, about three shops, and a dozen other houses. It is called a town, being the only collection of houses in the district, the nearest other towns being Newcastle and Utrecht, each about 30 miles off; they are a little bigger than this place...The country is very thinly populated. I only passed two houses, and three small Kaffir villages, yesterday during my ride from Utrecht.'[12] Woodgate went on to fight in the Anglo-Boer War (1899–1902) as Major General, and was fatally wounded at the famous Battle of Spioenkop.

7

THE BATTLE OF INYEZANE

Most people tend to associate the Anglo-Zulu War more with epic battles such as Isandlwana and Rorke's Drift, and the skirmish on the Ityotyosi River in which the Prince Imperial of France and son of Napoleon III met an unfortunate and untimely death. The importance of the Battle of Inyzane, however, should not be underestimated. It in fact took place on the same day as the bloody events at Isandlwana and Rorke's Drift. Today, the old battlefield lies in the heart of KwaZulu Natal's sugar cane belt and much of it has unfortunately been ploughed under.

Mention has already been made of the expiry of the ultimatum to Cetshwayo, and the deployment of the various columns commanded by Lord Chelmsford. Of these columns, the First Column (also called the Coastal Column), under the command of Colonel Charles Knight Pearson, invaded Zululand upon the expiry of the ultimatum, at the Lower Drift across the Tugela on Sunday 12 January 1879. Heavy rains had turned the river into a wide and sluggish expanse of muddy water and the crossing turned out to be a difficult exercise. Their first mission was to construct a large earth-walled fort on the Zulu side of the Tugela, opposite Fort Pearson, the headquarters of the colonial troops' coastal division. Fort Pearson itself was situated on top of a high cliff face overlooking the Tugela River and the crossing that was used by the British troops. From this high point the soldiers had excellent views over the river, the ocean and a large part of what was then Zululand territory.

The new fort on the Zululand side of the river was named Fort Tenedos after the British warship that was anchored off the mouth of the Tugela, the crew of which formed part of the column's Naval Brigade. The fort was built under the supervision of Captain W. R. C. Wynne, Royal Engineers, and it was large enough to shelter the entire column under Pearson in the event of a possible Zulu attack.

At the time, eighteen-year-old William John Sawdon Newmarch of the Natal Hussars wrote to his father, George William Newmarch, a colonist who came to South Africa in 1849. The letter was dated a day before they were to cross into Zululand. 'We got down from Grott Spruit and we will cross over into the Zulu country in a day or two. The Barrow horse and the Victoria Mounted Rifles cross tomorrow morning [12 January]. This morning a lot of niggers gathered together opposite the fort and as it was a nice chance for the Blue Jackets to try their Armstrong guns they fired two shells at them. The first shell dropped a little beyond them and exploded, the second dropped in the midst of them but did not explode. But for all that it sent them running off like mad. I am in very good health at present and have quite recovered from the fever I had in Durban.'[1]

After crossing the Tugela River on the 12th, young Newmarch and his comrades were involved in a skirmish with the Zulus. Cavalry patrols penetrated 10 miles into the countryside without encountering any opposition, before Major Barrow stumbled on a dozen warriors who threw down their shields and assegais and tried to run as he pounced on them with the Natal Hussars. He captured five of them; 'One complained bitterly that 200 mounted men were not fair odds for a dozen men afoot, and he promised them better sport further along.'[2]

The Pearson Column consisted of the 2nd Battalion of the East Kent Regiment (the 'Buffs'), the 99th Regiment (the Duke of Edinburgh's Lanarkshire Regiment), the Naval Brigade from HMS *Active* and HMS *Tenedos*, two guns from the Royal Artillery, two 7-pounder guns with the Naval Brigade, a Gatling gun, various local imperial units consisting of the Natal Hussars, the Durban Mounted Rifles, Alexandra Mounted Rifles, Stanger Mounted Rifles and the Victoria Mounted Rifles. The Natal Hussars were a unit founded in 1865 for the protection of the districts of

Greytown, York and Noodsberg in the Natal Midlands, and would have been well suited for their scouting duties.[3] There were also around 2,200 Natal natives formed into two battalions of the 2nd Regiment, Natal Native Contingent, and a company of Col Durnford's Natal Native Pioneer Corps.

Col Pearson set out from Fort Tenedos in the early morning of 18 January, en route to the Zulu stronghold Ulundi, via Eshowe. Due to the fact that the rivers were in flood, he made slow progress from the Tugela, and it was only possible for one wagon at a time to get across. His column spent the night encamped on the banks of the Inyoni River. On the 19th, they crossed the Umzundusi and on the 20th, the advance party of the column reached the Amatikulu River, which was the largest since the crossing of the Tugela. As some of the wagons were still crossing the Inyoni River, Pearson decided to camp there to allow the rest of the column to catch up. Considering the difficulty of the drift, he ordered Capt. Wynne and his Royal Engineers to improve the approaches, and spent the entire day in camp.

The column crossed the Amatikulu on the following day, 21 January, and Pearson made sure that his route ahead was thoroughly scouted. Pearson's advance parties reached the old Zulu kraal Gingindlovu, which was established by Cetshwayo after his victory over Mbulazi at the Battle of Ndondakusuka in 1856. The British soldiers, who had problems with the Zulu pronunciation, liked to call it 'gin, gin, I love you!' As the kraal was deserted, the soldiers set fire to it. Pearson established a camp nearby, about 4 miles from the Inyezane River.[4]

The column crossed the Inyezane on 22 January, the same day that Chelmsford's main column found itself at Isandlwana. The mounted troops under the command of Major Percy Barrow, 19th Hussars, scouted the land across the Inyezane River and on returning informed Pearson that they had found a reasonably flat area where the column could halt until the wagons had been brought across. This position lay below the Wombane Hill, which formed the right spur of a high E-shaped ridge, in the foothills of the high range of hills upon which Eshowe is situated.[5] At Eshowe, a mission station was established in 1861 after permission was obtained from Cetshwayo by the Norwegian missionary Reverend Ommund Oftebro. The station later became the KwaMondi Mission Station after the Zulu name that was given to Oftebro.

Pearson's men had their breakfast (bully beef and biscuits) here near the Wombane Hill, and whilst the troops were having a break and the first of the wagons were crossing the Inyezane River, a number of Zulus were seen on the summit of the centre spur. Pearson immediately ordered Lt Reginald Hart, Royal Engineers, to take his company of the Natal Native Contingent (NNC) up this ridge to pursue them. These men set off, but the NNC were armed with only ten rifles, half of them obsolete, and the remainder of the troops carried assegais. To make things worse, there was a serious communication problem between officers and their men, none of them being able to converse in the other's language.

Hart's men went up the hill along the wagon track to Eshowe but before they could reach the top, the Zulus disappeared off the centre spur and moved through the ravine separating the side spurs. They only reappeared some distance away on the right spur, Wombane. Leaving the track, Hart sent his men charging through the dense bush into the ravine to ascend the right spur, where they regrouped. Now a large number of Zulu impi appeared, hardly a hundred yards ahead, causing Hart's men to rush back into the ravine and scramble for the centre spur, and then the campsite.

Intent on attacking the campsite from the flanks and then overrunning the wagons, the Zulus rushed headlong into the white officers and some of the black NCOs still left on the right spur, who still tried to make a stand. In this brief whirl of fighting, Lts J. L. Raines, G. Platterer and six NCOs were killed, while Lt Webb and one NCO were wounded. Raines's body was so riddled with stab wounds that 'It would have been impossible to place your hand anywhere on his body without covering one,' an observer noted later.

At the time that the first Zulu warriors had reached the foot of the right spur, the rear were still spread out along the crest; these men were now targeted by the infantry and the men of the Naval Brigade, under Commander Campbell. Maj. Barrow's mounted troops turned their fire upon the head of the impi, which had swung right at the bottom of the spur and was closing in on the rest of the column, and were joined in timely fashion by Capt. Wynne and his Royal Engineers who had earlier been working on the drift.

The guns under the command of Lt Lloyd had also been brought into action and were firing devastating volleys onto Zulus still on the spur, while the Gatling gun, manned by a few sailors under nineteen-year-old Midshipman Lewis C. Coker, started spraying death at 300 rounds a minute into the now less aggressive Zulus. In the meantime, another group of Zulus had taken up position in a kraal further up the track on the centre spur, and Commander Campbell, supported by Lt Hart's white survivors, directed his fire at these Zulus, with supporting fire from Lt Lloyd's guns, which had ceased firing on the Zulus on the right spur. The bombardment eventually set the kraal alight and in the resulting confusion the Naval Brigade and one company of the Buffs succeeded in occupying it.

Some fifty years after the war, chief Zimema of the uMxapho *ibutho*, recalled how frightening it had been for the Zulus to face these bombardments: 'They brought out there by-and-by [artillery] and we heard what we thought was a long pipe coming through the air toward us ... We never got nearer than 50 paces to the English, and although we tried to climb over our fallen brothers, we could not get very far ahead because the white men were firing heavily closer to the ground while the by-and-by was firing over our heads into the regiments behind us ... The battle was so fierce that we had to wipe the blood and brains of the killed and wounded from our heads, faces, arms and legs and shields after the fighting.'[6]

Once these Zulus lost heart they retreated and, along with those fellow warriors who were retreating up the right spur, disappeared into the surrounding hills. These men, totalling some 6,000, had consisted of five regiments, the veteran iziNgulube, the iQhwa, the umxhapho, izinGwegwe and the inSukamgeni. Led by the aged uMatyiya, they apparently intended to ambush Pearson's Column as it crossed the Inyezane Drift, employing a three-pronged attack from the three spurs of Wombane Hill. Fortunately, because of Lt Hart's reconnaissance, the intended ambush was sprung prematurely; the loins and left horn had been checked, while the right horn that had to attack from the left spur was not yet ready. It was estimated that some 350 Zulus died in the battle. Many of their wounded lay in the open until they died of loss of blood, shock or exposure, and members of British convoys still found men alive several days afterwards.

Colonel Pearson ordered the ceasefire at around 9:30. His column halted briefly for the ten men who had been killed in the battle to be buried; there were also sixteen men wounded. They continued up the difficult track and near the summit of the range made one more halt to allow the forces – strung out over a distance of 5 miles – to regroup. The column reached Eshowe on the morning of 23 January, where Pearson chose Revd Martin Oftebro's deserted mission station, named KwaMondi, as his camp site. Two days later, they started to erect earthworks according to a plan drawn up by Capt. Wynne, which were completed some days later. The oblong-shaped fort was 200 metres long, 50 metres wide, with 2-metre-high earth walls and surrounded by a ditch over 2 metres deep. The buildings of the mission station were also incorporated into these defences.

On the morning of 25 January, two companies of the Buffs and the 99th Regiment escorted forty-eight wagons out of the fort to collect supplies from Fort Pearson. Hardly had they left before Pearson received information of the massacre at Isandlwana and the death of Col Durnford. The last time Pearson had heard of Durnford, the latter had been at Middle Drift. Pearson had the impression that the Second Column at Jamieson's Drift, about 55 miles upstream from Fort Pearson, had been attacked with disastrous consequences, and it dawned on him that a massive Zulu force lay between him and Kranskop, as was reported, and that there was nothing to stop this Zulu force from invading Natal.

On the 28th, Pearson received a message from Lord Chelmsford in Pietermaritzburg with the details of the disaster at Isandlwana. Chelmsford also advised Pearson to prepare himself for an attack by the entire Zulu army, and if he decided to stay at Eshowe at all, his men should strike their tents and use the wagons for shelter. Consequently, Pearson called his officers together and it was then decided to withdraw from Eshowe. However, while this meeting had been in progress, Pearson received another message that wagonloads of supplies were close by and that he would then have sufficient stores and ammunition to withstand a major Zulu attack, or a prolonged siege. To lighten the burden of his supplies, Pearson began to send unnecessary equipment back to Fort Pearson, and on 29 January, Major Barrow returned to Fort Pearson with all the mounted men and the 2nd Regiment, NNC.

The *Natal Mercury* columnist expressed relief at being back on the Natal side of the border with Zululand: 'Early this morning the Victoria, the Stanger and the Hussars were punted over to Fort Pearson. We are now bivouacking on the heights above Fort Pearson. The heat was something intense, and we were all literally scorched. Thank goodness the volunteers are in Natal. The satisfaction expressed at our being on this side of the border is immense. It is no use denying it; to a man we are heartily thankful to be back here again all safe and well. What is yet before us it is idle to conjecture, but we shall be defending our own soil and not invading a savage country.'

Young William Newmarch (Natal Hussars) wrote to his mother on 2 February, telling her about their fight at Inyzane.

As soon as Colonel Pearson heard the news of Col. Glynn's men being killed he sent all the Volunteers and Mounted Inf[antry] back to Natal; and remained at Eshowe with with all the infantry comprising the 3rd Buffs, the 99th Regiment, the Naval Brigade and a company of Engineers. At Eshowe, Col Pearson can defy the whole of the Zulu nation, as he has had large earth works thrown up and deep ditches dug all round, and further he has set dynamite all around the fort connected by an electric battery. The Naval Brigade have 4 large guns and 2 Rocket tubes and a couple of Gatlings with them, which are now on the walls of Fort Eshowe. At Eshowe they have provisions for two months.

In my last letter of either the 23rd or 24th of Jan I told you of our having a battle with the Zulus in which 8 white men were killed being officers of the native contingent and soldiers, and that 13 were wounded out of which 3 have died since. Over three hundred (300) of the Zulus were killed.[7]

The countryside was swarming with pockets of Zulus who followed the force back but made no attempt to attack. Due to lack of grazing within the confines of the fort at Eshowe, Pearson decided to send back the more than 1,200 oxen gathered earlier by Chelmsford, but within an hour of leaving the camp, 900 were captured by the Zulus. In the following days, fewer messengers were arriving from Fort Tenedos and Fort Pearson; but Pearson was still able now and then to heliograph back to Fort Pearson from Mbomboshana, a hill south of the fort at KwaMondi.

Pearson's force now consisted of about 1,300 white fighters and 400 black drivers and conductors. In the light of his situation, Pearson sent a message to Lord Chelmsford to advise him of his predicament. At the same time he requested reinforcements of seven additional companies of infantry. Chelmsford replied a week later that he had no reinforcements available and that Pearson should withdraw from Eshowe. Pearson was aware that it would be impossible to withdraw all at once and therefore asked permission to withdraw the bulk of his force in stages, and then to leave a group small enough to guard the fort and subsist on the rations available. Pearson's message never reached Chelmsford, however, as the Zulus had effectively sealed off all access to and from Fort Eshowe. This was the only time during the Zulu War that the Zulus – armed mainly with assegais – were able to pin down a British force armed with rifles and even a Gatling gun.[8]

The siege was destined to last for another two months, before Pearson was to be relieved by Lord Chelmsford and Major General Henry Hope Crealock on 3 April. Details of this period, however, will be described later.

During the long months of the Zulus' siege, many members of the garrison died of dysentery, enteric, and other fevers. There was also the occasional skirmish, of which the most notable was the one that took place on 13 February, when Pearson's men turned around and pursued the Zulu attacking force as far as the military kraal at Entamedi.

Colonel Wilford Neville Lloyd's Report: Action at Inyezane

'On the morning of the 22nd January 1879, No.1 Column, under the Command of Colonel C. K. Pearson, crossed the Inyezane River, prior to stopping for breakfast, and to feed and rest the oxen. At 8:00 a.m., as Colonel Pearson was giving orders about the pickets and scouts required, and as the wagons were being unloaded, the leading company of the Native Contingent, who were scouting in front, discovered the enemy advancing rapidly over the ridges to the front of the British position, and making for the bushes on either side. The Zulus at once opened a heavy fire on the men of the company who had shown themselves in the open, with the loss to the scouting party of one officer and seven men killed. As soon as the firing began, Colonel Pearson ordered the Naval Brigade, under Commander Campbell; the Division of Guns under Lieutenant Lloyd; and the Companies of the East Kent Regiment under the commands of Captain Jackson and Lieutenant Martin, to take up a position on a knoll close by the road, from where the whole of the Zulu advances could be seen and dealt with. With all the wagons now parked, and the length of the column sufficiently decreased, Colonel Pearson ordered two Companies of the East Kent Regiment, under the commands of Captain Harrison and Captain Wyld, and guided by Captain MacGregor, D.A.Q.M.G., to drive the approaching Zulus back into the open, thus exposing the enemy to the rockets, shells, and musketry from the knoll. This movement released the main body of the Mounted Infantry and Volunteers, who, with the Royal Engineers, had remained near the River Inyezane, to protect that section of the convoy of wagons. When thus released, both the Royal Engineers and the Mounted Troops moved forward with the infantry. At this stage the enemy was observed by Commander Campbell to be trying to outflank the British left, and he led a party from the Naval Brigade to drive away a body of Zulus who had got possession of a kraal about 400 yards from the knoll, and which was helping their turning movement. The Naval Brigade was supported by a party of the officers and non-commissioned officers of the Native Contingent under Captain Hart. With the kraal taken, the Naval Brigade, together with Colonel Parnell's company of the Buffs, attacked the heights beyond the kraal, upon which a considerable body of Zulus were still posted. The action was a complete success, and the Zulus fled in every direction. 'The practice made by Lieutenant Lloyd's guns, and by the rockets of the Naval Brigade, directed by Mr. Cotter, boatswain of H.M.S. Active, was excellent, and no doubt contributed materially to the success of the day.' (Colonel Pearson's despatch, dated 23.1.1879, refers). British casualties were 10 killed and 16 wounded. Zulu casualties were estimated at 300 killed out of a total force of about 4,000. The action was over by 9:30 a.m., and the stage was set for the rest of the day's events: the catastrophic defeat at Isandlwana, and the heroic defence of Rorkes Drift.'[9]

8

DISASTER AT ISANDLWANA

The backbone of Lord Chelmsford's British force consisted of twelve regular infantry companies – six each of the 1st and 2nd Battalions, 24th Regiment of Foot (2nd Warwickshire Regiment). These were hardened and experienced troops. In addition, there were about 2,500 local African auxiliaries of the Natal Native Contingent, of whom many were exiled or refugee Zulu, and serving under the command of European officers. They were generally considered by the British as of poor quality as they were prohibited from using their traditional fighting methods and were insufficiently trained in the European method, as well as being improperly armed. There were also some irregular colonial cavalry units, and a detachment of artillery consisting of six field guns and several Congreve rockets. Along with the wagon drivers, camp followers and servants, No. 3 Column numbered more than 4,000 men, but not including Colonel Durnford's No. 2 Column. Eager to accomplish their scheme, Sir Bartle Frere and Lord Chelmsford began the invasion of Zululand during the Natal rainy season, which had the serious drawback of slowing down the British advance considerably.[1]

The Zulu army organisation has already been discussed earlier, but suffice to say here that Zulu warriors were armed primarily with assegais, the *iklwa*, knobkerries, some throwing spears and shields made of cowhide. Some Zulus also had old muskets and antiquated rifles stockpiled, but their marksmanship was very poor, as was the quality and supply of powder and shot. The

British had timed the invasion to coincide with the Zulus' harvest, hoping to catch the Zulu warrior-farmers dispersed. Fortunately for Cetshwayo, the Zulu army had already begun to assemble at Ulundi for the yearly First Fruits ceremony when all warriors were obliged to report to their regimental barracks near Ulundi.[2]

On 17 January, Cetshwayo sent some 24,000 Zulu impi from near the present-day Ulundi across the White Umfolozi River with the command to 'March slowly, attack at dawn and eat up the red soldiers.'[3] The next day, some 4,000 warriors were detached from the main body to attack Charles Pearson's No. 1 Column near Eshowe, while the remaining 20,000 Zulus were gathered at the isiPhezi ikhanda. The main force arrived on the 19th, camped near Babanango Mountain and then moved to a camp near Siphezi Mountain. On 21 January they advanced into the Ngwebeni Valley where they were hiding with the plan to attack the British two days later. The next day, however, they were discovered by a British scouting party. The Zulu army was led by Ntshigwayo kaMahole and had marched in two columns within sight of each other, but far enough apart to prevent a surprise attack. A screening force of mounted scouts, supported by parties of warriors 200–400 strong, moved ahead with the task of preventing the main columns from being sighted. Their speed stood in stark contrast to that of the British; where the Zulu impi had advanced over 50 miles in five days, Chelmsford had only advanced about 10 miles in ten days.[4]

Chelmsford's force pitched camp at Isandlwana on 20 January. Isandlwana Hill itself is a remarkable shape, small in size by comparison with the hills round about, but standing out well from its surroundings. The camp was pitched along the eastern declivity and extended across the road, the tents of the 1st Battalion, 24th, being on the eastern slope of Black's Kopjie; next on their left, but on the other side of the road, those of the mounted infantry, Mounted Police and volunteers; then the Royal Artillery with six guns; next to them the tents of the 2nd Battalion, 24th; and on the extreme left the two battalions of the 3rd Natal Native Contingent. The tents of each corps were pitched in front of its wagons. The hospital and headquarters' tents were a little in rear of the wagons of the mounted troops and artillery. The camp thus faced the Izipezi Hill, having a slope in front intersected by water courses, wet and dry, and with broken ground on the flanks. Its line of picquets extended from a spur of the Ingutu range on its left to the right rear of Black's Kopjie on its right. While the position might have been good against European troops, it afforded no protection whatever against Zulus, who would move with a surprising agility and to whom the rocky broken ground on the flanks was no serious obstacle.[5]

Inexplicably, Chelmsford ignored standing orders to entrench. He also did not see the need for creating a laager, a circle of wagons for defence as the Boers used to employ, declaring that it would take too long. It was more the logistical arrangements which occupied Chelmsford's thoughts, as could be understood with a British force of this size. Rather than any fear that the camp might be attacked, his main concern was managing the huge number of wagons and oxen required to support his forward advance.

It appears at the same time that he had seriously underestimated the Zulus' fighting capabilities, based on the British experience of various colonial wars where the firepower of relatively small groups of troops with modern firearms and artillery had been too much for the poorly armed natives. Chelmsford must have reckoned that a force of over 4,000, including 2,000 British infantry armed with Martini-Henry rifles, as well as artillery, would have more than sufficient firepower to repel any attack by Zulus, who were only armed with spears and a few outdated firearms, such as Brown Bess muskets. He neither expected to remain at Isandlwana for long, nor that the Zulus would dare to attack his force.[6]

Chelmsford was later criticised for his choice of campsite at Isandlwana. The hill constitutes an isolated spur of the iNyoni ridge that frames it to the north, and rises some 300 feet above the plain. Dominating the landscape for several miles around, it offered a clear view should an enemy approach. At the same time there was no lack of water and firewood. However, his flanks remained a problem. Towards his left, the iNyoni heights obscured his view hardly a mile from his camp, although the surface of the heights was fairly open. On the right flank stood a high rocky hill named Malakatha, which blocked his view towards the Mzinyati downstream, while the Hlazakazi plateau stretched from the camp towards the head of the Mangeni Gorge. Chelmsford was aware that the Zulu army could sneak into the Mangeni Gorge and proceed down to the Mzinyati under cover of the hills.[7]

By the time he arrived at Isandlwana, the first reports reached him that the Zulu army had left oNdini three days before, with a substantial number advancing in his direction. While his troops were still unpacking their equipment from the supply wagons, Chelmsford set out with some of the staff to inspect the Mangeni Gorge from the shoulder of the Hlazakazi. Towards the horizon lay hills upon hills, but below them, the country seemed deserted. They nevertheless knew that it was possible for a whole army to hide in the wild and bushy countryside.[8]

Back in the camp, Chelmsford prepared to reconnoitre the Malakatha and Hlazakazi areas. For this task he depended on a squadron of regular mounted infantry and a few experienced Natal volunteers, including the Natal Mounted Police and Natal Carbineers. They were backed by two smaller units of the Newcastle Mounted Rifles and Buffalo Border Guard. Major John Dartnell, Commander of the Mounted Police, was instructed to thoroughly scout the heights. He was to be supported by the 3rd Regiment, NNC, commanded by Commandant Rupert Lonsdale, a veteran of the Cape Frontier Wars.

They set out at dawn on 21 January. Having looked for signs of the enemy in the hills, they were to rendezvous at the head of the Mangeni Gorge before returning to the camp before dark. The NNC had a difficult march over rough and broken country of large boulders and thick bush in hot temperatures. Disappointingly, they only succeeded in capturing a few herdboys and girls. At the top of Mangeni Gorge they met up with Dartnell's mounted men as planned. The latter had been scouting the hills towards Siphezi and further towards oNdini. Here one group encountered a group of several hundred Zulus, who retired quickly and disappeared among the hills. Dartnell now ordered the NNC onto a secure position on the Hlazakazi ridge, while he took his mounted men into the hills at the head of the Mangeni Gorge. However, the horsemen had only covered a few hundred yards when a group of several hundred Zulus suddenly appeared over the skyline facing them. They advanced rapidly with the horns on either side, then halted and disappeared over the hill as soon as they had appeared.

Wisely, Dartnell decided not to pursue them as he suspected that they were luring him into a trap. As it was getting dark and marching back to Isandlwana could expose his men to an attack in the rear, Dartnell decided to join the NNC with his cavalry and sent a message back to Chelmsford, explaining that he had to stay out overnight in the light of what he had seen of the Zulus. The message reached Chelmsford at 1:30 in the morning, confirming his suspicion that the Zulus were where he expected them to be.[9]

Realising that he could not expect to advance his entire force to confront them in time, he ordered more or less half of his command to march out, with himself in charge. His force consisted of most of the 2/24th Regiment and four guns from the N/5 Battery. With nothing to slow him down, he left behind the camp equipment with a strong force to guard it, only taking ambulances. He was hoping to reach Dartnell at daybreak.

Chelmsford also ordered one of his columns under the command of Colonel Durnford at Rorke's Drift, previously positioned at the Middle Drift on the Tugela, to move up to Isandlwana. Chelmsford's group moved out around 2:30 in the morning of 22 January, leaving behind in the camp five companies of the 1/24th Regiment, two guns under the command of major Stuart Smith, about 130 mounted men and several companies of the 3rd NNC, although under the command of Lieutenant Colonel Henry Pulleine of the 1/24th. While Pulleine had served through much of the last Frontier War, he had never commanded troops in action before.[10]

Chelmsford's reached the Mangeni Valley just after dawn, but by now the Zulus had disappeared, only small groups to be seen here and there on the hilltops. The rest seemed to have moved in the direction of the Siphezi Mountain. Dartnell's mounted men were sent to scout the surrounding hills, with the NNC and 24th companies in pursuit of the remaining Zulus. It resulted in only sporadic skirmishing here and there.

At about 6 a.m., back at the camp at Isandlwana, a large body of the Zulus suddenly appeared on the crest of the Inyoni ridge to the left of the camp, but they made no attempt to advance down the escarpment to attack. Pulleine immediately ordered the 1/24th to form up on the parade grounds in front of the camp tents. After a while, the Zulus disappeared out of sight beyond the crest. Pulleine sent scouts onto the ridge, who informed him that the Zulus were heading north-west.[11]

About 10:30, Colonel Durnford arrived at the camp with some 250 men of the Natal Native Horse and a section of two Royal Artillery 9-pounder rocket tubes, and supported by infantry of the NNC. He allowed his men to off-saddle and suggested to Pulleine he allow his 24th to stand down. Durnford was technically superior in rank to Pulleine, but Chelmsford's original order was unclear on this point with no new orders waiting for Durnford here at the camp.

Durnford considered Chelmsford's situation, fearing that the Zulu presence on the iNyoni heights might pose a danger, with the Mangeni Gorge 12 miles away across the plain and a large body of Zulus that may try and cut off Chelmsford from the camp at Isandlwana. The latter had no supplies or reserve ammunition with him. Durnford now decided to take his own men out to search the iNyoni range, hoping to drive any Zulus away from Chelmsford, as well as the camp. He also asked for a company of the 24th, but Pulleine was reluctant to agree since his orders had been specifically to defend the camp.

Durnford left the camp at about 11:30, an hour after his arrival. His baggage wagons only arrived at the camp after he had left. Durnford divided his command in two, sending two troops of the NNH under lieutenants Raw and Roberts onto the ridge at a spur closest to Isandlwana, while a company of the 24th under captain Cavaye came up to the top of the escarpment to support Durnford. Durnford moved straight across the plain with the rest of his command, along the foot of the escarpment curving to the left. The strategy was that the two groups would join up again north-east of Isandlwana.[12]

When they were up on the heights, Lieutenants Raw and Roberts looked across several miles of grassy plateau, spotting small groups of retiring Zulus here and there. These were pursued by the mounted men. Catching sight of a group of Zulu herdboys trying to drive some cattle over a rocky rise, Raw's men gave chase. But having crossed the rise, they got the shock of their lives. Looking down into the valley below, they saw about 24,000 Zulu warriors, of which the closest were only 200 to 300 yards away. These men had left their camping site at the foot of Siphezi early on the 21st, and made their way here in small groups. They did not intend to attack that day, but with Raw's men suddenly showing up they sprang into action, running up the slope. Raw's men fired a volley into the onrushing warriors, retreated to join Roberts's group who was coming up behind, and both troops rushed back to the camp at Isandlwana.

At the same time the Zulu army poured out of the Ngwebeni Valley, soon adopting the traditional chest and horns formation. Some 4 miles away, at the foot of Isandlwana, Pulleine was unaware of the mighty force advancing on him and his men. Raw immediately sent out messengers to both Pulleine at the camp and Durnford, several miles out around the foot of the escarpment. On receipt of the message, Pulleine sent a further company of the 1/24th under Mostyn to support that of Cavaye now positioned on the ridge. These men being out of sight, Pulleine had no idea of the extent of their engagement with the Zulus. Captain Edward Essex, one of the few officers to survive the Battle of Isandlwana, went up there on to the hills with Mostyn, and later described that from the crest of a rise he had seen Cavaye's men in open order on the slope below him, firing at a line of Zulus coming around from behind a hill and moving across their front. Even though the 24th kept up a sustained fire, the Zulus' advance was not checked and they moved rapidly around their flank, deploying their right horn manoeuvre.[13]

Colonel Durnford found himself miles away from the camp, his rocket battery and escorting NNC infantry still lagging behind and out of his sight. He was rounding the foot of the escarpment when Raw's messenger found him. He had hardly received the report when a large body of warriors, actually the left horn, suddenly appeared only a few hundred yards away. Durnford immediately ordered his men into line, who dismounted and started firing a volley into the advancing Zulus. They then mounted up and started retreating back in the direction of the camp at Isandlwana. They had to stop and repeat the manoeuvre every few hundred yards, with the enemy at times only 50 yards away.

In the meantime, Major Russell with the rocket battery were also at the foot of the escarpment when they heard the news of the Zulu approach. Durnford was already out of sight and Russell decided to move up onto the escarpment. Starting up the slope, he encountered the first groups of the Zulus on the crest above. He set up to the rockets on the rise nearby and one rocket was fired over the heads of the warriors, without inflicting any damage. These Zulus ran into a donga and appeared again only a few yards to the left of Russell's position. They shot at Russell's men at close range, and Russell himself was wounded. His command immediately disintegrated. Several of the crew were killed or wounded, the NNC broke ranks and the mules panicked and ran off. As they tried to carry Russell off to safety, he was hit again and killed. As the Zulu vanguard saw Durnford's men coming into view, they went to ground to wait for the Zulu main body to come up behind them.

Durnford now collected the survivors from the battery and moved on towards Isandlwana. Here at the camp, Pulleine sent Major Smith's two guns out onto a slight rise some several hundred yards from the tents, which overlooked the iNyoni escarpment. He also sent out two companies of the 1/24th, under Wardell and Lieut Porteous, in support, which then deployed on either side. Beyond their position the ground dipped into a hollow and from the rise just above it, Pullein's men had a good line of fire. No Zulus were yet visible from the camp at this stage. To the right of the guns' position a company of the NNC and one of the 2/24th under Lieutenant Pope were formed; they had been out on piquet duty, and were facing across the plain, anchoring the right of the defensive line.

When the first groups of the Zulu onslaught spilled over the escarpment into view of the camp, Pulleine for the first time became fully aware of the extent and danger of the attack. Realising the threat of Mostyn and Cavaye's men being cut off from the camp, he sent out Lieutenant Melvill of the 24th to recall them. Positioned at the tail of Isandlwana hill, the company of Captain Younghusband could cover their retreat. Retreating down the slope, they got mixed up with Raw's and Roberts's men rallying close to them, but regrouped at the bottom. Mostyn and Cavaye took up position next to Porteous, the Native Horse lining up between them and Younghusband. The Zulu chest advancing down the escarpment met with both heavy rifle and shellfire, so that their right was forced to retire behind the skyline, before attacking again from a less vulnerable position.

At this stage, Durnford's men showed up as they retreated across the plain, pursued closely by the left horn of the Zulu army. They reached a large donga, the Nyogane, about 1,000 yards from the camp, and here Durnford decided to make a stand. A piquet of mounted men from the camp was already in position at the donga. Durnford's men left their horses at the bottom of the gully and lined its lip to fire on the onrushing enemy. Spurred on by their commander, they kept up such heavy fire that they drove back the warriors directly attacking them, though a more experienced regiment followed up, advancing in short bursts of rising and ducking. The Zulu chest had also stalled descending from the heights and occupying the dongas below the British line, as the intense British fire made it difficult to regain their momentum and advance up the exposed slope.

The British line, however, was ominously overstretched. The Zulu left horn was threatening Pullein's rear, and was only checked by Durnford, while on his right, Pope's company drew back to get in line with Durnford's men. A serious gap of several hundred yards stretched between the two sections of the British force. Some groups of Zulus probed the gap, but were held back by firing from Pope's and Durnford's flank. At this stage, Durnford was in danger of being outflanked to his right, and worryingly his supply of ammunition was beginning to run low. The mounted men he sent into the camp were refused supplies from the 24th's wagons, as they had instructions to look after themselves first. On top of it they could not find their own wagons that had arrived after they had left the camp, so they had to leave empty-handed.

Realising the danger of the gap, Pope's company moved to its right to strengthen Durnford's left flank. During this move, however, Durnford left his position and retired on the camp, telling an officer that he could no longer hold his overextended position. He conferred with Pulleine, and it was agreed that the 24th line was in serious danger. They were ordered to retire to regroup in a more compact position nearer the camp.

Shortly before, the Zulu command had become worried that their attack was experiencing setbacks; below the iNyoni escarpment, along a line of dongas, the men were bogged down under heavy fire. So they sent one of their *izinduna* (headmen), a warrior named Mkhosana, to fire them into action. Reminding them of their duty to their king Cetshwayo, he stung them into rising and running forward, and along the line the other *amabutho* (regiments) took heart and also rallied. At the forefront, the heroic Mkhosana fell dead, but from here there was no stopping the Zulu attack.

The 24th maintained their formations at first, steadily retiring, but the NNH and NNC retired at a quicker pace; by the time they reached the camp they were running, having opened up gaps in the 24th's line. Before any attempts to stop them could be made, the Zulus swarmed into their midst. Major Smith's guns position was overrun, and between the firing line and the camp the British position disintegrated – a distance of a few hundred yards. The companies of Younghusband, Mostyn and Cavaye were driven through the tents from the north, and those of Porteous and Wardell from the front. One Zulu regiment broke past Pope into the tents, slaying cooks, servants, wagon drivers, anyone in sight, also oxen, horses, mules and dogs.

An officer in advance from Chelmsford's force recalled the final stage of the battle thus: 'In a few seconds we distinctly saw the guns fired again, one after the other, sharp. This was done several times – a pause, and then a flash – flash! The sun was shining on the camp at the time, and then the camp looked dark, just as if a shadow was passing over it. The guns did not fire after that, and in a few minutes all the tents had disappeared.'[14] Nearly the same moment is described in a Zulu warrior's account: 'The sun turned black in the middle of the battle; we could still see it over us, or should have thought we had been fighting till evening. Then we got into the camp, and there was a great deal of smoke and firing. Afterwards the sun came out bright again.'[15] The time of the solar eclipse on that day was calculated as 2:29 p.m.

A horde of NNC, mounted men and civilians had made a run for the rear, but the 24th still tried to hold their line. The runaways crossed the neck and into the Manzimnyana Valley behind Isandlwana, but straight into the Zulu right horn, which had already cut off the wagon track to Rorke's Drift. The latter swarmed over the neck and into the camp from behind, extinguishing any hope of the 24th taking up a new position.

In the meantime, Durnford had joined a small group of Natal Volunteers fighting valiantly against the left horn, with most of these African followers already gone from the scene. Here, on the neck beside the wagon track, and in the Manzimnyana Valley further down, the fiercest combat took place. Durnford, with the use of only one arm, was killed along with all the Natal Volunteers, who had simply been overrun by the mass of Zulu warriors. The remainder of two or three companies, with Pulleine among them, managed to make a stand near the wagons for a while, but they were eventually broken up and all killed. The company of Captain Younghusband had to fall back behind the tents and took up a position on the shoulder of Isandlwana. It was a good position – while the ammunition lasted – as the Zulus had to attack up the slope, but the time came when there were no more bullets. As a last resort Younghusband led his men in a charge to where the remaining British soldiers were fighting desperately on the neck. It was all in vain, and the body of Younghusband was later found near that of Pulleine.

A group of the 24th that had retreated over the neck, hoping to make it to Rorke's Drift, was confronted by the right horn as they entered the Manzimnyana Valley and was driven away from the track. Retreating down a series of dongas, they lost men along the way until they were trapped on the banks of the stream and finally overrun. For an hour or so after the collapse of the camp, small numbers of soldiers carried on fighting with broken rifles, bayonets, bare fists, whatever was available, but no life was to be spared. A report on the burial of the dead by Lieutenant Colonel Wilsone Black later appeared in the *Belfast Evening Telegraph*, which gave a good indication of the final actions of the battle.

As I reported in March last, the bodies of the slain lay thickest in the 1/24th camp. A determined stand had evidently been made behind the officers tent, and here an eyewitness told me that while he was escaping from the camp he saw a compact body of the 24th men fighting surrounded by Zulus. 70 dead lay here. Lower down the hill, in the same camp, another clump of about 60 laid together, among them captain Wardell, lieutenant Dyer, and a captain and a subaltern of the 24th, unrecognizable. Near at hand were found the bodies of Colonel Durnford, Lieutenant Scott, and other carbineers and men of the Natal Mounted Police, showing that here also our men had gathered together and fought in an organized body. This was evidently a centre of resistance, as the bodies of the men of all arms were found converging, as it were, to the spot, but stricken down ere they could join the ranks of their comrades. About 60 bodies lay on the rugged slope under the southern precipice of Isandlwana, among them those of Captain Younghusband, and two other officers unrecognizable. It looked as if these had held the crag, and fought together as long as ammunition lasted. Three soldiers were lying by as many dead Zulus. Zulu and white man confronted each other as living they had stood. Many did lay on the Buffalo side of the wreck, and I think it will not be out of place to describe how the line of retreat led here. When our two lines of infantry – one facing to the left of the camp in the position naturally taken up after retiring before the main body of the Zulu army as it swarmed over the Ngulu Hill, the other facing more towards the front, and parallel to the donga, making head with the two mounted volunteer troops against the Zulu left wing – when the two separate lines of skirmishers, outflanked on both sides, ammunition well nigh expended, retired almost at the same time to rally in the camp, form square around the ammunition wagons, and there refilled their pouches, some of those then present tell me that the attention of all being fixed on their own front, none had realized how it fared behind them. Once they turned towards the tents they saw that all was lost. The camp was full of Zulus, swelling round the flanks all of the isolated lines, following through the gap between them made by the retreating Natal natives. The Zulus' were already masters of the place of refuge, while those who made the frontal attack now stormed behind the retreating lines. The order of battle was over.

All that disciplined men could do had been done. The lines melted into groups, groups into files; coherence ceased; friend and foe mingled in one mass – a surging, stabbing crowd. The very numbers prevented the Zulus from making an immediate end of the horsemen, who escaped. The footmen struggled through the tents. The very guns moved at a walk whenever a gap opened in the mass, and slowly won their way towards the neck. Once here – once onto the road – the hope of escape arose only to be quenched at the next glance, for circling round Isandlwana road the right horn of the Zulu horde barred the way to Rorke's Drift.'[16]... Colonel Black goes on to say that there is strong evidence of how dearly our countrymen sold their lives, and it concludes by saying that from the spot 800 yards from the camp, where the guns were found, the bodies are even more and more apart, until about 2 miles from the camp the last one lies, and marks the limits reached by the white men on foot. The fatal trail begins again near the river bank, where Stewart, Smith, and others rest, a river's breadth from Natal. Across the river it runs until the graves of Melvill and Coghill nearly mark its limit.[17]

The Flight to Fugitive's Drift

Although little could be done by the Zulu commanders to coordinate the attack, the Undi Corps and the uDloko regiment had been held back and under the command of Dabulamanzi were ordered to move to the western end of the plateau, go behind Isandlwana and cut off the retreat to Rorke's Drift. Reaching the track they spread across it but took no part in the actual battle.

The bulk of the NNC had fled from the field at an early stage, about 12.45 or 13.00, but by this time the Undi Corps were already across the track to Rorke's Drift so that they were forced to follow a more direct route to the Buffalo River, which led under the slopes of Black's Koppie. Observing this, Dabulamanzi sent the inDluyengwe to attack them in the flank and although many had already cast away their weapons, headbands or any other signs of allegiance to the British in the hopes of becoming unrecognisable, most were discovered and killed, although some managed to escape.

To the fleeing whites, the route offered many obstacles. The first was the so-called rocky torrent, or stony stream bed, which hampered the horses and brought the guns to grief. The latter had got through the camp but were upset on the bank of the stream bed and the horses, suspended by the traces, were killed by the Zulus. The fugitives who negotiated this feature were then confronted by what some accounts called a 'chasm', a donga some 4 metres deep and apparently only fordable near its junction with the Manzimyama stream. One rider put his horse to jump the chasm but was crushed when it fell to the rocks in the bottom. The Manzimyama has very steep banks and a rocky bed. It was described as a gorge and many were killed trying to cross it. Some respite was given in climbing the slopes of the Mpete ridge, which is capped by a marsh where P. Brickhill (interpreter) lost his spectacles, but from here the descent into the Buffalo River valley is steep and difficult. On the Zululand side there is a small flat area where the fugitives congregated. As the river was running in spate, the crossing was a dangerous operation. At the point where the fugitives reached it, it was flowing turbulently but in a straight course. About 100 metres downstream there was a rocky island of boulders around which the water boiled. Below this was a whirlpool from which several horses were vainly struggling to escape, while further downstream the water roared through a boulder-strewn gorge where man and animal would be battered to death. After the NNC had crossed very few men on foot managed to escape the Zulus and by 13.30 it would seem that the inDlu-yengwe were in control of the route and the inGobamakhasi and uMbonambi had crossed Black's Koppie to close it from the east. The number of the NNC who escaped is unknown but about seventy-four whites survived.

Several tales of individual courage emerged after the battle. A soldier from Younghusband's company had retreated up the slopes of Isandlwana and hid in a cave at the foot of a cliff. For several hours after the camp had fallen, the desperate man defended himself, shooting and stabbing any warrior who confronted him. Finally the Zulus had had enough of him and blasted a volley into the cave that killed him. In another incident, a seaman from HMS *Active* and servant of a naval officer on Chelmsford's staff had found himself isolated, finally with his back to a wagon. He fought the warriors one at a time with his cutlass until one of them crept under the wagon and fatally stabbed him through the wheel spokes.[18]

Lieutenant Newnham Davis of the 3rd Buffaloes was one of the lucky ones to escape death at the hands of the Zulus. When he saw that things were really falling apart, he made a dash for it and had to fight his way out of trouble:

When we saw that the camp was gone, and that our men began to try to get away by twos and threes, I said to to Henderson, 'What are we going to do? Our only chance now is to make a run for it and dash through.' We started; he took to the right and I to the left, and rode slap at the enemy. One fellow seized hold of my horse's bridle and I made a stab at him with my rifle (a foolish thing that has a 9-inch knife attachment); but the man caught hold of it and pulled it out of my hand, which at the same time made my horse rear and shy and cleared me of the man. I then had only my revolver, and I saw a Zulu right in my course, and rode at him and shot him in the neck. My horse got a stab, and many assegais were thrown at me; but, as I was lying along my horse, they did not hit me. The ground was stony that I was going over, and I soon came to grief; but, as there was no time to think, I was soon up and away again, and took the river in front of me. Many were then escaping, but not being accustomed to take horses across rivers, they fell and rolled over, as the current was strong. I have had a good deal of experience in swimming horses, and I kept mine from falling, and directly he was in the water I threw myself off and caught hold of the stirrup. The Zulus followed us down and fired at us crossing. Some of the Zulus took the water after us, as our natives stabbed two Zulus just as they reached the Natal side. I never saw Colonel Durnford or George Shepstone after we left the gully or water-wash, and I did not see Henderson after we began our race until I met him next day at Helpmekaar.[19]

Another one of the fortunate men to escape the bloodbath was young officer Wallace Erskine of the 1st Regiment, Natal Native Contingent. In a letter to his father, Major D. Erskine, he gave an account of his escape:

We arrived at the Buffalo River on the night of the 21st. On the morning of the 22nd Colonel Durnford told us to saddle up, after which he gave us the order to march. We started at about 7:00 a.m., and marched as far as the Bashee, a stream about 7 miles from the Buffalo, and about three from Isandlwana. He ordered my company to stop there to escort the wagon, while he rode on to Isandlwana with the Edendale Kaffirs, Basutos, and the other company of foot Kaffirs. As soon as we were off saddled we heard the cannon firing at Isandlwana, and after about an hour's waiting, we were ordered two proceed to the front.

When we had gone about 2 miles farther, Captain Stafford ordered to me to take 16 men and go back and wait for the wagons and to escort them to camp, and to hurry them on as fast as possible, as the Zulus were trying to cut them off. I accordingly took the Kaffirs and met the wagons, and took them safe to the front, and told the Kaffirs to fire low while I went back to the wagon to fetch a gun. I got one, and went back until we got to camp, when we made another stand, and fired harder than ever. When the cannon fired, the Zulus would either lie down or break away, and leave a lane down the middle, so that the shell had very little effect. When they got about 100 yards off, the fire was so heavy that they could hardly come on. We were then suddenly surprised to hear a rush on our right flank, and on looking round saw that we were surrounded, and that it was the left horn of the Zulu army that was in the camp.

During this momentary pause the chest-guard found time to charge, and then the confusion began. It was impossible to stand the Zulus with their short assegais, which were awful. We were overpowered and driven back. The confusion was horrible. Soldiers, Kaffirs, horses, oxen, dogs, bucks, grasshoppers, wagons, etc., etc., all flew in the same direction. The slaughter was awful. The yells of pain from sundry horses and mules made it fearful.

I started off to run, but soon got blown, with the weight of my ammunition, gun, sword-bayonet, etc., and was obliged to throw everything away except my sword-bayonet and gun, with five cartridges. At last I could not run any father – so I sat down on an ant-heap, determined to fight it out to the last. Suddenly I heard a rustling behind me, and looking round, I saw the Zulus, within five yards of me, killing soldiers right and left, and off I started again, forgetting my gun in my haste. I had now nothing left except my sword-bayonet, which I stuck to. After running some distance, I saw my captain with two horses, one of which he was riding and the other leading. I called out to him to give me a horse, which he did. I jumped on, and on looking round for him, he was gone. I thereupon looked which way the Kaffirs were going, and followed them.

I found that the horse I was riding was merely done up, and would not go out of a walk.

After proceeding thus for about half a mile, I was watching a soldier who seemed very nearly at the end of his breath, when suddenly a Zulu appeared behind him, and calling out 'U yong assi venlunga' (where are you off to, white man?), he sent his assegai in between the soldier's shoulders, and then finished him with a stab in the side. To my dismay, I saw him come after me, and all at once I saw him throw his assegai at me; it went into my leg. He then pulled out another, and let fly, and sent it into my horse, behind the flap of the saddle. On looking for the next assagai to come, I could not see the Zulu anywhere, and do not know what became of him. A little farther on, up jumps another 'Johnny' Zulu, and catches hold of the reins of my horse, and presents an assegai at my chest, but he was too slow, for I cut the top of his head nearly off with my sword-bayonet.

On I went again, and then Colonel Durnford's horse passes me, with his saddle under his belly. I managed to catch him, and gave him to a soldier, who was so done that he could not get on to him. Wiley was trying to get onto it, the Zulus assegaied him, and the horse flew past me. Then I suddenly found that I had left the trail and got on top of a precipice about 12 or 15 feet high, and while I was turning back to look for a road down, the Zulus came up to me – so sooner than to be assegaied, I jumped my horse over, and fortunately neither myself nor my horse were hurt by the jump.

So off I went again, my horse going slower than ever. Then into the river we went helter-skelter; nine out of every 10 were washed down – horses and all. I suddenly found that my horse was fast, and on looking round to see what was the matter, I found five men hanging onto his tail and the flap of the saddle, while I was calling out to them to let go and hold on to some one's horse that was fresh. The Zulus came and assegaied them all, and then my horse, relieved of the burden, swam through safely. Then whizz came a bullet, and missed me, but killed poor Dubois, who was just in front of me; my horse stepped over his body, and I continued my flight to Helpmekaar, where I stayed two weeks before returning to

Pietermaritzburg. My wound took six weeks or more to heal. Then I left for Blood River, to finish my six months under 'Offy' Shepstone.

Wallace B Erskine.[20]

Smith-Dorrien's Escape Account

The most well known of these Isandlwana survivors was Horace Smith-Dorrien, who became a general in the First World War and wrote an account of the battle and his escape. He also talked about Lieutenants Melvill and Coghill, who escaped with the Queen's Colour of the 1st Battalion, 24th, but were killed by the Zulus.

I jumped on my broken-kneed pony which had had no rest for 30 hours, and followed it, to find on topping the nek a scene of confusion I shall never forget, for some 4,000 Zulus had come in behind [Isandlwana Mountain] and were busy with shield and assegai. Into this mass I rode, revolver in hand, right through the Zulus, but they completely ignored me. I heard afterwards that they had been told by their King Cetshwayo that black coats were civilians and were not worth killing. I had a blue patrol jacket on, and it is noticable that the only 5 officers who escaped – Essex, Cochrane, Gardner, Curling and myself – had blue coats. The Zulus throughout my escape seemed to be set on killing natives who had sided with us, either as fighting levies or transport drivers.

After getting through the mass of Zulus busy slaying, I followed the line of fugitives. The outer horns of the Zulu army had been directed to meet at about a mile to the southeast of the camp, and they were still some distance apart when the retreat commenced. It was this gap which fixed the line of the retreat.

Again I rode through unheeded, and shortly after was passed by Lieutenant Coghill wearing a blue patrol and cord breeches, and riding a red roan horse. We had just exchanged remarks about the terrible disaster, and we passed on towards Fugitive's Drift. A little farther on I caught up Lt Curling and spoke to him, pointing out to him that the Zulus were all round and urging him to push on, which he did. My own broken-kneed transport pony was done to a turn and incapable of rapid progress.

The ground was terribly bad going, all rocks and boulders, and it was about 3 or 4 miles from camp to Fugitive's Drift. When approaching this drift, and at least half a mile behind Coghill, Lieutenant Melvill, in a red coat and with a cased Colour across the front of his saddle, passed me going to the drift. I reported afterwards that the Colour was broken; but as the pole was found eventually whole, I think the casing must have been half off and hanging down. It will thus be seen that Coghill and Melvill did not escape together with the Colour. How Coghill came to be in the camp I do not know, as Colonel Glyn, whose orderly officer he was, was out with Lord Chelmsford's column.

I then came to Fugitive's Drift, the descent to which was almost a precipice. I found there a man in a red coat badly assegaied in the arm, unable to move. He was, I believe, a mounted infantryman of the 24th, named Macdonald, but of his name I cannot be sure. I managed to make a tourniquet with a handkerchief to stop the bleeding, and got him halfway down, when a shout from behind said, 'Get on man, the Zulus are on top of you.' I turned round and saw Major Smith RA who was commanding the section of guns, as white as a sheet and bleeding profusely. In a second we were surrounded and assegais accounted for poor Smith, my wounded M[ounted] I[nfantry] man, and my horse.

With the help of my revolver and a wild jump down the rocks, I found myself in the Buffalo River, which was in flood and 80 yards broad. I was carried away, but luckily got hold of the tail of a loose horse, which towed me across to the other bank, but I was too exhausted to stick to him. Up this bank were swarming friendly natives, but I only saw one European, a Colonial and Acting Commissariat Officer named Hamer, lying there unable to move. I managed to catch a loose horse, and put him on it, and he escaped. The Zulus were pouring in a very heavy fire from the opposite bank, and dropped several friendly natives as we climbed to the top.

No sooner had I achieved this than I saw that a lot of Zulus had crossed higher up and were running to cut me off. This drove me to my left, but 20 of them still pursued for about 3 miles, and I managed to keep them off with my revolver.

I got into Helpmakaar [Helpmekaar] at sundown, having done 20 miles on foot from the river, for I almost went to Sandspruit. At Helpmakaar I found Huntley of the 10th who had been left there with a small garrison, and also Essex, Cochrane, Curling and Gardner, from the field of Isandlwana, all busy placing the post in a state of defence. We could see that night the watchfires of the Zulus some 6 miles off, and expected them to come on and attack, but we knew later they had turned off to attack Rorke's Drift.

I at once took command of one face of the laager, and shall never forget how pleased we weary watchers were when, shortly after midnight, Major Upcher's 2 companies of the 24th, with Heaton, Palmes, Clements, and Lloyd, came to reinforce. These two companies had started for Rorke's Drift that afternoon, but had been turned back to Helpmakaar by Major Spalding, a staff officer, as he said Rorke's Drift had been surrounded and captured, and that the two companies would share the same fate. Luckily his information proved to be wrong.[21]

Saving the Colours

Before Colonel Pulleine was killed, he is believed to have charged Melvill to escape with the Regimental Colour of the 24th. Information supplied by Lieutenant Curling, Royal Artillery, who gave evidence at the Court of Enquiry held at Helpmekaar on 27 January, sheds further light on the event. After losing two guns from N. Battery, Curling returned to the camp, only to find the enemy in possession. He then fled towards Natal along the Fugitives' Road.

'We saw Lieutenant Coghill, the A.D.C., and asked him if we could not rally and make a stand; he said he did not think it could be done,' said Curling. A little later he again met Coghill, who told him that Colonel Pulleine had been killed. Curling only saw Melvill once. 'Near the river I saw Lieutenant Melville (sic) 1st Battalion 24th Regiment with a colour, the staff being broken.'[22] General Sir Horace Smith-Dorrien (at the time a subaltern in the 99th Foot) survived to tell of his nightmarish experience along the road to Fugitive's Drift. 'After the desperate combat at Isandhlawana a scene of utter confusion seems to have occurred – horse and foot, black and white, English and Zulu, all in a struggling mass, making through the camp towards the road, where the Zulus had already closed the way of escape. The ground there down to the river was so broken that the Zulus went as fast as the horses, killing all the way.'[23]

Fifty years later Smith-Dorrien recorded: 'I was passed by Lieutenant Coghill of the Twenty Fourth, wearing a blue patrol jacket and cord breeches, and riding a roan horse ... When approaching Fugitive's Drift, and at least half a mile behind Coghill, Lieutenant Melvill of the 24th, in a red coat, with a cased colour across the front of his saddle, passed me going to the Drift ... It will thus be seen that Coghill (who was orderly to Colonel Glyn) and Melvill (who was adjutant) did not escape together.'[24]

The two reached the drift together with Lieutenant Higginson (1/3rd NNC). He recalled: 'I put my horse into the river and poor Melvill was also thrown; he held on tightly to the Queen's Colour, which he had taken from the field of battle when all was over, and as he came down towards me he called out to me to catch hold of the pole. I did so and the force with which the current was running dragged me off the rock to which I clung but fortunately into still water. Coghill, who had got his horse over all right, came riding back down the bank to help Melvill, and as he put his horse in, close to us, the Zulus who were 25 yards from us on the other bank commenced firing at us in the water. Almost the first shot killed Coghill's horse, and on his getting clear of him we started for the bank and managed to get out all right ... When we had gone a few yards further Melvill said he could go no further and Coghill said the same (I don't think they imagined at this time there was anyone following us.) When they stopped, I pushed on reaching the top of the hill. I found four Basuto with whom I escaped by holding on to a horse's tail.'[25]

While the defence of Rorke's Drift by the garrison under Lieutenant Chard halted any possible invasion of Natal, Chelmsford's shocked forces were in disarray – the annihilation at Isandlwana was the worst since the massacre at Chilianwhalla in 1849. It was only on 4 February that Colonel Glyn felt sufficiently confident of his situation to send a patrol out to search for survivors of the disaster, and to look for the missing colours. The staff officer to Commandant Lonsdale, Lieutenant Henry Charles Harford, accompanied a party led by Major Black. He recorded in his diary: 'and as there was still sufficient of the afternoon left, Major Black suggested that we should go a little further down ... when suddenly just off the track to the right of us, we saw two bodies, and on going to have a look at them found that they were those of Lieutenant Melville (sic) and Coghill. Both of them were clearly recognisable. Melville was in red, and Coghill in blue uniform, both were lying on their backs about a yard from each other. Melville at right angles to the path and Coghill parallel with it, a little above Melville and with his head uphill, both assegaied but otherwise untouched.'[26]

While the media, the public and the officers of the regiment took solace in the sacrifice of Melvill and Coghill, not all were as happy about their actions. Sir Garnet Wolseley, future Commander-in-Chief of the British forces in Zululand, noted in his journal: 'I am very sorry that both these officers were not killed with their men at Isandhlana (sic) instead of where they were. I don't like the idea of officers escaping on horseback when their men on foot are killed ... Heroes have been made of men like Mellville (sic) and Coghill who taking advantage of their horses, bolted from the scene of the actions to save their lives ... It is monstrous making heroes of those who saved or attempted to save their lives by bolting.'[27] Such opinions, however, would never have been able to surface in the newspapers.

When the patrol could not find the colour, they continued the search the following day, and Harford found the colour and its case in the Buffalo River, some 500 yards downstream. Harford and his companions broke into spontaneous cheering and the colour was ceremoniously saluted by the rest of the search party before they returned to Rorke's Drift, Major Black carrying the cased colour aloft. There the colour was met by a guard of honour and the whole garrison. It was then carried to Helpmekaar, and Harford was privileged to be standard bearer. It was a peculiar occasion in that an officer of another regiment (the 99th) carried the Queen's Colour of the 24th. When the colour returned to England with the 24th Regiment, Queen Victoria crowned it with a wreath of Immortelles, and the following message was sent to the Adjutant-General: 'As a lasting token of her act of placing a wreath on the Queen's Colour to commemorate the devotion displayed by Lieutenants Melvill and Coghill in their heroic endeavour to save the Colour on January 22nd, 1879, and of the noble defence of Rorke's Drift, Her Majesty has been graciously pleased to command that a silver wreath shall in future be borne on the peak of the staff of the Queen's Colour of the Twenty Fourth Regiment.' This colour is now laid up in Brecon Cathedral in Powys in the Diocese of Swansea and Brecon.[28] The *Manchester Evening News* reported in 1894 that 'nearly sixteen years after the event and in a foreign capital thousands of miles from the scene of the disaster one of the colours – the regimental colour of the second battalion, in defence of which so many noble fellows fell – has within the last few days been recovered. The flag came into the possession of Baron St. George, of Paris, and was handed over by him to Colonel Talbot, our military attaché in Paris. How the colour came to be preserved and to reach the French capital is a mystery.'[29]

Military Mistakes

Major (Dr) Felix Machanik stated that the success or failure of any force is dependent mainly on its firepower and would rest on the following considerations:

  i) Number of men defending the position;
 ii) Adequacy of the weapons in use and a sufficient supply of good ammunition; and
iii) Adequate training in the use of the weapons.

Regarding the defence of the camp, he states: 'The site appeared suitable and wood and water were available. The space seemed adequate to contain the large force of approximately 4,313 men, 2,747 British troops and 2,566 or so Natal Native Contingent. In addition there was space for the large wagon park at the saddle, for the 220 wagons, 82 carts, 346 conductors, room for 1,500 oxen, hundreds of mules and horses, and indeed the whole camp stretched for 800 yards, with units spaced at a greater distance at the base of the Nqutu escarpment. 2,500 men left the camp with Col Glyn on the morning of the 22nd January, 1879; thus only 1,800 men remained in the camp for its defence.'

On the other hand, the site was unsuitable, as the ground was hard and rocky for the digging of trenches; no laager was formed and there were not enough wagons to contain the large numbers of men, oxen, horses, mules or stores; no sangars were constructed or deemed necessary; and indeed no defences at all were made.[30]

Looking at experience and weaponry, the British forces had experienced officers and NCOs and the men were well trained and disciplined, and were armed with the sturdy Martini-Henry rifle. The Martini-Henry was a modified American Peabody (Patent 1862) single-shot, hinged falling-block rifle, and was supplied to all troops at Isandlwana, Rorke's Drift and Ulundi.

The early coiled brass case was irregular and thus could jam in the breech after firing, when it would then have to be pushed out of the barrel with the ramrod supplied with each rifle. At Isandlwana and Rorke's Drift extraction problems occurred frequently, diminishing the firepower of the troops. At Rorke's Drift where the fire was heavy and persistent, the barrels overheated and the cartridge cases frequently jammed. The bayonet supplied was the 1876 Enfield triangular pattern, 25.25 inches long. Durnford's Edendale Horse were issued with Martini-Henry Carbines without the bayonet lug.[31]

Unlike the British troops, the Natal Native Contingent were badly trained, undisciplined and poor shots, and had little experience of battle conditions. Some were armed with the long Martini-Henry rifle, some with the Westley Richards Carbine. Durnford's Natal Native Horse had the Westley Richards carbine rifle, which used the black-powder paper cartridge. The capping percussion lock breechloader used a paper cartridge with a lead bullet at the tip and a felt wad behind. The black powder fouled the barrel and the breechblock lever and rapid fire was thus hindered and slowed down. Some of the Natal Native Contingent still had the early muzzle-loading, percussion Enfields, using black powder, wad and lead bullet rammed down the muzzle with the ramrod; others had the modified Enfield muzzle loader, and the rate of fire of both was slow.[32]

The Zulus, on the other hand, were armed mainly with assegais and large ox-hide shields, though they also had a few muzzle-loading percussion smoothbore muskets as at Isandlwana. Having captured Martini-Henry rifles at Isandlwana, they also used these the same afternoon and evening at Rorke's Drift. Fortunately for the British, the Zulus were poor shots.

A great drawback was that the camp was widely spread out and that concentrated firepower behind a fixed defence was not employed. The 1,800 men from ten separate units were thinly spread for a distance of about 1,800 yards. They fell into two ranks, one behind the other, but the line was ragged with gaps between, allowing the enemy to rush through and attack the defenders from the rear. This especially occurred when the Natal Native Contingent early in the battle broke and fled, leaving a gap in the defence line, 300 yards (275 metres) wide.

Furthermore, any concentrated firepower of the main force was drastically reduced and thus weakened by the absence of a large body of men who had left the camp. Firstly, some with the Commanding General, Lord Chelmsford; secondly Major Dartnell with his mounted troops; and thirdly Colonel Durnford with his dismounted native horsemen, who were isolated away from the main force in a donga, where he halted and held up the Zulu left horn, until eventually, when his ammunition ran out, he had to vacate his strongpoint and retreat to the saddle. He made his second stand here, but being surrounded was overwhelmed and died fighting.

Of approximately 900 British troops, 858 were killed and only 55 escaped, and of approximately 850 Natal Native troops, 471 were killed, the rest escaped but many I am certain were killed later, or died of their wounds. The Zulus had approximately 25,000 warriors, under experienced leaders and they were well trained and hard fighters; about 2.000 were killed and many more died later from their wounds. It is estimated that on the battlefield at Isandlwana and down the Fugitives' Trail, a distance of 15 miles, (24 km) there were scattered 3,500 bodies.[33]

On the same day that Colonel C. K. Pearson's column in the coastal sector defeated the Zulu attack at Nyezane, elsewhere in Zululand, Colonel R. Glyn's Central Column also experienced Zulu attacking tactics for themselves. At Isandlwana the main Zulu army overwhelmed a force of six companies of British infantry and two artillery pieces with colonial mounted and infantry support. In a classic demonstration of the 'beast's horns' attack the British force was held in position, surrounded and destroyed.

Horace Smith-Dorrien, 95th Regiment, another Transport Officer, one of the few to escape, saw the attack develop: 'It was a marvellous sight, line upon line of men in slightly extended order, one behind the other, firing as they came along. For a few of them had firearms, bearing all before them ... They were giving vent to no loud war-cries, but to a low musical murmuring noise, which gave the impression of a gigantic swarm of bees getting nearer and nearer.'[34]

Lieutenant H. Curling, Royal Artillery, another officer fortunate to survive the battle, watched the Zulus as they closed on the British position: 'The Zulus soon split up into a large mass of skirmishers that extended as far around the camp as we could see. We could get no idea of numbers but the hills were black with them. They advanced steadily in the face of the infantry and our guns ... Very soon bullets began to whistle about our heads and men began to fall.'[35]

The Zulu attack charged home and with retreat prevented by the outflanking 'horns', most of the British force died in desperate last stands close to the base of Isandlwana hill. Part of the Zulu army continued on towards the British supply depot at Rorke's Drift where it launched an attack against the heavily outnumbered garrison. Private J. Waters, 1/24th Regiment, working as a hospital orderly, witnessed the leading Zulus appear around the shoulder of Shiyane Hill: 'The Zulus came over the hill and I saw about fifty of them form a line in skirmishing order, just as British soldiers would do. Their main body was in their rear over the shoulder of the hill. They came about twenty yards, and then opened fire on the hospital.'[36]

A gentleman in Natal, whose son belonged to the Natal Carbineers with Lord Chelmsford, forwarded a letter dated 29 January to the *Thames Advertiser*.

Since my last letter there has been, as you will long ago have seen in the English papers, a terrible disaster to our arms. In England you will not be able to realise the extent of the misfortune as we do here; hardly a house in the colony but has to mourn the loss of some friend or relation. While sympathising with those who have lost, I cannot say how thankful I am that my boy, being with the Carbineers who were with Lord Chelmsford, was absent during the massacre. I will try and give you a few particulars that will, perhaps, not be mentioned in the papers. Our loss this day week was, as near as can be made out from different reports, about 909 whites, the rest natives. Camp and wagons were left in charge of Colonel Pulleine, who had been all through the Cape war, and was an experienced officer. Lord Chelmsford had, I believe, given him written instructions on which to act. Just as the Zulu army hove in sight, up rode Colonel Durnford, who was superior officer to Colonel Pulleine, and took the command out of his hands, and, contrary to instructions to act strictly on the defensive, engaged the enemy by advancing skirmishers without parking his wagons.

The Zulus extended their flanks for three miles on each side, and gradually closed in upon our men, who stood back to back and fired until the guns they held blistered their hands. Some who were near the spruits dipped their rifles into the water to cool them. They had seventy rounds of ammunition each man; as long as this lasted they kept the Zulus at bay, but when it came to an end the poor fellows saw their end was come too. The last order that was heard given was, 'Fix bayonets, men, and die like English soldiers do' and so they died. I was told by a man present, one of the mounted police who escaped, that in some places the bodies of the Zulus were several feet deep. They went down by hundreds at every volley, but still came on like wave succeeding wave, and dashed against a few white troops as the breaking of the sea against a rock. Some few men were seen to kill themselves, but the great majority sold their lives dearly.

My boy and his companion spent that weary night on the battle-field among the bodies of his dead, and in many cases mutilated, friends. Six out of his tent had been killed. He says he has roughed it since leaving home, but nothing could come up to the horrors of that night. He and some of his corps under Major Dartnell had been away with the General about twelve miles, engaged with another part of the Zulu army, which had easily been defeated. News came to them from the camp, and they hastened back. A party of the Carbineers were sent on a-head to report, and they found the camp in possession of the Zulus, who were busy loading up the dead in our wagons (120), and making off with them. They got everything, even to Lord Chelmsford's decorations and medals. They had stripped the dead, and what wagons they could get away had burnt with their contents. They got Martini-Henry rifles, ammunition, two cannons, shells, and 2,000 oxen. The guns will be of no use, as they were spiked. Of course, when the main body arrived at camp, they had no ammunition beyond the few rounds in their pouches, and had the Zulus attacked them that night they must have killed the lot. The Native Contingent gave no end of trouble with false alarms. One young fellow of the Carbineers was shot in the chest; as he reeled in the saddle, he turned round and said, 'Tell mother...' – but the poor boy got no further with his message. During the fight or massacre, which lasted four or five hours, Cetewayo sat on his horse on a neighbouring kopje. He held 5,000 men in reserve in case of need; but 15,000 were enough for our small force.'[37]

Casualties

Out of more than 1,700 British troops and African auxiliaries, some 1,300 were killed, most of them Europeans. Among them were the field commanders Pulleine and Durnford, and only five imperial officers survived. The fifty-two officers lost was the greatest such loss by any British battalion at that point. Included in the death toll was Surgeon Major Peter Shepherd, a pioneer of first aid. The Natal Native Contingent lost around 400 men, and a staggering 240 of the 249 amaChunu African auxiliaries died. One of the casualties of the Natal Native Contingent was Gabangaye, chief of the amaChunu, who was given over to be killed by the *udibi* (porter or carrier) boys. The captured NNC soldiers were seen as traitors by the Zulu and executed. Most of the survivors were from the auxiliaries.

There was no attempt by the British to count the Zulu losses since they abandoned the field, and the Zulus didn't count their dead either. Modern historians reject the older estimates, which are considered to be unfounded. The historians Lock and Quantrill estimate the Zulu casualties as 'perhaps between 1,500 and 2,000 dead'. The well-known Zulu war historian Ian Knight wrote: 'Zulu casualties were almost as heavy. Although it is impossible to say with certainty, at least 1,000 were killed outright in the assault.'

Some 1,000 Martini-Henry rifles, the two field artillery guns, 400,000 rounds of ammunition, three regimental colours, most of the 2,000 draft animals and 130 wagons, provisions such as tinned food, biscuits, beer, overcoats, tents and other supplies, were taken by the Zulu or just abandoned on the battlefield.[38]

When things had settled down somewhat, Private John Morgans of the 2/24th Regiment wrote to his brother about the disaster and his luck in escaping death:

> I am very sorry to tell you that on the 22nd of January 1879 I had a narrow escape of my life, also the regiment. We went out early that morning, before daybreak, to attack the Zulus; we went about sixteen miles from camp and, whilst we were away the Zulus came around the hill and about 7000 of them attacked the camp while we were away looking for them, and they killed about 100 of ours and five companies of the 1-24th Regiment, about 400 men altogether. So when we were coming back to camp, on half way the general came to meet us and he made us to sit down while he was speaking to us. He told us that our camp was attacked by the Zulus and that our men fought like warriors in the camp trying to save it but the Zulus were too strong.
>
> Also, he told us that we must gain our camp back before morning, so we started away on time, the big guns (cannons) in the centre. The 24th was formed in line with fixed bayonets. The big guns fired about twelve shells and we fired a volley and, after we had done that, we charged in double march up to the old camping ground. It was dark at the time and we heard the enemy retiring. The first thing I came across when I came to the ground was four dead bodies with their inside out and when we came a little closer to the spot, the tents were burnt and torn to pieces, and when we formed a piquet, I found a dead man and when I looked about it was a friend of mine, old P.Q. as I used to call him. There was about sixteen of my draft killed. So we had to retire back across the river (Buffalo River) and back to Natal colony; we went in about forty miles to Zululand and had to retire back to Natal colony … There is about 16,000 Zulus waiting for us the other side of the river. So I hope I won't die out in this country

but reach my old home. Give the news to my relations near. So I leave you now and hope that all are well. Don't vex about me if I die like a soldier.[39]

About ten days after the catastrophe, Private Francis Ward, also of the 2/24th, wrote to his aunt in Aberdare, Wales, about the battle. He did not bother to spare her the mention of the brutal mutilation of his comrades. He also wrote about his regret for signing up for the Army while under the influence of alcohol, and about the death of a relative, Tom Jones, of the same regiment during the battle.

I am glad to say that I enjoy capital health and hope to continue so. I am fully aware that you know that I have enlisted. I am now indeed sorry for it. I was under the influence of drink when I did so. I have already served fifteen months ... and I must go through it the best way I can. Ever since we arrived in this country we have been on active service and, most likely, operations will not be over for the next twelve months. I hope and trust that God Almighty will guide me safe through all, so that I may return to my dear native country once more.

I daresay that you are aware that Tom Jones, Aunt Betsy's son, was in the same regiment as myself. It is with very deep emotion and regret that I have to acquaint you of his sad death. He was killed on the 22nd of January at Isandula Camp in Zululand, the territory we invaded. There were lost on our side 993 men. I can assure you, dear aunt, it was a most ghastly sight to witness. After our poor fellows were shot, they were brutally mutilated. Kindly write to poor Tom's mother and let her know of his death. I was speaking to him the night before and he requested me to write home if anything should happen to him, also he said he would do the same for me ...

He was on guard this day and the company he belonged to went out with five other companies, we having been acquainted that the enemy was not far distant. We left camp at daybreak. In the meantime, the enemy was watching our movements and marched on our right flank towards the camp, which they captured after a terrible struggle. They cut up every man of ours, except three that managed to escape. The enemy brought a force of about 15,000 against our

handful of men. Our aide-de-camp was sent out after the
column to fetch them back with all haste, the reason being
that the enemy had captured our camp. We arrived near camp
when it got dark. We opened into skirmishing order and we
had four seven-pounders in the centre of the column. They
throwed some shells and rocket to the left of the camp; also
we fired a few volleys as well before we advanced towards
the camp. We had our bayonets fixed; we captured the camp;
but the enemy had disappeared – but before they retired, they
burnt all things that belonged to us and took away with them
one million rounds of ammunition and the colours of our
battalion; and the first battalion of ours lost five companies
of men and officers; also the artillery and volunteers lost every
man; indeed, it was a terrible calamity.

Dear Aunt, I wish I had listened to your good advice and
give up the drink, I would not be where I am at present.
If I should have the same fate as poor Tom, tell Mary, my
youngest sister, to claim what belongs to me to the War Office
but I sincerely hope that I shall be spared to return home
again. There will be many poor fellows yet will have their
heads laid low before the war is over. Also tell poor Tom's
mother to write to the War Office for his money.[40]

Edward Evans of Llawrglyn, Wales, managed to escape with
his life from Isandlwana with two of his comrades by charging
through the centre of the Zulu line. In a letter dated 3 February, he
told his mother and brother about his ordeal: 'You know nothing
of the horrors of war and if I was to write from now till Christmas,
I could never explain half what I have seen or how I was saved.
Myself and two more comrades rode our horses through the centre
of their line of fire and hundreds of guns pointing at us; but I can
assure you it was a ride for life. Many of our noble heroes that
escaped from the hands of the enemy lost their lives in crossing the
Buffalo River. Thank God for learning me to swim. My horse fell
in the water and both of us went down together and both swam
out again – but a very hard struggle. I had to let go my rifle and
ammunition and everything I had …'[41]

Private Thomas Thomas wrote to his uncle and aunt about
Isandlwana and mentioned that 'the Zulus killed about 1,841

of our fellows altogether but we ourselves killed some of the volunteers because they were running away and the colonel in command [referring to either Pulleine or Durnford] shot himself because he knew he had done wrong.'[42]

The British had a tremendous problem in supporting the troops in Zululand. The stores and equipment upon which the soldiers depended had to be transported in ox wagons, and soon the rough tracks of Zululand broke down under all the strain; drifts collapsed, tracks became waterlogged, and grazing for the trek animals consumed. In addition, the trek oxen were overworked and killed by disease. As more and more wagons and trek animals had to be brought in to replace the lost ones, the cost of the war slowly but surely mounted. Chelmsford wrote soon after the disaster at Isandlwana: 'Unless the Swazies come down and help us I do not see how we are to make any impression in Zululand. The country is quite impracticable for a force which must take ox wagons about with it and it is not possible to guard properly the line of communications. We might all march straight through the country taking a month's provisions with us, but having done so, what should we have gained?'[43]

The Fate of the Drummer Boys

One of the most gruesome tales by men who had been part of Lord Chelmsford's reconnaissance after the battle and perpetuated in book after book concerns the fate of the so-called 'little drummer boys', who were said to have been tortured, slaughtered and ritually mutilated by the Zulus.

Samuel Jones of the Newcastle Mounted Rifles told a newspaper reporter in 1929, fifty years later: 'One sight, a most gruesome one, I shall never forget. Two lads, presumably two little drummer boys of the 24th Regiment, had been hung up by butcher's hooks which had been jabbed under their chins, then they were disembowelled. All the circumstances pointed to the fact that they had been subjected to that inhuman treatment while still alive.'

Zulu War author James Bancroft is quoted as saying that 'the Zulus had seized five band boys and either tied them to wagons by their feet or hung them on butcher's hooks by their chins, sliced them up and then cut their privates off and put them in their mouths.'

Drummer W. Sweeney of the 2/24th said he noticed on 29 April 1879: 'Two drummer boys, Anderson and Holmes, and five little boys of the band about 14 years of age. They were butchered most awfully indeed. One little chap named McEvery they hung up by the chin to a hook.'

'There is no doubt that the Zulus practised ritual mutilation after a battle, and the packs of young dibi boys roaming the area after the battle must have had a field day looting and despatching the wounded,' wrote Zulu War expert Pat Rundgren. 'But there is little evidence to show that the Zulus restricted their attentions particularly to the youngsters or that, indeed, there were very many of them there in the first place.'[44]

He lists 'bandsmen/drummers/boys' who were killed in action at Isandlwana by age[45] and in summary concludes that only nineteen soldiers who might have been classified as bandsmen or boys of the 24th Regiment were killed in action. Of the nineteen, three were aged between fifteen and seventeen; four were aged between eighteen and twenty; eight were aged between twenty-one and thirty; three were aged over thirty; and one of unrecorded age. Therefore, if the 24th Regiment lost a total of twenty-two officers and 590 men, the percentage of bandsmen and boys was only 3 per cent. Of those 3 per cent, only three might be classified as 'little drummer boys' (i.e. aged fifteen and seventeen). The remainder were grown men.

Drummer Sweeney is way out as Anderson and Holmes were in their mid-twenties, and the five little boys of about fourteen years of age must have been a figment of his imagination as there weren't that many there. Visiting the site three months later, what with the heat, humidity and scavengers, most bodies would have totally decomposed by then and would be unrecognisable.

Rundgren concludes that 'Most, if not all bodies, were probably mutilated in typical Zulu style; drummer boys would not have escaped such a fate, but their numbers were a minute fraction of the overall total of killed in actions; so it's probably not fair to single 'bandsmen' out considering their paucity of numbers overall; visitors some months afterwards would definitely not have been unable to identify decayed corpses as belonging specifically to bandsmen.'[46]

The Burial of the Dead
The British did not revisit the Isandlwana battlefield until 17 May, but the burial party of the Dragoon Guards spent four days there from 21 to 24 May. Some bodies, which had been disemboweled,

dried up but others had decomposed. During the months before the revisit, vultures, crows, hyenas and jackals had also attacked many of the bodies so that large numbers were unrecognisable. Also, in many cases the tunics had been removed by the Zulus, making identification even more difficult. British and Zulu dead were lying together in some areas, and could not be identified separately. Due to lack of time and tools, as well as the hardness of the soil there, no graves were dug, but the bodies pulled together in heaps and stones piled over them – leaving a battlefield covered by cairns. It is known that attention was paid to the battlefield after the annexation of Zululand and the cairns were probably whitewashed during the early 1900s, and later several regimental monuments were erected.[47]

The body of Durnford was recognised by the waistcoat he had worn and a pocketknife with the colonel's name on it. Two rings were also taken from the corpse. These relics were to be sent to his father. Durrant Scott of the Carbineers had his patrol jacket on. 'His face was like life, all the hair being on it, and the skin, though dried up, still perfect,' the *Lakes Visitor* reported. Durnford's body was wrapped in canvas and buried in 'a kind of water-cask'.[48]

Captain Percival Tatham Armitage[49] was a member of the burial party. In a letter to his mother, written from Koppie Alleen, Zululand, he describes the scene they found:

Dearest Mother ... I stayed at Koppie Allein (sic) about three weeks and then received orders to join my own company at Rorke's Drift. First, though, I must tell you, the second day after arriving at Koppie Allein (sic) we heard of the Princes death [Prince Napoleon] ... we were, in fact, almost within sight of where the Prince was killed. His body was brought down in an ambulance wagon escorted by a few lancers & we had to furnish an escort half way to Landman's Drift ... it was very sad.' It goes on: 'Major Black commanded at Rorke's Drift ... there were 3 companies there. Up to this time the bodies of the poor fellows who were killed at Isandlwhana (sic) were lying unburied but Major Black received permission to go in and bury them. Shortly after I arrived there a force composed of 2 companies 2/24th, 1 squadron of dragoons, half dismounted and about 500 native contingent commanded by Major Black marched in to fulfil the melancholy duty that had been so long delayed. I had command of a burying party, composed of some of our own men & some natives, with picks and shovels. We started at 3 o'clock in the morning & crossed the Buffalo into Zululand. It was bitterly cold & we marched the 11 miles to Isandlwhana (sic) getting there about day break. The scene was frightful. Bodies lying about in every direction ... This is the dark side of war. After burying for about 2 or 3 hours we marched back to Rorke's Drift. It took about 4 days to bury the dead but altogether I have been in 9 times to Isandlwhana with Major Black, bringing out the wagons & other things. We brought out £6,000 worth of wagons and ought to get salvage for them but I am afraid there is no chance of doing so. I found 2 or 3 officers' bodies, amongst them that of poor [Lieutenant Edgar Oliphant] Anstey, instead of whom I came out. I found poor [Lieutenant Charles Walter] Cavaye's diary on the field. After I had been about a month at Rorke's Drift, orders came one day that William's Company was to proceed to Koppie Allein. Next morning we started & after 3 days marching arrived here, where we are still. Your affectionate boy, Percy.[50]

Letters from those men who returned to the battlefield of Isandlwana in May as members of the first burial party would reveal something of the final moments of the bloody battle, as this one from a soldier in the 17th Lancers and published in the *Sheffield Daily Telegraph* showed: 'I enclose you a card of four of diamonds which lay close to the colonel of the 24th (i.e., Lieutenant Colonel Pulleine). They had evidently been playing cards, for a whole pack was kicked about, lots of music, too, I picked up.'[51]

The correspondent of the *Daily News*, Archibald Forbes, described the scene as it was when British troops finally returned to the field of Isandlwana on 21 May 1879: 'Some were almost wholly dismembered, heaps of yellow clammy bones ... Every man had been disembowelled. Some were scalped, and others subjected to yet ghastlier mutilations'.[52] Melton Prior, of the *Illustrated London News*, filed a similar report: 'The sight at Isandlwana is one I shall never forget. In all the seven campaigns I have been in ... I have not witnessed a scene more horrible'.[53]

9

THE AMMUNITION CONTROVERSY

One of the most contentious issues around the catastrophe at Isandlwana has been that of the organization and supply of the rifle ammunition. Some historians, like F. W. D. Jackson, believed that there was no reliable contemporary evidence that the regular soldiers had run out of ammunition while in the firing line. A young transport officer at the time, H Smith-Dorrien,[1] on the other hand, stated that there had been no rounds in the firing line with thousands in the ammunition wagons some 400 yards in the rear at the camp. All the ammunition in the firing line had been used up.

A chronic failure in the supply of ammunition to the regular soldiers as a key factor in the massacre has been a predominant view until the 1960s, and culminated in D. R. Morris's classic publication *The Washing of the Spears: the Rise and Fall of the Zulu Nation*. It was supported by contemporary accounts, including that of Lieutenant Smith-Dorrien and Captain Edward Essex (75th Regiment). Smith-Dorrien's account suggests that there had been a breakdown in the regimental supply line during the mainly Zulu advance and that he had rounded up 'camp stragglers such as artillery men in charge of spare horses, officers' servants, sick etc.' and had taken them to the ammunition boxes, which they broke open and sent packets of rounds to the firing line. He also referred to the difficulty in opening these boxes, which were screwed down; according to Morris the crate lids were held down by two copper bands, fastened with nine large screws. Smith-Dorrien also suggested that the stubbornness of the regimental quartermaster Edward Bloomfield contributed to fatal delays. He was severely reprimanded by Bloomfield when he broke open his battalion's boxes. 'For heaven's sake don't take that, man, for it belongs to our battalion!' Bloomfield allegedly shouted.

A fresh view was offered from F. W. D. Jackson that the collapse could be ascribed more to the over-extended lines, which, after the collapse of Durnford's right wing, were critically outflanked. The well-known Zulu War author Ian Knight supported his line of thought and added that the boxes in question would have been the Mark V version that could be opened by removing one screw only, or by a sharp blow to the edge of the panel in an emergency. Knight also dismisses a major breakdown of the supply lines to the regular infantry in view of all the runners coming and going.

Military historian Edmund Yorke analysed the obstructive action of at least one of the two regimental quartermasters and the general disorganisation of the supply network at the time of the Zulu entry into the camp. He concluded that at the commencement of the battle there was clearly little concern about the ammunition supply. Secondly, there was continued reliability of ammunition supply as the detachments of Mostyn, Cavaye and Dyson retreated to the bottom of the spur and were reinforced by C Company of Younghusband and the other three imperial companies of Wardell, Porteous and Pope to the front and left front of the camp to face the main Zulu attack. Both Smith-Dorrien and J. A. Brickhill confirmed consistent and effective firing along the line so that the battle stabilised in these final set positions. The Zulus were at this stage feeling the full force of the British Martini-Henry rifle at close range. Captain Edward Essex, one of the few survivors, recalled that the men had been in good spirits at the time, while firing one volley after the other into the black mass.

Yorke points at two disastrous breaks in the British line, one on the extreme right flank as Durnford retreated, leading to the outflanking of the central line of defence and exhaustion of the ammunition supply. One of Durnford's mounted colonial force, Yabez Molife, recalled that the colonel was encouraging his men left, right and centre, 'but at last our cartridges were nearly done'. This indicates a delay in securing fresh ammunition. Durnford asked for more from the camp but none arrived. Eventually he took some men into the camp to their own wagons, but while they were getting their ammunition, the Zulus swept around the upper camp and cut them off.

Bloomfield's refusal seemed not to have been an isolated incident, as Captain Barton stated that his mounted Amangwane had fought well until all the ammunition was exhausted, and they had to fall back on the camp for fresh ammunition. However, this was refused them by the officer in charge, who told them that everything would be required by the infantry themselves.[2]

What about the ammunition supply for the six imperial companies in the centre and left of the British lines? The companies of Mostyn and Cavaye had been the longest in the firing line and furthest away from the camp, and had used the bulk of their rounds. This was confirmed by Captain Hallam-Parr, who said that these companies 'were very short of ammunition'. He stated, 'The men were as cheery as possible, those belonging to the two companies on the left, retiring coolly and quite convinced in their own minds that they had come back for more ammunition and would turn the tables on the Umcityu when they had refilled their pouches and could fire more rapidly; for the ammunition of these two companies had been rapidly expended owing to the hot fire they had been forced to sustain to keep the Zulus from closing upon them while they were retreating on the camp.'[3]

It seems obvious that against this background, Smith-Dorrien and Essex would gather casuals to plug the gap in the ammunition supply line. Smith-Dorrien's fallout with Bloomfield had occurred when the 1/24th had fallen back to where they (Smith-Dorrien's men) were.[4] Another officer, Lieutenant F. H. Macdowel (or McDowell), was seen rounding up 'bandsmen, gunners and others' and bringing up reserve ammunition to the 24th's fighting line, before being killed near the general's tent.[5]

Yorke argues that the collapse of the left, which created panic and confusion, and the resultant disruption of the central ammunition supply lines may well have damaged the central defensive position far more than Durnford's retreat from the right. One of the 1/24th survivors, Private H. Grant, stated that arriving back in camp, he found that the companies on the left were completely surrounded by the Zulus and everyone 'was making the best of their way out of the camp'.[6] The companies of Mostyn and Cavaye were most likely the first to be virtually annihilated. It was possibly the panic-stricken flight resulting from the fast Zulu advance from the camp's left, rather than from the right, that sealed the extinction of the centre. Along with large numbers of European casuals, the NNC were involved in the rush to escape via the neck of Isandlwana. In their defence it has to be said that they were poorly equipped and armed, and not nearly as experienced as the imperial regular soldiers, who had just completed a campaign on the Eastern Cape frontier. The NNC's flight, nevertheless, heavily disrupted the ammunition supply lines to the rear of the three centre companies of Wardell, Pope and Porteous.

This disruption of the supply line was confirmed by private John Williams of the 1/24th. 'The men in camp, Bandsmen and men on Guard etc were trying to take ammunition to the companies but the greater part never got there as I saw horses and mules with ammunition on their backs galloping about the camp a short time afterwards.'[7] One of the 1/24th's stretcher bearers, Private E. Wilson, stated, 'When the idlers and men among the tents were now making the best of their way out of camp the doctor told us we were no longer likely to be of any use and the Band Sergeant told us we had better get away as best we could.'[8] Once the quartermaster Bloomfield had been killed by a Zulu rifle, it could only have heightened the confusion around the ammunition supply. Another 1/24th survivor, Private J. Bickley, recalled that the companies that had been out skirmishing were apparently running out of ammunition, and that the Native Contingent, together with most of the transport and other employed natives, were fleeing out of camp towards the road to Rorke's Drift.[9]

Considering the extent and intensity of the Zulu attack, with leading warrior formations hardly 100 to 150 yards distant, the rate of fire would have increased dramatically, with the demand eventually exceeding supply. Heavy fighting along the southern crest line, where the centre companies of Pope, Wardell and Porteous were positioned, took its toll in this respect. Once the ammunition supply lines were permanently broken, they had hardly a few minutes to escape a rout as they joined the chaos of the camp site with the Zulus hard on their heels.

By now Bloomfield was already dead, with quartermaster James Pullen of the 1/24th their last hope with regard to logistical support for the returning regular soldiers. Pullen, however, had already decided to abandon his post by their ammunition wagon, and tried to rally the running soldiers to turn the Zulu right horn. Amidst the confusion he asked Mr James Brickhill to go and ask Colonel Pulleine to send them help as they were being outflanked on the right. He then went off towards the front of Stony Kopje (Hill) with several of the soldiers.[10] Yorke asks the question whether Pullen would not have been of more value at the ammunition wagons, enabling the soldiers with him, as well as others, to make a much more credible stand. Large numbers of men from the three centre line companies had survived the retreat into the tent area. Lieutenant Higginson of the NNC mentioned 'the number of men coming in from the outlying companies searching for ammunition'. He said that although the 2nd Battalion of the NNC were fleeing, the 24th were retreating 'but very slowly', while at least two companies were seen still intact kneeling and firing even in the camp area.[11]

Out of ammunition, these men had to fight for their lives in little groups and individually – sadly doomed and killed off within minutes. There were, apparently, last-ditch attempts to reach the ammunition wagons. One party of soldiers appeared from among the tents and formed up a little above the ammunition wagons. Another group on the slope under the cliff behind the camp may well have been making a dash for it, but coming down the slope they got surrounded and along with a group of white men on the neck were the last to perish.[12]

Norris-Newman, a government conductor of wagons, wrote, 'When I left the camp Colonel Durnford was still alive, as well as a small remnant of the regulars, but they were so hemmed in that escape was impossible, and their ammunition seemed expended, for artillery men were trying to break open the cases on the wagons to supply them but it was too late.'[13] When the Zulus searched the pouches of the 24th soldiers after the battle, 'some had a few cartridges, most of them had none at all; there were very few found … Some had cartouche boxes, others cartridge belts; the belts were all empty, but a few cartridges were found in a few of the cartouche boxes.'[14]

Yorke concludes that 'a chronic failure in the organization of the ammunition supply, not only to Durnford's right wing but also to the imperial firing line both immediately before and after the final retreat, did play a key role in the disaster at Isandlwana.' This was due to a combination of human error and poor logistical planning. These factors were:

1. The inflexible nature of the regimental quartermastering procedures;
2. The unexpected mass panic around the central wagon supply area which fatally undermined the ammunition lines of the surviving imperial companies as they redeployed to the camp area;
3. An overall failure to anticipate the scale, spread and intensity of the final Zulu advance.

'This, in turn, meant that, in the final critical minutes, cartridge demand grossly exceeded supply. For the latter problem one can only return again to the tactical shortcomings of the camp commanders, Durnford and Pulleine, both of whom had allowed a gradual over-extension of the British lines during the two hours preceding the final collapse.'[15]

Military historian Major (Dr) Felix Machanik also mentions the main reasons given for the massacre at Isandlwana that appeared in numerous publications and following the official inquiry as being:

i) The inadequate organisation of the ammunition supply.
ii) The available ammunition boxes could not be easily opened, because they were surrounded at both ends with copper bands, securely fixed with multiple screws.
iii) There were not enough screwdrivers and thus not enough boxes had been opened before and during the action.
iv) The copper bands had to be forced open, using anything at hand from stones to bayonets.
v) The tinplate lining of the ammunition boxes (used to keep the cartridges dry by preventing moisture seeping through) was not easily torn open to get to the packets of cartridges inside.

vi) The Martini-Henry cartridges could not be easily extracted, as they frequently jammed in the breech. The extractor was inadequate, and thus valuable time was lost during the action; the ramrod had to be used via the muzzle of the rifle to push the cartridge case out of the breech, thus the overall firepower of the troops was reduced, especially as the Martini-Henry was a single-shot rifle. The other firearm used by the British troops was the Westley Richards capping breech-loading, single shot carbine, using a paper cartridge with black powder which fouled frequently and the barrel had to be cleaned often.[16]

At the second alarm the men were at lunch and when they came rushing out of their tents, they only had forty rounds in the pouches on their belts; a few brought their haversacks, which had two extra packets of cartridges, and some did not wear the pouch, which contained the loose ten rounds. Most of the men only had forty to fifty rounds when in fact each soldier should have had seventy rounds. Cavaye's 'A' company actually did. Each battalion quartermaster had an ammunition reserve of thirty rounds per man and there were 480,000 rounds in the ammunition wagons parked on the saddle.

The first half hour of the battle was static, the mass of warriors was stopped and the Zulus suffered heavily, but they still advanced. Slowly but surely the ammunition pouches emptied and the messengers were sent back for extra supplies to the 1st Battalion's ammunition wagon behind the tented camp, 1,000 yards from the 1st Battalion companies in the firing line. Cavaye's A' company was 1,800 yards away from his ammunition supply. QM James Pullen was inundated with demands for ammunition. The 2nd Battalion's ammunition QM Edward Bloomfield was actually only responsible for Pope's 'G' company, 1,100 yards away.

There was chaos at the wagons with the ammunition boxes being closed. Each box had the middle third top section as a sliding lid, held in position with only one cheese head brass screw, which when removed allowed the lid easily to slide out, revealing the tinlining, which was easily opened by pulling on a tin strap in one corner. The whole procedure took a few minutes, and according to Major Machanik the complaint made later by the few survivors that 'the difficulty in opening the ammo-boxes was the cause of the men not obtaining enough cartridges is blatantly incorrect. The main cause was the fact that each company or section did not have its own ammunition supply readily at hand, and thus the long distances of many of the companies from their ammunition wagons resulted in the loss of valuable, and as it turned out, vital time, before a trickle of supplies arrived.'[17]

As the available ammunition dried up, the firepower dropped and the Zulu impis rushed through the available gaps in the line, attacking the isolated companies from both the front and the rear. They overran the camp itself, by which time all supplies of ammunition were completely cut off, the wagons having been surrounded and all personnel slaughtered.

10

THE HEROISM OF
RORKE'S DRIFT

Rorke's Drift where the British garrison was stationed was named after a trader named James Rorke, who purchased a tract of land on the banks of the Buffalo River in Natal in 1849. The river formed a natural border between British-governed Natal and the independent kingdom of the Zulu. On the river at the point close to where Rorke settled was a natural ford (drift), which in time would bear his name. Rorke traded his merchandise across the Buffalo to his near neighbours the Zulus. In July 1875, the Norwegian missionary Karl Titlestad was anxious to purchase Rorke's trading post with a view to using it as base to preach the gospel to the Zulus. Rorke was keen to accept the offer, but he died on 24 October 1875, at the age of forty-eight, at his trading-post after a very short illness. His widow eventually sold the trading post to the Norwegian Missionary Society in 1878. A Swedish missionary, Otto Witt, took up the incumbency and Rorke's store was transformed into a makeshift church. Witt also decided to rename Shiyane Hill, which he called Oskarberg in honour of the King of Norway and Sweden.

In March, soon after his arrival at Oskarberg, Witt witnessed the negotiations that the British conducted with Sirayo, one of Cetshwayo's most powerful chiefs, over the boundary dispute between Natal and Zululand. The presence of between twenty and thirty tents accommodating British soldiers at Rorke's Drift, however, led him to believe that 'this means the certain eclipse of the Zulu people, and there should not be any doubt that within a short time Zululand will be an English colony'. It therefore did not surprise him to see missionaries from Zululand cross the Buffalo River in anticipation of imminent hostilities.[1]

At the outbreak of the war, Oskarberg was serving as a field hospital for the British forces. Witt had been compelled to lease its modest buildings to the Crown for the first three months of 1879. In addition, the mission was to get paid for the use of its punts and ferry at Rorke's Drift for the same period. On the eve of the Battle of Isandlwana, thirty-six patients were occupying the stone and brick manse, although only three of them were actually wounded. Witt was then obliged to live in a tent on the property. He had sent his wife and three children to Gordon Memorial station a few days earlier.

During the fortnight immediately preceding the battle, more than 5,000 troops had passed through the area. In spite of the strategic location of the station, which was ten minutes' walk from Rorke's Drift, nothing had been done to fortify it. The location of the hospital so close to a point where the Buffalo River could easily be crossed made it all the more vulnerable.

Witt saw little if any of the extermination of the British army at Isandlwana, and by the time the Zulus attacked at Rorke's Drift, he and his family had taken flight from the hostilities.[2]

After the main British force had moved off to Isandlwana, the garrison at Rorke's Drift got busy with the improvement of the roads, the maintenance of the punt and the handling of the supplies. There were two important buildings on the Rorke's Drift site: the former house of Witt, which had been converted into a hospital, and the old store built by the trader Rorke. The house had eleven rooms and a verandah but like many colonial houses of the period, some of the rooms could only be entered from the outside. Not all had windows, but those that did exist were small and shuttered. The outside walls were constructed of round stones and homemade bricks, but the interior ones were of mud bricks. The roof was thatched, and was therefore high and steep. The store built by Rorke and later converted to a chapel by the Swedish missionaries, was built of stone, with a very high roof. It was used as a commissariat store. To the west of the house stood a toilet, to the south a cookhouse and ovens, and to the east were two kraals and a 1-metre-high wall in the garden, which lay below the 1.5-metre-high rocky outcrop on which the buildings stood. The soldiers' tents of the garrison were pitched below the garden to the north.

On the morning of 22 January, Major H. Spalding from Helpmekaar was at the drift making arrangements to move troops forward and he gave Lieutenant John R. M. Chard, Royal Engineers, permission to ride to Isandlwana with Lieutenant H. L. Smith-Dorrien. On hearing that there were Zulus to the north of the camp, Chard returned to Rorke's Drift as he feared that the road might be threatened. He arrived back at the drift at midday, and shortly after, distant firing could be heard while a black mass moved across the col. As no messages were received, Major Spalding returned to Helpmekaar and left Chard in charge of the camp. While Chard was busy at the punt, Lieutenants J. Vane and Josef Adendorff came galloping along to bring news of the disaster at Isandlwana. Lieutenant Vane had been amongst the survivors; he had become separated from them and rode north along the river for some 5 miles before he met Adendorff, who had 'escaped by the road', although how this was possible has never been explained. The two delivered the message to Lieutenant G. Bromhead at the station and then rode off.

Lieutenant Chard went up to the station where he found that Bromhead, who had received a note of the disaster from Captain E. Essex, had struck the tents and unloaded two wagons near the hospital with the intention of evacuating the sick to Helpmekaar. They consulted with Quartermaster (Acting Commissariat Officer) James L. Dalton and concluded that any evacuation would be overtaken by the Zulus, that an attempt to hold the punts would be futile and that the only hope was to fortify the station, for which no defensive measures had been taken. A start was made on a mealie bag wall along the rocky ledge between the kraal and the house, while on the south side the corner of the commissariat store was connected to the house by a similar wall incorporating the two wagons. In the process, heaps of mealie bags, which weighed about 100 kilograms each, and biscuit boxes weighing about half of that were stacked in front of the store. They made loopholes in the walls of the buildings and barricaded all the outside doors and windows. But it was felt that the perimeter was too long to be defended by the men available, which comprised one company of the 2nd/24th Foot Regiment and one company of the NNC. Thus the arrival of a company of Durnford's Horse was met with great relief. These men were posted at the drift and instructed to hold it as long as possible if attacked, and to fall back if the situation demanded. Some other survivors from Isandlwana also rode by the drift but none of them bothered to stay.

By 16.30 that afternoon, the Zulus were seen from the top of Oskarberg, but at that stage the company of Durnford's Horse rode off and were followed by the NNC. This of course reduced the strength of Chard's group drastically and they found themselves in a grave situation. Chard then decided to divide the defences into two by means of a wall of biscuit boxes, but they had only completed part of the wall when the Zulus started to attack. At this stage the strength of the garrison was: Royal Engineers, Lieutenant Chard and one man; 24th Foot, Lieutenant Bromhead and 109 other ranks, but of whom twenty-two were ill; other units twenty-seven, of whom thirteen were sick. That made up a total of 139 men, of whom thirty-five were sick. Of the latter, fortunately, fifteen were walking patients and could help to defend. That meant that there were 120 men to defend the post. In the barricaded rooms in the house were six able-bodied men, four walking patients and twenty bed patients.

In the meantime, the 1,500-strong uThulwana and the 2,000-strong uDlobo turned aside from the col at Isandlwana and made their way to the bend of the Buffalo River, which they then crossed and advanced towards Rorke's Drift on the Natal side. The inDlu-yengwe, led by Usibebu, had been following the fugitives in their wake, and killed officers Melvill and Coghill, then turned north, burning kraals on their way. Their leader Usibebu, however, had been wounded and had turned back.

The two Zulu groups met on a small knoll and, now under the command of Dubulamanzi, advanced on the garrison at Rorke's Drift. At the time, Revd George Smith and missionary Otto Witt and Private Wall had been posted on the Oskarberg, and observing these development they rushed down the hill to warn the soldiers at the post. Missionary Witt did not wait to see the outcome of all of this but abandoned his property and left to join his wife and children at the Gordon Memorial station, to where he had sent them five days earlier.[3]

The inDlu-yengwe swung round the western flank of the Oskarberg, deployed under the hill terrace and attacked the rear of the military post where they suffered heavily from the concentrated British fire. They were followed by the uThulwana and the uDloke, who attacked the western end of the post, but their losses were so heavy that they withdrew to regroup behind the trees in the garden. From here they stormed the south side of the post, with the fight reaching a climax, Zulus storming over their own dead to scale the ledge and the wall of mealie bags. At the same time, some Zulus positioned themselves on the terrace of the Oskarberg and fired down into the post; this caused some casualties to the British at the south wall. The soldiers in front of the hospital, especially, came under severe pressure, so Lieutenant Chard pulled them in, closing the gap between the front wall and the building with a short wall. The Zulus then poured into this space, which had been evacuated and threatened the house, which had empty rooms in front but no loopholes for the defenders.

During the first attacks many Zulus had taken up position against the walls and tried to smash down the doors or grab the rifle barrels protruding from the loopholes. Their onslaught was fierce and something had to give, and the first door to give way was the one to the middle room on the west face of the building. Inside the room, Private John Williams had cut a hole through the wall while Private Joseph Williams and Private William Harrigan – one of the walking sick – were holding the Zulus at bay. They managed to evacuate two patients but Privates Joseph Williams and Harrigan, as well as two patients, were overcome and killed by the attackers. In the room on the south-west corner of the building, Private Thomas Cole, who was suffering from claustrophobia, ran out of the front of the house and into death. That left Private Henry Hook alone with the Zulu wounded at the attack on Sihayo's kraal. With the Zulus battering at the door, Hook went into the next room alone where he found Private Williams and the two patients coming through the other door. There were now two soldiers and eleven patients in the room. Hook held the doors against the attacks while Williams dug a hole into the next room, where the only occupant was Private John

Waters, a walking patient (Private Waters' account of the fight is provided later). Williams again did the digging and Hook held the defence until they were all into the next room, except for Waters, who was hiding in a cupboard and later escaped.

In the last rooms, Private Robert Jones helped four patients to escape through the window and when Privates Hook and Williams brought the other patients in, all got through the window except Sergeant Robert Maxfield. Because he was delirious from fever, a helpless Maxfield could not be moved in the helter-skelter and was an easy prey for the Zulus, who stabbed him to death. Gunners Arthur Howard and A. Evans of the Royal Artillery were in the room on the north-west corner of the building, with the door opening on to the space occupied by the Zulus. Evans seized the opportunity to race around the front of the hospital to reach the safety of the entrenchment, but when Howard charged out he went the wrong way. He vaulted the breastwork and crawled into the bush where 'in company with a dead pig and four of our horses (which had been shot where they were tied up), he lay unobserved all night, and came in unharmed at daylight.'[4]

With the evacuation having shortened the perimeter to be defended, it nevertheless released many Zulus from the attack on the house to circle round to the eastern side. The British lost a few lives getting the wounded across the open space to behind the biscuit box wall, but they built up a redoubt of mealie bags in which the sick could be accommodated while it afforded a vantage point for the riflemen. Most of the patients who eventually reached the entrenchment were attended to by Dr Reynolds, and some were able to take up position among their fellow soldiers defending the inner fort with all their might. Corporal William Allen of the 24th hardly had his arm bandaged when he helped Reverend Smith to distribute the ammunition. 'A missionary worked hard keeping the men supplied with bullets, and then prayed for victory,' survivor Henry Martin recalled some fifty years later. 'Victory came but the soldiers thought it was the missionary's bullets rather than his prayers that brought it about!'[5]

Private E. Savage was lying on his side firing through a gap in the boxes, while Trooper H. Lugg manned a position below the eaves of the storehouse's roof. ACO J. L. Dalton also kept firing with great effect until he was wounded in the right-hand side of his chest and had to be bandaged and moved to the inside of the mealie bag redoubt.[6]

While this hospital evacuation was taking place, the Zulus set fire to the thatch on the building, and with the flames lighting up the surrounding area, it gave the British soldiers some advantage. Surgeon Major Reynolds said years later that 'the bright light enabled the men to fire with terrible effect, and the enemy obtained no cover in the garden, which otherwise would have enabled them to get close in without being seen'.[7] In an interview with the *Sunderland Daily Echo* on 6 March 1879, the Swedish missionary Witt also said: 'That the hospital was put on fire was certainly a personal loss to me, as all my property was burnt, but it was of great importance to the whole colony, and especially for the people in the commissariat store, as the flames of the burning house enabled them to aim properly on the Zulus, and thus keep them at a fair distance. If the Zulus had known they would never have put fire to the house; the heavy darkness of that dreadful night would have made our troops unable to defend themselves as they did.'[8]

The Zulus concentrated on the eastern side of the defences and were eventually able to occupy both cattle kraals but despite heroic efforts were unable to break into the last defence. Around midnight, Lieutenant Chard led an attack to drag the water cart near the biscuit box wall to quench his men's thirst. The Zulu attack then started to slacken, and by about 04.00 on the morning of 23 January they withdrew. Chard sent out patrols about an hour later, but around 07.00 the Zulus reappeared at the western end of the Oskarberg, where they sat down and took snuff. Chard's men had to take up their posts again, but after a while the Zulus skirted wide round the post and then withdrew by way of the drift. By that time, the men at the post were all exhausted, having fought for the better part of ten hours and were running low on ammunition. Of 20,000 rounds in reserve at the mission, only 900 remained.[9]

Considering the circumstances, the British losses were relatively low. The British lost seventeen dead, who were buried just south of the post, and the Zulus some 400 or 500. When Chelmsford's force arrived, the house was broken down and the material used to build a loopholed fortification, 3 metres high, which incorporated the commissariat store. Shortly after, a start was made on the building of Fort Melvill, an extensive system of fortifications overlooking the drift and the punt moorings that was occupied until the end of the war.

The Account of Private Frederick Hitch, VC

We did not expect any fighting that day, and were occupied in our usual duties, little thinking that a horde of Zulus – the pick of the Zulu Army, in fact – were marching on us, determined to kill every man at our little post.

About one o'clock two men galloped to the Drift, bringing the news that the Zulus had annihilated our force at Isandlwana, and that they were now marching on to attack our post at Rorke's Drift. Lieutenant Bromhead, who was in charge of the post, and Commissioner Dalton at once held a conference. The position was a difficult one: our little force only consisted of a handful of men, whilst the approaching Zulus, mad with success, must have numbered at least four thousand. And many of them, moreover, were armed. At first it was thought the better part of valour to desert the post, but fortunately this decision was altered. We were to defend the post, and hold it at all costs.

With us were four hundred friendly natives, and these men we at once set to work carrying mealie (corn) bags and boxes of stores, which we placed in position as barricades, making an enclosure or laager of which the mission house, used as a hospital, and some out-buildings formed a part. Just before the barricades had been completed the friendly niggers began to funk it, and as soon as they found out that the Zulus were really coming down upon us in great force they commenced to sneak away.

We tried to rally them, but it was of no use. Then their captain went after them with the intention of bringing them back; but he disappeared too. Just to show these black gentlemen what we thought of their conduct, some of us, including myself, sent a few shots after them, which brought down dead one of their white non-commissioned officers.

While the men were still barricading the place, Lieutenant Bromhead asked me to climb to the top of a building, which I believe had been used as a church, and keep a look-out for the enemy. Having got to the top of the building I could plainly see the Zulus forming up just over the brow of a hill. 'They are ready to attack, sir,' I called out to Lieutenant Bromhead, 'and I think there are about four thousand of them.' A little fellow named Morris, who heard me, remarked: 'Oh, if that's all there are, we can manage that lot all right!' Presently I saw a Zulu, evidently one of their chiefs, who was standing on the summit of a hill, gave the signal by extending his arms, and immediately the whole force commenced to advance on us. They seemed to work on a pivot, the pivot being only about three hundred yards distant, when the final advance began; so that, in order to attack us on all sides at once, the other end of their line had come on at a tremendous pace.

My position on the housetop was a pretty good target for them, but none of their shots hit me. As soon as I saw them on the move, I dropped down into the laager and fixed my bayonet. I was only just in time, which will give you some idea of the rapidity of their movements. On they came with a rush. With one hand the warriors held their shields, and in the other hand they carried their deadly assegais. A few were armed with rifles, just taken from the poor fellows whom they had annihilated at Isandlwana. We volleyed into the mass as they advanced, but there was little hesitation. Our bullets accounted for many, but there were hundreds to fill their places.

They still came on right up to the barricades, and were only turned by the good cold steel of our bayonets, for which they had far more respect than for bullets. Then it was load and fire and bayonet just as fast as we could. The niggers would retire and come on again in rushes, each rush being announced by a short war cry. This war cry, by the way, was very useful to us: we knew what to expect. Even when darkness came upon us they continued to use their war shout, which was not altogether wise on their part, because it at once put us on the alert. However, we didn't complain on that score. Fortunately those of the Zulus who had rifles knew very little about their weapons or how to use them. Their shots appeared to go either much too high or too low. I suppose they did not understand the sighting. Had there been a few marksmen amongst them I fear myself and many more would have gone under at Rorke's Drift.

Soon it was discovered that it was impossible to defend the laager which we had made, so Major Chard [*Chard was given a brevet Majority after Rorke's Drift*] gave an order to make a second line of barricades, inside the outer one. This work was carried out under great difficulties and under heavy fire from a cave close by, where a few Zulus had taken cover. Had the four hundred friendly native troops not bolted, the larger laager would have been none too roomy. This second line of barricades proved a great success, as it meant that we had less ground to cover. There was a certain space of about nine yards where the barricading was uncompleted. It was, of course, the weakest link in the chain, and the Zulus were not long in discovering this fact. In this position eight of us – Bromhead, Nicholls, Fagan, Cole, Dalton, Schiess, Williams, ands myself – made a stand, and it was here, I think, that the hardest work was done. Though the situation was so uncomfortable, there was no bungling. Each man in a businesslike manner singled out the nigger who was nearest him, and dealt out death if he could. In one of these nasty rushes three Zulus were making for me; they seemed to have specially marked me out. The first fellow I shot; the second man I bayoneted; the third man got right into the laager, but he declined to stand up against me. With a leap he jumped over the barricade, and made off. A few yards from the barricade lay a wounded Zulu. We knew he was there, and that he had only been wounded, and so wanted watching. At the moment we were far too busy with the more active members to find time to put him right out. Presently I saw him, with rifle in hand, taking aim at one of my comrades. It was too late to stop him; he fired, and poor Nicholls fell dead, shot through the head. I practised a little ruse upon a Zulu at which I had to smile even at the time. This particular Zulu had got through the barricades into the laager, and was in the act of throwing an assegai at Lieutenant Bromhead, whose attention was directed elsewhere. At that moment my rifle was unloaded, and there was no time to reload. I shouted to the Zulu, and brought my rifle up to my shoulder as if to fire. My Zulu soldier didn't wait. With a duck of the head and a mighty leap he bounded over the barricades and made off in a manner worthy of any eminent acrobat. In one of the many rushes a nigger, who had missed our bullets, came full tilt at me, and seized my bayonet with both his hands. This was quite a new experience for me. There was no time to lose: I had to settle up with him quickly or not at all. For a few seconds we struggled for possession of the rifle; then I managed to point the barrel at his stomach, and fired whilst he still clutched the bayonet. He was a brave fellow. Parson Smith, our chaplain, kept us well supplied with ammunition. Now and then he would ask our men not to swear so much. But the men continued to swear, and fight the harder. Now the Zulus had set fire to the roof, which was of thatch, and the patients had to be taken away. In order to reach the laager the patients and their defenders had to cross an undefended space, which was swept by the enemy's fire.

We knew that the poor fellows in the hospital were fighting against great odds for their lives, but we could not see what was going on there. Jones, Williams, Hook, and their comrades had kept the enemy off for some time, by bullets. One by one the poor fellows scrambled out of the burning building, and ran the gauntlet. We covered them as much as we could, but many of them went under. When the Zulus set fire to the hospital the other company of the battalion, for which we had been so anxiously waiting, appeared in sight. But they didn't march to our rescue. Seeing the hospital on fire, they came to the conclusion that we had all been annihilated, and with drooping spirits we saw our comrades turn back and retire. It was at this time that the Zulus made one of their most desperate charges, and Rorke's Drift was all but lost. Lieutenant Bromhead encouraged the men. 'Don't lose heart,' he called out; 'Our men will return as soon as they find we are holding out.' The hospital fire became more fierce. This fire turned out to be our salvation, for as darkness came on it lit up the ground on all sides of the laager, and enabled us to see the Zulus whenever they approached the barricades.

The fighting went on desperately. Rush after rush had been repelled. Of the eight who held the unbarricaded position only two of us were left, Lieutenant Bromhead and myself. Nicholls, Fagan, and Cole were killed, whilst Dalton and Williams were wounded. So Bromhead and I went on together for about an hour, and a rough time we had too. More than once the Zulus got inside the laager, but were beaten back or killed. We were both very busy with Zulus in front when one of the niggers managed to pass us and get inside. I knew he was there. I was just about to shoot down a Zulu in front, when the Zulu inside shot me through the right shoulder, carrying away the scapula. Turning round quickly, Bromhead at once shot down the man who had wounded me. I got up again, and attempted to use my rifle, but it was no use; my right arm wouldn't work, so I strapped it into my waist belt to keep it out of the way. Then Bromhead gave me his revolver to use, and with this I think I did as much execution as I had done before I was wounded. Seeing how badly wounded I was, one of my comrades, a man named Deacon, asked me whether he should 'put me out' when it came to the finish. He could see that my strength was fast failing, and that if the devils got through I would be quite unable to strike a blow for myself. 'No, I don't think I want any,' I said, I had no desire to have my life ended, but it was kind of my friend Deacon to think of me in this way. It was about ten o'clock. Four hours I had been bleeding from the wound in my back, and I was getting very faint from loss of blood. I knew that I was losing consciousness, the last of my recollection being that Bromhead still held his post. Then I went down where I had been fighting for seven hours. I was told that later on they dragged me inside the inner laager.

It was not till the next morning that I came to, when I found we had just been relieved by a column under Lord Chelmsford. My chum was one of the relieving force. He, good chap, came and changed my shirt, which was saturated with blood, and did what he could for me. Later on in the day towards evening Lord Chelmsford himself came to me, and, bending down beside me, said: 'Mr. Bromhead has given me an account of your excellent services. I will recommend you for the V.C., and, if you only survive, you may be sure I will do everything that lies in my power for you.[10]

Private Hitch also spoke to the *Aberdeen Journal* later that year. The newspaper reported:

Private Frederik Hitch states 'The first news I had of what had happened at Isandula was when one of the mounted infantry named Evans came galloping up to the mission house and said that a part of the camp across the river had been destroyed by the Zulus; that two guns had been taken as well as all the ammunition; and that the enemy was advancing in force to attack Rorke's Drift. This was about 3:00 in the afternoon. I was ordered by Lieutenant Bromhead to mount the roof of the stores to watch for the Zulus. The big mob of the enemy soon came up, extending from the right; and the column appeared to me, as I watched them from the roof of the house, to be about a mile and ½ in length. They were then just beyond gunshot, but were perfectly quiet. They then made a right wheel, and the extreme right moved into the caves on the adjoining hill; and as I was about the only man they could see, being on the roof, they took a potshot at me, but missed.

I reported the movements to my comrades below, and fired three shots – these being the first that were fired at the Zulu at Rorke's Drift. The enemy made a yell, and came at the little fort with a rush, and I then got down and took my position with the rest of the company on the right front, Mr. Bromhead being close to me. The sun was just beginning to set at the time. The Zulus came close up to the front, and after they had taken the hospital and were burning it, Lieutenant Bromhead and three privates, with Colour-sergeant Bourne, kept the deposition in the right front, in order to keep the enemy from getting a line of fire at the men of the 24th, who were firing to the front from behind a line of biscuit boxes. I was here for about an hour, being all the time between these crossfires. I saw one of my comrades, Private Nichols, killed.

He was shot through the head, his brains being scattered all about us. He had up to his death been doing good service with his rifle. Another, Corporal Sheath, of the Natal contingent, was shot on my left. I myself kept on shooting into a good mob of the enemy, who were very quiet in all they did. About a quarter to seven I was shot from the left, the ball striking me under the right shoulder blade, and came out through the shoulder. I did not come to before the morning, just at the peak of day, and I then found myself in a stable.'[11]

Private Waters was another to be interviewed by the *Aberdeen Journal* on the battle:

I was special orderly at the hospital at Rorke's Drift, and at this time have seen 21¼ years service. I was in the hospital when Private Evans rode into the camp and reported that the Zulus had massacred the whole column at Isandula. We would hardly believe this at first, but very soon had reason to understand it was only too true.

We got as many patients as possible out of the hospital, but we had not time to remove them all. It was an utter impossibility to do that. Between half past four and five, as near as I can remember, the Zulus came over the hill, and I saw about 50 of them form a line in skirmishing order, just as British soldiers would do. The main body was in their rear, over the shoulder of the hill. They came about 20 yards, and then opened fire on the hospital. I stopped there, firing at the enemy through holes made by other men, and others did the same, but were not able to prevent the enemy coming right up to the hospital. Some of them came in and set fire to it. While I was there I took refuge in a cupboard, and Private Beckett, an invalid, came with me. As they were going out I killed many of them; and as I could not stay there long, the place of being so suffocating, I put on a black cloak which I had found in the cupboard, and which must have belonged to Mr Witt, and ran out in the long grass and lay down. The Zulus must have thought I was one of their dead comrades, as they were all round about me, and some trod on me. Beckett had gone out half an hour before, and he, poor fellow, was assagaied right through his stomach. I went into laager next morning. Dr. Reynolds did all he could to save him, but did not succeed.

I got up at daybreak, having expected every minute my life would be taken, and then saw my comrades on the top of the mealie sacks, and I said, 'Thank God, I have got my life.' I had been shot early in the engagement in the shoulder and knee, and here's the bullets which were taken out next morning by Dr. Reynolds. I knew many poor fellows who fell at Isandula. I saw Private Harrigan killed. Poor Beckett was buried next morning properly. Around the hospital dead Zulus were piled up in heaps.[12]

The commander at the post, Lieutenant John Chard, later compiled a report for his superiors in the Royal Engineers, which is given in full below:

Rorke's Drift
25th Jan: 1879

Sir

I have the honor to report that on the 22 Inst: I was left in command at Rorke's Drift by Major Spalding who went to Helpmakaar to hurry on the Co. 24th Regt. ordered to protect the punts.

About 3.15 p.m. on that day, I was at the ponts when two men came riding from Zululand at a gallop, and shouted to be taken across the river – I was informed by one of the, Lieut Adendorff of Lonsdale's Regt. (who remained to assist in the defence) of the disaster at Isandlwana camp, and that the Zulus were advancing on Rorke's Drift. The other, a carbineer, rode off to take the news to Helpmakaar.

Almost immediately I received a message from Lieut. Bromhead, Commg. the company 24th Regt. at the Camp near the Commt. Stores, asking me to come up at once.

I gave the order to inspan, strike tents, put all stores & c into the wagon and at once rode up to the Commt. Store and found that a note had been received from the third Column to state that the enemy were advancing in force against our post, which we were to strengthen and hold at all costs.

Lieut. Bromhead was most actively engaged in loopholing and barricading the store building and hospital and connecting the defence of the two buildings by walls of mealie bags and two wagons that were on the ground.

I held a hurried consultation with him and with Mr. Dalton of the Commt. (who was actively superintending the work of defence, and whom I cannot sufficiently thank for his most valuable services), entirely approving of the arrangements made. I went round the position and then rode down to the ponts and brought up the guard of 1 sergt. and 6 men, wagon &c.

I desire here to mention the offer of the punt man Daniells and Sergt. Milne 3rd Buffs, to moor the ponts in the middle of the stream and defend them from their decks with a few men. We arrived at the post about 3.30 p.m. Shortly after an officer of Durnfords Horse arrived and asked for orders; I requested him to send a detachment to observe the drifts and ponts, to throw out outposts in the direction of the enemy, and check his advance as much as possible, falling back upon the post when forced to retire and assisting in its defence.

I requested Lieut. Bromhead to post his men, and having seen his and every man at his post, the work once more went on.

About 4.20 p.m. the sound of firing was heard behind the hill to our south. The officer of Durnford's returned, reporting the enemy close upon us, and that his men would not obey his orders, but were going off to Helpmakaar, and I saw them, apparently about 100 in number, going off in that direction.

About the same time Capt. Stephenson's detachment of Natal Native contingent left us, as did that officer himself.

I saw that our line of defence was too extended for the small number of men now left us, and at once commenced a retrenchment of biscuit boxes.

We had not completed a wall two boxes high when about 4.30 p.m. 500 or 600 of the enemy came in sight around the hill to our south and advanced at a run against our south wall. They were met by a well sustained fire, but notwithstanding their heavy loss continued the advance to within 50 yards of the wall, when they met with such a heavy fire from the wall, and cross fire from the store, that they were checked, but taking advantage of the cover afforded by the cook house, ovens &c kept up a heavy fire. The greater number however without stopping, moved to the left around the hospital and made a rush at our N.W. wall of mealie bags, but after a short but desperate struggle were driven back with heavy loss into the bush around the work.

The main body of the enemy were close behind and had lined the ledge of rock and caves overlooking us about 400 yards to our south from where they kept up a constant fire, and advancing somewhat more to their left than the first attack, occupied the garden, hollow road and bush in great force.

Taking advantage of the bush which we had not time to cut down, the enemy were able to advance under cover close to our wall, and in this part soon held one side of the wall, while we held the other, a series of desperate assaults were made extending from the hospital along the wall as far as the bush reached, but each was most splendidly met and repulsed by our men with the bayonet, Corpl. Schiess N.N.O. greatly distinguishing himself by his conspicuous gallantry.

The fire from the rocks behind us, though badly directed, took us completely in reverse and was so heavy that we suffered very severely, and about 6 p.m. were forced to retire behind the retrenchment of biscuit boxes.

All this time the enemy had been attempting to force the hospital and shortly after set fire to its roof.

The garrison of the hospital defended it room by room, bringing out all the sick who could be moved before they retired, Privates Williams, Hook, R. Jones and W. Jones 24th Regt. being the last men to leave, holding the doorway with the bayonet their own ammunition being expended.

From the want of interior communication and the burning of the house it was impossible to save all – With most heartfelt sorrow I regret we could not save these poor fellows from their terrible fate.

Seeing the hospital burning and the desperate attempts of the enemy to fire the roof of the stores, we converted two mealie bag heaps into a sort of redoubt which gave a second line of fire all round; Asst. Comy. Dunne working hard at this though much exposed, and rendering valuable assistance.

As darkness came on we were completely surrounded and after several attempts had been gallantly repulsed, were eventually forced to retire to the middle and then inner wall of the kraal on our east. The position we then had we retained throughout.

A desultory fire was kept up all night, and several assaults were attempted and repulsed; our men firing with the greatest coolness did not waste a single shot; the light afforded by the burning hospital being of great help to us.

About 4 a.m. 23rd Inst: the firing ceased and at daybreak the enemy were out of sight over the hill to the South West.

We patrolled the grounds collecting the arms of the dead Zulus, and strengthened our defences as much as possible.

We were removing the thatch from the roof of the stores when about 7 a.m. a large body of the enemy appeared on the hills to the South West.

I sent a friendly Kafir, who had come in shortly before with a note to the Officer commanding at Helpmakaar asking for help.

About 8 a.m. the third column appeared in sight, the enemy who had been gradually advancing, falling back as they approached. I consider the enemy who attacked us to have numbered about 3,000 (three thousand).

We killed about 350 (three hundred and fifty).

Of the steadiness and gallant behaviour of the whole garrison I cannot speak too highly.

I wish especially to bring to your notice the conduct of Lieut. Bromhead 2/24th Regt. and the splendid behaviour of his company B 2/24th.

Surgeon Reynolds A.M.D. in his constant attention to the wounded under fire where they fell.

Act. Commt. Officer Dalton, to whose energy much of our defences were due, and who was severely wounded while gallantly assisting in the defence.

Asst. Commy. Dunne
Acting Storekeeper Byrne (killed)
Col. Sergt. Bourne 2/24th
Sergt. Williams 2/24th (wounded dangerously)
Sergt. Windridge 2/24th
Corpl. Schiess 2/3 Natal Native Contingent (wounded)

1395 Private Williams 2/24th
593 Private Jones 2/24th
Private McMahon A.H.C.
Pte Beckett, 1/24th Regt.
making a total killed of 17

* List already forwarded by Medical Officer.

Herewith is appended a plan of the buildings showing our lines of defence, the points of the compass referred to in this report are as shown in sketch approximately magnetic.

To Col. Glynn C. C/o Commt. 3rd Column
I have the honour to be your obedient servant
Jno R.M. Chard
(John) Lieut. R.E.[13]

Private Henry Hook, B Company, 2nd/24th Regiment wrote from Rorke's Drift in an undated letter to his mother, Mrs E. Hook, Drybridgestreet, Monmouth, some time after the battle:

After the enemy had fled from the general's camp [Isandlwana], they came across the river here and attacked our commissary stores but fortunately we got an hour's warning and made a fort. By-and-bye down they came in thousands – one black mass – so many we did not know where to fire first, they being so many and we were about 100 all told. But, thank God, after a night of great fighting, we drove them off and we saw the general's forces coming over the hill and that gave us great relief, I can tell you. There were four Monmouth men killed, viz. Sergeant Maxfield [Cinderhill Street], Private Hopkins [formerly a servant at Gibraltar House, Monmouth and later a policeman stationed at Llanarth], Private Charles [Penalt near Monmouth] and Thomas Bennet [Monnow Street]. Sergeant Maxfield was burnt alive in the hospital; the enemy swarmed around and burnt the place before we could save him and, as he was raving mad with fever, he could not save himself. Hopkins and the others were killed in the fight at the general's camp. I had a very narrow escape, for I was

in the hospital and when the enemy set fire to it, I had to get
out of the window and fight my way through them ... I am
now servant to Major Black [his man having been killed] and
a nice gentleman he is and I like him very much ...[14]

Corporal George Howe was one of sixty sappers of 5 Field
Company, Royal Engineers, who was marching from Greytown to
Mooi River the day before the Battle of Isandlwana, and on the
22nd received a note with the message, 'Push on for Mooi River;
rumours of a reverse.' 'That was all we could learn,' he wrote.
'Push on we did, we almost ran. We got to Mooi River about one.
All we could learn there was that the camp had been captured, and
every man was cut off.' Their dilemma now was whether to return
to Greytown, which they thought would be attacked, or dig in
where they were? They settled for occupying a farmhouse, where
they were to spend a nerve-wracking night.

'About a hundred yards from the river where we had first crossed
stood the house of a settler,' he recorded. 'We took possession of
this. Along one side and down towards the river we drew up the
wagons in line. On the other two sides we threw up a shelter
trench. We were hard at work until dusk, when we broke our fast.
At night we turned into the trenches ... The eyes were coming
out of our heads with trying to pierce the gloom. About twelve a
Dutchman came in, and said he had seen the enemy. Hour after
hour we stood, but no enemy. The least noise brought the rifle to
the ready. We all knew we had to deal with an enemy who did
not know what mercy was, and should have to fight to the bitter
end. I took one cartridge and put it in my breast, determining if
it came to the worst to blow out my own brains rather than fall
into their hands. At last day broke, and never did we welcome it
with such joy.'[15]

Having covered another 14 miles, and about to camp, a
messenger arrived with the news that thirty wagons filled with
ammunition stood undefended at Sandspruit. On they marched to
Sandspruit, and on 24 January built a makeshift fort where they
had a Zulu attack that lasted about twenty minutes. Four days
later they marched to Helpmekaar, and then on to Rorke's Drift.
At the drift they had to assist in the construction of another and
much stronger fortification.

The month of February saw Rorke's Drift turned into a hellhole. Hundreds of rain-drenched soldiers, commanded by Colonel Glyn, found themselves without shelter in the old fortifications, to emerge each day to work on the new fort. Of these circumstances, Corporal Howe wrote: 'To guard from surprise, we fall in and stand to our arms until daybreak. When we can see the coast clear we march out and pile arms, and then go to work. We work till 5 p.m. At six the bugle sounds and we all go into fort. We are not allowed to take off our things, but lie down in them, our rifles near our sides. We have no tents, we have a rug and take the open air. Sunday we have a church parade at nine, and go to work at ten.'[16]

A sergeant of the 2/24th Regiment recorded their forlorn and verminous plight: 'It is not safe to get a drink of water without our rifles at present. We have lost all our tents and cooking utensils, we have only what we stand up in. The Zulus destroyed everything belonging to us. We are literally in rags and will soon be carried about, for we are getting plenty of companions and can't keep them away. You would laugh to see the regiment, some with no boots, some with their jackets and trousers patched with sheepskins and all kinds of things.' By 14 February he had not taken off his clothes or pouches since the day of Isandlwana, three weeks before.[17]

Ralph Busby had joined Chelmsford's column as a civilian surgeon, and also witnessed the massacre at Isandlwana. He was stationed in the fort built at Rorke's Drift after the fight there on 22 January, and less than a fortnight later recorded: 'All the farmers seem to have gone into laager, and left their houses. I had a five and twenty miles ride to one – Fort Pine [between Rorke's Drift and Dundee] – a few days back to see some who were sick there; the few farms passed on the road were all deserted and cattle driven off to near the laager. It's a queer sight inside, cramful of wagons, women, and children. But I got a good square meal, some tender mutton, fresh milk, with my coffee and butter, and had a good sleep in a covered wagon … It's very hot and cooped up in this place [Rorke's Drift], very much troubled with flies which swarm everywhere; they worry the horses frightful, I have now lost both mine. I expect the expense to the country before this war is over will be enormous; and of all the useless lands I have ever been in, South Africa is the chief.'[18]

Private Thomas Thomas of Ystalyfera, Wales, wrote to his uncle and aunt from Rorke's Drift about their hardships while based at the drift. 'I am very sorry to tell you that we see very hard times of it out here now. We are on the march all the time and we have not seen a bit of bread this last two months, only biscuits all the time and we are often on the road for two or three days at a stretch, that we don't get coffee or tea, only dry biscuit; it is an awful place for water. Another thing, we have to write with powder and water and I had to pay fourpence for this sheet of paper and envelope.'[19]

Corporal Thomas Davies of the 2/24th wrote to a friend: 'Since the great misfortune we had, I have not had my clothes off. We haven't had any attack since but we are living in great misery for we haven't any opportunity of getting anything yet in the way of clothes for change. We are at Rorke's Drift holding our position in a commisariat fort where we shall remain, I believe, until they have got more troops from England … I am happy to inform you that I am made full corporal since the great disaster. I wear two stripes on my arm and one good conduct badge below… P.S. You must excuse my writing as this ink is made of gunpowder.'[20]

A cousin of Owen Ellis, whose letters were mentioned earlier, Private Richard Owen of 2/24th Regiment wrote from Helpmekaar to his mother in Caernarvon: 'My time will be completed twelve months next July and I hope to be home before long, as I am tired of this life, as we have been nearly four years lying out on the Velt. Our Regiment is now up in Natal Colony at war with the Zulus. We have had some very hard times up in the Transkei [during the 9th Frontier War] but it is a great deal worse up here … We are getting very hard times since the fight [at Isandlwana], as there are only a few of us left. As we are only a few miles from the Zulu King's country, we are on the look-out day and night. We have not pulled our clothes off since the 21st of January, and we are expecting another attack before long, as the General has sent home to England for six or eight regiments to come out. As soon as they arrive out here, we will advance on the Zulu King's residence but the Zulus are a great deal stronger than us.'[21]

A few months after Rorke's Drift, Lieutenant Bromhead (by then Major) was presented with a special revolver by the residents of Thurlby Estate 'as a token of our esteem and admiration for your gallant conduct, which has brought honour to the name of England, and especially to Thurlby, your native place'.[22]

11

BRITISH DEFENCE AFTER ISANDLWANA

It is a misconception that after its defeat at Isandlwana, the British army in northern Natal remained passive and that it was only months later that they had resumed the offensive after the arrival of reinforcements from Britain. The reality was that the consternation after Isandlwana lasted only a few weeks, and that about two months later the British went over to an active defence. Therefore, from the end of March, the British forces demonstrated and raided along the border of Natal and Zululand, and during April and May the British gained ascendancy in the northern sector, as was proven by the withdrawal of the Zulus from the exposed country on the left bank of the Buffalo River.

Within a fortnight after the battles of Isandlwana and Rorke's Drift on 22 January 1879, the British forces in northern Natal had recovered from the shock of defeat and introduced regular patrolling and occasional scouting on their front. On 14 March, a small party also made a quick visit to the Isandlwana battlefield.[1] In the meantime, the bulk of the Imperial forces, which was garrisoned at Helpmekaar, Rorke's Drift and near Msinga, immediately set about fortification and maintenance. Settler units at these posts and at Fort Pine, and the Native Border Guard near the Buffalo River, also restored their confidence and discipline. The situation along the northern border soon stabilised, where Lord Chelmsford would resume his offensive in due course, but first there was a big task in the south that he had to attend to. The Zulus' siege of Colonel Pearson's British force at Eshowe neccesitated him to lead a relief column to Eshowe at the end of March, and in order to facilitate his advance he ordered a demonstration all along the border to distract the Zulus.

On 27 March Major Wilsone Black of the 2/24th Regiment crossed the Buffalo River at Rorke's Drift with thirty-five Natal Mounted Police and ten officers who remained from the now defunct 3rd Regiment, Natal Native Contingent. They rode 10 miles into Zululand, going round the Zulu chief Sihayo's kraal but not engaging any enemy; for a while though, they did observe a Zulu force moving along a ridge some 2 miles off. At the same time Major Harcourt M. Bengough, commanding the 2nd Battalion of the 1st Regiment, Natal Native Contingent, led most of his men from Fort Bengough near the Msinga Magistracy to the Buffalo downstream. They were joined by part of the Native Border Guard, but the river level was too high for them to cross.

Lord Chelmsford's column to relieve the force at Eshowe consisted of 3,390 Europeans and 2,280 natives and had a range of artillery, including two 9-pounders, four 24-pounder rocket tubes and two Gatling guns. The progress was slow as the rivers they had to cross were swollen by heavy rains, and in addition they had to take a roundabout route to avoid ambush. By the evening of 1 April, the relief column was laagering on the south bank of the Inyezane, where they fought the victorious Battle of Gingindlovu, before continuing on to Eshowe. They entered Eshowe on 3 April, thus ending the two-month siege. Chelmsford concluded that Eshowe did not need to be retained, and had the constructed defences demolished.

Encouraged by this success, Chelmsford ordered the demonstration along the Zululand border to continue, and authorised raids across it where practicable. He assembled a force of over 2,000 men at Rorke's Drift, which consisted of Natal Mounted Police, Natal Carbineers, and some mounted natives from Helpmekaar; the 2/1 Natal Native Contingent from Fort Bengough, two detachments of the Native Border Guard from downriver, and a mounted native detachment from the Msinga Magistracy. They were led by Major John G. Dartnell, commander of the NMP and commandant of colonial defence in Klip River County. On 9

April at about 05.00 Dartnell's force crossed the Buffalo River and dispositions were made against an enemy surprise. The NMP, the NNC and some of the mounted natives then advanced into the Batshe Valley and burnt Sihayo's kraal and several others, as well as crops. A strong Zulu force was rumoured to be at Isandlwana, but the party saw only two Zulus who tried their luck at firing a few shots from long range. The force returned to the Natal side of the border in the afternoon without mishap.

These raids across the border led to a fall out between Lord Chelmsford and Sir Henry Bulwer, the Governor of Natal. Chelmsford argued that British raids would throw the Zulus off balance and reduce their resistance, but Bulwer on the other hand argued that the British would benefit little and only provoke retaliation. Eventually the home authority ruled in favour of Lord Chelmsford, who doubted whether the colonial troops really were suitable for the purpose. Chelmsford ordered one more general effort to disconcert the enemy on the eve of his second invasion of Zululand, and Major General Frederick Marshall, commander of the cavalry of the column forming in the north, determined that the demonstration would culminate in an expedition directed to Isandlwana.

On 13 May, Bengough's battalion, which had moved to Landman's Drift, crossed the Blood River near Koppie Alleen and scoured Itelezi Hill, said to be the lair of a hundred Zulu spies, with detachments of the 17th Lancers and the Natal Horse deployed in the movement. Three days later, Colonel D. C. Drury Lowe made a similar reconnaissance with two squadrons of the 17th Lancers from Landman's Drift, crossing the Blood River and burning a large number of kraals.

Just the previous day, on 15 May, Lieutenant-Colonel Black (promoted from Major) and a small party had moved out to Isandlwana, and were followed by a Zulu force of thirty to forty as they returned via Fugitive's Drift; their crossing was covered by part of Bengough's battalion. On 19 and 20 May, General Marshall concentrated the mounted imperial and colonial units at Rorke's Drift. The imperial units were comprised of the Lancers and the King's Dragoon Guards, a section of N Battery, 5th Brigade, Royal Artillery, and some of the Army Service Corps; while the colonial units were the Natal Mounted Police, the

Natal Carbineers, Carbutt's Rangers, probably the Buffalo Border Guard, the Newcastle Mounted Rifles, and some native scouts.

Very early on 21 May, Colonel Drury Lowe led a wing of the Lancers and another of the Dragoons, along with ten Carbineers and some scouts across the drift and up the Bashee Valley, then over the Nqutu Ridge into the valley beyond, in a wide sweep around and on to the Isandlwana battlefield. Not long after, Marshall led the rest of the Lancers and Dragoons, Bengough's battalion, and some of the colonial troops across the drift, following the advance as far as the high ground, then sweeping down to a junction with Drury Lowe's cavalry on the battlefield. The return route was in the meantime secured by Lieutenant Colonel Black, who posted the four companies of the 2/24th Regiment at the head of the Bashee Valley. Having reached Isandlwana, the main forces' troops searched the site and buried some of the dead, and also burnt abandoned kraals in the area.

They encountered no opposition, although it was reported later that a Zulu force had gone to confront them, but had arrived too late. Marshall returned with the troops in the early afternoon, and the next day returned to Dundee with the troops remaining at Rorke's Drift and a squadron of the Lancers scouting across Fugitive's Drift. The units returned to their original posts on 23 May. Within the week, those which comprised the invading column gathered at Landman's Drift and moved across the Buffalo River to Koppie Alleen, from where they advanced into Zululand on 31 May.

These British demonstrations and raids along the Buffalo River during the months of March to May 1879 indicate that they had at least regained the initiative along the northern border of Natal and Zululand. To what extent it had contributed to the relief of 'Eshowe and the Second Invasion of Zululand is arguable, but it did dispel the perception that the British forces did little or nothing during the long interval between the two invasions.[2]

12

GINGINDLOVU AND
THE RELIEF OF ESHOWE

After the disaster at Isandlwana, plans were gradually evolved for a second invasion of Zululand from the lower drift of the Tugela River, so colonial units were reorganised and, in some cases, revived. Oxen and wagons were gradually obtained to replace those lost up to that time. Lord Chelmsford also gained the alliance of the well-known trader John Dunn, with his official title in this role to be Chief of Intelligence. Over the next several weeks, Chelmsford prepared for the second invasion and set about his task with ruthless precision. He was hindered, though, by a reluctant Natal Government whose colonists disapproved of his policy of rearming the Natal natives, and their ranks being reinforced by men of the Natal Native Contingent.[1]

In the meantime Colonel Pearson was still besieged in Eshowe and waiting for the advance of the relief column, keeping his men occupied by strengthening the fortifications, which surrounded the Mission Station at Kwa Mondi and executing the occasional raid on nearby kraals. All the British fortifications in Zululand were fieldworks, constructed for purposes of temporary entrenchment only, unlike the stone laagers erected by the colonial government in some of Natal's towns, and by the white settlers themselves in rural areas near the frontiers; they were not intended as permanent fortifications.

A problem facing a British column advancing into Zululand was how to defend a large amount of stores in its rear with the fewest possible men. Army standing orders laid down that companies were never to be broken up into detachments, so the least garrison in any one case had to be one company. At the same time, experience in the field had shown that for a garrison's defensive rifle fire to be effective, the men should be ranged quite densely along the parapet of a fort, and these considerations resulted in an average-sized garrison of two companies per fort in Zululand and determined the size of the works. As temporary fieldworks, they were mainly built of earth, though stone was used when it was available. This meant that they have not stood up well to the ravages of the elements.

To serve its primary and typical function of protecting stores, the fort at Eshowe had to be built around the existing church and other buildings of the Norwegian Mission on the site, which had been selected to contain No. 1 Column's supplies. It had a healthy position and an ample supply of water from a nearby stream, and outweighed the disadvantage of the fort being commanded by hills on the northern and southern sides, and the problem posed by a wooded kloof and the valley of a stream on the western and northern flanks, which could not be thoroughly commanded by fire from the fort's parapet.

A parapet, such as at Eshowe, was formed artificially, the earth for its construction being derived from the ditch, dug immediately in front of and parallel to it. The construction of such works required heavy labour on the part of the soldiers, not made easier by the inadequate 'intrenching tools' with which they had been issued. Access to the fort across the ditch was by three bridges: a rolling bridge with a 'wagon roadway' and two drawbridges for 'foot passengers'. Seven-pounder guns were mounted at the four salient angles.

The ditch was filled with sharpened stakes and other obstacles and at Eshowe there were also wire entanglements – officially considered the best form of accessory defences – and trous-le-loup ('wolfpits'). The latter were holes in the ground in the form of inverted cones 6 to 8 feet in diameter and 6 feet deep, and at the bottom was fixed a sharp stake 3 feet long, sharpened branches of a tree, or other sharp obstacles like 'Crows' Feet'.[2]

With the soldiers being cooped up within the confines of the fort, it was not long before dysentery began to take its toll on the men. By the end of March, already, the food position had become critical and the draft oxen had to be slaughtered, as well as the slaughter cattle, for food. Fortunately, by this time the relief column had already crossed the Tugela River and was nearing Wombane Ridge.

Lord Chelmsford's preparations for the proposed relief of Eshowe had virtually been completed by the middle of March. He took personal command of this column, which was once again based at Fort Pearson. By 28 March all the troops and impedimenta had been transferred across the flooded Tugela River where Fort Tenedos was similarly used as a headquarters while the men were encamped in the area north of the precincts of the fort.

At this stage the force was made up of two divisions, an advance and a rear division. The former was commanded by Lt Col T. A. Law of the Royal Artillery and consisted of two companies of 'the Buffs', five companies of the 99th Regt, and the entire 91st Regt, and, in addition, 350 men of the Naval Brigade.[3]

The Rear Division was commanded by Lt Col W. L. Pemberton of the 3rd Battalion, 60th Rifles. Under him were the 57th Regt, six companies of his own 3rd/60th Rifles, commanded by Lt Col F. V. Northey, 190 sailors, and a company of the Royal Marine Light Infantry. In addition, the remnants of the Natal Native Contingent had been regrouped and posted to what was now referred to as the 4th and 5th Battalions, NNC. The artillery for the invasion consisted of two 9-pounder guns, two 24-pound rocket tubes, and two Gatling guns. Finally, Maj. Percy Barrow commanded some seventy mounted infantry, which included a newly established unit called the Natal Volunteer Guides, commanded by Capt. Friend Addison, 130 Natal natives, and 150 blacks supplied by John Dunn.

This new force totalled over 3,300 whites and almost 2,300 blacks. In view of the lessons learnt at Isandlwana, ammunition was more evenly distributed throughout the column and strict laagering instructions were given for overnight stops, with both out- and inlying pickets posted in strength around the camp. The long convoy of wagons and animals stretched out Chelmsford's column to well over 5 kilometres, but on the march this occasionally became more than 10 miles, usually because of holdups at the numerous drifts along the route. Had his enemy been more tactically minded, the situation could have caused serious problems for Chelmsford.

The column's march began early in the morning on 29 March, but made slow and steady progress because of all the crossings to be negotiated. The Advance Division crossed the Amatikulu River and then proceeded for approximately 1.5 mile past the drift and established a camp to await the arrival of the Rear Division. The crossing had taken the column almost an entire day. On 1 April, Capt. W. C. F. Molyneaux and John Dunn rode out to select a laager site for that night, and chose one on a slight rise near the south bank of the Inyezane River and close by the burnt-out Gingindlovu military kraal. By the evening, the wagons had been formed into the laager and the men settled down to a wet, miserable night.[4]

Maj. Barrow's scouts had reported the presence of Zulus in the vicinity of the Umisa Ridge, which stretches from the Amatikulu River in the West to Umisa Hill. Col Pearson also heliographed Chelmsford from Eshowe that he could clearly see a Zulu impi approaching the Inyezane Valley. Dunn and Capt. Molyneaux again rode out on the night of the 1st in the direction of the Inyezane River to check the presence of any Zulus across the stream. They later reported that they saw a large number of Zulu camp fires burning, and it was generally expected that the Zulus would attack the next day.

And so it turned out. At first light on 2 April, the outlying pickets galloped in to announce an imminent attack by the Zulus, amidst a heavy mist shrouding the surrounding countryside, which limited visibility. But it was not even necessary to position the men, for they had all been prepared for the attack and had taken up their posts as follows:

North (front) face – 60th Rifles
Right flank face – 57th Regiment
Left flank face – 99th Regiment and 'the Buffs'
Rear face – 91st Regiment.

Each angle was manned by the Naval Brigade, Bluejackets from HMS *Boadicea* and Marines. The Gatling from *Boadicea* was mounted in the north-eastern corner and the two rocket tubes under Lt Kerr were positioned on the north-west corner, whereas the two 9-pounder guns under Lt Kingscote covered the south-west. The second Gatling and two more rocket tubes under Commander Brackenbury covered the south-eastern approach.

Then, at 05.45, the outlying pickets of the 60th and 99th Regiment galloped in to herald the arrival of the Zulus and fifteen minutes later the attack had commenced on the north front, where the Zulus had first been observed. They were commanded by Somapo and Dabulamanzi, who had been given strict instructions by Cetshwayo to prevent the column from joining up with Col Pearson in Eshowe – orders they disregarded.[5]

Even before they had crossed the Inyezane River, the impi had begun to split up into the traditional Zulu horn formation, with the two horns running ahead of the chest or loins. As they drew opposite the laager, it entered the river and splashed across, the right wing and loins split up again and ran over the Umisa Hill to the west. It became clear to the column that it was facing no less than six Zulu regiments, totalling over 10,000, as well as a reserve in excess of 2,000. Most of these had fought at Isandlwana, the regiments being the Uve, in Gobamakhosi, umCijo, umHlanga, uMbonambi, and the head-ringed uThulwana.

The Gatling gun from HMS *Boadicea* fired the first shots at a range of 1,000 metres, and the Zulus dropped into the long grass and reappeared some 300 metres from the shelter trench, from where heavy fire in volleys checked their advance to some extent. This prompted Lord Chelmsford to order Maj. Barrow to make a somewhat premature charge with his mounted infantry to check the advance of the Zulu left horn. Realising that Barrow's men were dangerously far from the laager, the Zulus were quick to try and cut him off in the rear. Chelmsford ordered him back to the safety of the laager but the men still had to fight their way in.

Despite determined assaults, the Zulus were unable to advance to within more than 20 yards of the laager. Although the British were well entrenched, they nevertheless suffered some serious casualties. Lt Col Northey was hit in the shoulder, and although the naval surgeon extracted the bullet, the slug had severed an artery and put him out of the fight; he died some days later. Capt. Barrow and Lt Col Crealock were also slightly wounded and Lt Courtenay and Capt Molyneux had their horses shot from under them.

When the Zulus realised that the Gatling gun had checked any further advance from the north, they turned their attention to the west of the laager, resulting in Lt G. C. J. Johnson of the 99th Regt being killed. At the same time another attack developed from the direction of Umisa Hill, in the rear, and throughout the Zulus kept up a withering fire from behind the cover of bushes or tall grass.

Chelmsford now again ordered Maj. Barrow to attack with his mounted infantry. They had been clearing the front face of the laager from the outside and redirected their attention to the impi's right flank. The manoeuvre finally broke the Zulus' resistance, who also realised that they were unable to penetrate the laager from the rear, which they had thought was poorly defended. At the sight of Barrow's men, the Zulus broke and started their retreat, and were hotly pursued by the Mounted Infantry and the Natal Native Contingent. The pursuit was continued for several miles, resulting in the flight becoming a rout. The reserve impi on Umisa Hill joined the general retreat and an hour-and-a-half after the first attack, the Zulus had all but disappeared. Apart from the rifle fire casualties, many of the fleeing warriors were sabred by the Mounted Infantry. The Zulus lost heavily and more than 470 bodies were buried initially and more than 200 were subsequently found. The Gatling gun and artillery in particular took a heavy toll; in addition, scores were wounded and died in solitude later. Hundreds of Martini Henry rifles were recovered, most of which had previously belonged to the 24th Regiment and had been looted during the disaster at Isandlwana nine weeks earlier. On the British side, two officers and eleven other ranks were killed and about fifty wounded. The dead were buried close to the laager.

The soldiers still besieged in Eshowe – those who had not fallen ill with fever, including Col Pearson – observed much of the battle from vantage points overlooking the plain below. When it became clear to him that the Zulus had been routed, Pearson flashed his congratulations to Chelmsford by heliograph. Chelmsford replied that he anticipated arriving in Eshowe the following day.[6]

Captain Edward Hutton, 3/60th Rifles, was witness to the battle. He arrived in Natal with his battalion late in March 1879 and almost immediately received orders to march to the Tugela River and join the Eshowe Relief Expedition. He encountered the Zulu army for the first time at Gingindlovu on 2 April. The memory of the defeat at Isandlwana was a cause of some concern, but the tactics of the Zulu army were also a factor in the nervousness of the reinforcements. Captain Edward Hutton recorded how the speed of the Zulu troops forced a rethink of British tactics during the advance of the relief column to Eshowe: 'Lord Chelmsford told us to forget the drill ... the enemy was to be treated as cavalry. The impression left upon our minds was that the Zulus were very formidable foes ... Our men, especially the young soldiers, were not slow to share the general feeling of uneasiness which the disasters at Isandlwana and elsewhere had caused.'[7]

About the battle itself, he recalled:

Shortly after we were in our places large, streaming masses of the enemy were seen moving at a rapid rate through the bush that hid the Inyezane from our view. The Zulu impi was estimated at 12,000 men; contrary to precedent, they did not wear their full war costume, but carried rifles, assegais, and small shields. The dark masses of men, in open order and under admirable discipline, followed each other in quick succession, running at a steady pace through the long grass. Having moved steadily round so as exactly to face our front, the larger portion of the Zulus broke into three lines, in knots and groups of from five to ten men, and advanced towards us. Not a sound was heard...

The Zulus continued to advance, still at a run, until they were about 800 yards from us, when they began to open fire. In spite of the excitement of the moment, we could not but admire the perfect manner in which these Zulus skirmished. A small knot of five or six would rise and dart through the long grass, dodging from side to side with heads down, rifles and shields kept low and out of sight. They would then suddenly sink into the long grass, and nothing but puffs of curling smoke would show their whereabouts. Then they advanced again, and their bullets soon began to whistle merrily over our heads or strike the little parapet in front.[8]

Guy Dawnay, the gentleman adventurer who had managed to attach himself to the 5th Battalion, Natal Native Contingent, recalled: 'We could see large bodies moving round behind the first ridges ... The big bodies of Zulus broke up into skirmishing order before crossing the ridge, and the way they then came on was magnificent. We kept up a heavy fire at every black figure we saw, but they crawled through the grass, and dodged behind bushes, shooting at us all the time, and soon every bush in front of us held and hid two or three Zulus, and the puffs of smoke showed us they were there.'⁹

A newspaper correspondent writing for the *Natal Mercury*, also present at the battle, reported the Zulu method of attack to his readers, confirming the impression gained by Hutton and Dawnay: 'Two large columns of the enemy were seen coming down the Inyezane hills, while one came round the left by the Amatikula bush, and another smaller one from the direction of the old military kraal. In ten minutes' time our laager was completely surrounded, and the attack began. The enemy came up with a rush to within three or four hundred yards of our position, being favoured in many places by the nature of the ground. They then scattered more, and advanced skirmishing, under a hot fire, to about one hundred yards of the laager, all round. Unfortunately there was plenty of long grass and bushes to shelter them, and as they lay down immediately after firing, our men were not able to dislodge them.'¹⁰

It seems that the pursuit after the battle was prosecuted with vengeance for the massacre at Isandlwana in mind. A piper of the 91st Highlanders described the aftermath: 'When the Zulus commenced to retire, our natives and mounted volunteers went out after them; the natives assegaied all the wounded they could find. It was brutal work; still, it was nothing more than they would have done to us, if it were possible.'¹¹ Another first-hand account of the pursuit, written by Sergeant Edwin Powis of the Mounted Infantry to a lady friend, backs up this account: 'We were attacked by about 8,000 black devils ... [we] saddled our horses and made heavy chase out into the open field with sword in hand. We were cutting them down like cutting grass, they were that thick ... we caught [Zulus], who had been wounded, trying to make for the bush. We cut off their heads, the three of them, and let them lay.'¹²

Early on 3 April, a flying column left the camp at Gingindlovu and proceeded along the track to Eshowe, leaving the rest of the invasion force to prepare to advance along a route closer to the coast. Col Pearson rode out from the fort to meet them and the column trickled into the fort. The first regiment to enter was the 91st Highlanders and the last man arrived at about midnight. So, Eshowe had finally been relieved after a siege of some ten weeks. The Eshowe garrison left the fort and proceeded to Fort Pearson, by which time an additional two officers and two other ranks had died of fever. Lord Chelmsford followed Colonel Pearson out of Eshowe some twenty-four hours later and reached Gingindlovu on 7 April, where the command of the column was handed to Col Pemberton, who established a new advance base approximately 5 miles from Gingindlovu, overlooking the Inyezane River, and which was named Fort Chelmsford.[13] Of the battlefield today, little remains; apart from the small military cemetery, there is very little evidence of the trenches or their whereabouts.

Note: See under Appendices, 'The Defence of Ekowe [Eshowe]' by Lieut. W. N. Lloyd, R.H.A.

13

THE FIGHT AT
INTOMBE RIVER

The old village of Lüneberg, in the so-called disputed territories to the north of Zululand (still located on the Natal border with present-day Mpumalanga), was originally settled by German Lutheran missionaries in 1854, and named after the town of Lüneburg in Germany. From 1875 on, Zulu attacks against nearby farms increased, killing several baptized Zulu. The German settlers therefore built a low wall around the church, with a moat watered by an irrigation ditch, and the settlers retreated there when necessary. In 1877, the Zuid-Afrikaanse Republiek (ZAR) was annexed by British forces, and the Germans gained the protection of the British authorities. Colonel Evelyn Wood was deployed to the area with the 90th Regiment of Foot and he settled in Fort Clery in 1878; it never garrisoned troops in warfare but was used among other purposes as an ammunition depot.

During the Anglo-Zulu War in 1879, 120 citizens of all ages were trapped in the church fortress. When the disturbing news of the disaster at Isandlwana on 22 January reached the village, the settlers living there went into the laager. With the hot weather, conditions in the laager were poor and diseases spread. The settlers fears were not unfounded, as on the night of 10/11 February the Zulus attacked the area. As the British feared a repeat of the attack, they sent four companies of the 80th Regiment of Foot under Major Charles Tucker to garrison the village.[1]

In late February 1879, a convoy of eighteen wagons carrying 90,000 rounds of Martini-Henry ammunition, mealies, tinned food, biscuits, a rocket battery and other weapons for the 80th Regiment was sent from Lydenburg (on the wagon route to the port of Delagoa Bay) to supply the garrison. From the Transvaal border it was escorted by D Company under Captain Anderson, accompanied by Lieutenant Daubeney, of the 80th Regiment, from Lüneberg. They rendezvoused on the road from Derby on 1 March and by 5 March, having been hampered by rains, which caused the rivers to swell, the convoy was still 5 miles short of Meyer's Drift, which was 8 miles from Lüneberg.[2]

Fearing a Zulu attack, Major Tucker sent an order to Captain Anderson to reach Lüneberg that night 'at any cost'. The company commander took this literally, abandoned the wagons and returned to Lüneberg. In the meantime, the Swazi pretender Mbilini waMswati and his Zulu irregulars had been watching the convoy and as soon as the escort left the wagons were attacked by looters. The wagon drivers and *voorloopers* made a run for Derby, and soon afterwards, an advanced party from Hamu arrived and drove off the looters in turn, who came back as soon as Hamu's men departed. The raiding party got away with stores and forty oxen. When Anderson reached Lüneberg without the supplies, Major Tucker sent Captain David Moriarty[3] and 106 men to bring in the convoy. The escort had got six wagons to the far bank of the Intombe River, 4 miles from Lüneberg, while six other wagons were 3 miles further back. By the time Moriarty's party reached Meyer's Drift, the river had risen and a camp was established on the Lüneberg side. The men began to lash a raft of planks and barrels together with rope and a few men at a time were ferried across, except for a party of thirty-five commanded by Lieutenant Lindop. When Moriarty and the rest of the party went to recover the wagons on the far side, they found that most had been emptied by the looters.

It was only around noon on 11 March that they had managed to get all of the wagons to the Derby side of the river. The Intombi had risen again and was flowing far too fast to cross. Moriarty ordered the wagons to be laagered for the night. The Moriarty party, out for five nights, soaked through and unable to cook food, did not laager the wagons as tightly as possible, leaving gaps between them, in a 'V' with the ends at the river. By the afternoon, the river had subsided, leaving the laager wide open at the ends of the 'V'.[4]

When Tucker inspected the laager at the river he found it to be poorly constructed. There were other flaws in the arrangement; all in all, Tucker considered that it afforded 'no protection whatever in the event of the Zulus attacking in numbers'. The garrison was weakened by being divided by a river, with thirty of its number laagered on the other bank.[5]

On the night of 11 March 1879, two sentries were stationed some twenty yards from the laager. A rise in front of them restricted their range of vision to a mere fifty yards. At 3:30 the next morning, a shot was heard close to the camp, but the men returned to sleep after Moriarty decided that it was of no consequence. Then, an hour and a half later, a sentry on the far bank saw, through a clearing in the mist, a huge mass of Zulus advancing silently on the camp.

'He at once fired his rifle and gave the alarm,' Tucker recorded. 'The sentries on the other side did the same. Of course the men were up in a moment, some men sleeping under the wagons and some in the tents; but before the men were in their positions the Zulus had fired a volley, thrown down their guns ... and were around the wagons and on top of them, and even inside with the cattle, almost instantly. So quickly did they come, there was really no defence on the part of our men; it was simply each man fighting for his life, and in a few minutes all was over, our men being simply slaughtered.'[6]

Moriarty charged out of his tent with his revolver and killed three Zulus before being shot from the front and stabbed with an assegai from behind and was said to have shouted 'Fire away boys, death or glory! I'm done' as he fell.[7] Few of his comrades managed to put up any resistance and many were cut down. Survivors fled into the river, still flowing strong, in the hope that they would be washed to the far bank. The troops on the far bank provided as much covering fire as possible. Lieutenant Henry Hollingworth Harward, Moriarty's second-in-command, gave the order to withdraw upon seeing several hundred Zulus crossing the river. No sooner had he done this than he grabbed the first horse he spotted and fled, abandoning his men.[8]

The survivors at the drift were now under the command of Sergeant Anthony Booth. The Zulus pursued the group of around forty survivors for some 3 miles. Whenever they drew closer, several of the troops along with Booth stopped to deliver a volley. Four men who split up from the group to take a short cut to Lüneberg were killed, but the others made it to Raby's Farm, about 2 miles from Lüneberg. Fortunately for them, the Zulus broke off pursuit here. The wagons were looted and all the ammunition and supplies were carried off by the Zulus or destroyed. For his brave conduct, Booth was rewarded with the Victoria Cross.[9]

When Harward arrived at Lüneberg, he frantically told Tucker of what had happened and Tucker quickly ordered all his mounted troops with him to the camp, and ordered a further 150 infantry to follow. Tucker and his mounted men spotted dense masses of Zulus leaving the scene of the battle as they approached. At the camp, they discovered one soldier who had made a miraculous escape by being carried down the river and then making his way back to the camp. He and two African wagon drivers were the only survivors they found.

The disaster at Intombe again demonstrated the vulnerability of the cumbersome and awkward supply lines that the British Army was so dependent on. Eight months after the incident, Harward was brought from England, under arrest, charged with 'misbehaviour before the enemy and shamefully abandoning a party of the regiment under his command when attacked' and other lesser charges. Harward was acquitted, supposedly because he left to get reinforcements, which, by their promptitude, prevented Harward's party from total annihilation. Harward resigned his commission in May 1880.[10]

The bodies of Captain Moriarty and Surgeon Cobbins were found among the dead in the encampment. Casualty figures differ from author to author, but Donald Morris wrote of eighty men killed, sixty-two of the dead being British soldiers along with three conductors and fifteen African *voorloopers*.[11] The British also lost rifles, the 90,000 rounds of Martini-Henry ammunition and 225 lb of gunpowder.[12]

14

HLOBANE MOUNTAIN: MORE TRAGEDY

When Lord Chelmsford intended to invade Zululand with three columns and converge on the Zulu capital of Ondini, the No. 2 Column on the coast was to begin its advance at the Tugela River; No. 3 Column in the centre was to cross Rorke's Drift and advance 85 miles to Ulundi; No. 4 Column under Colonel Evelyn Wood had to advance the shortest distance, about 75 miles, but was to move slowly to enable No. 1 Column to catch up. Wood's Column consisted of eight infantry companies from the 13th and 90th Light Infantry, with about 1,500 men, four 7-pounder mountain guns of the 11th Battery, 7th Brigade (11/7) RA, roughly 200 cavalry of the Frontier Light Horse (FLH) and the civilian followers of Piet Uys and Wood's Irrregulars, 300 African infantry along with ox wagon transport and equipment, about 2,000 infantry and 200 cavalry all told.

No. 4 Column's purpose was to occupy the attention of those Zulus dwelling on the flat-topped mountains rising out of the plains of north-west Zululand. Chelmsford required these Zulus to be distracted so that they would not interfere with the operations of No. 3 Column during its advance to Isandlwana and onto Ulundi. Wood advanced his column north-eastwards on 17 January 1879, and three days later a laager was established at Tinta's Kraal, 10 miles south of a chain of flat-topped mountains. These mountains were Zunguin, Hlobane and Ityentika, which were connected by a nek and stretched for 15 miles in a north-easterly direction. While the camp was being fortified, Wood's scouts investigating the mountains were attacked from Zunguin by about 1,000 Zulu. At dawn the next day he mounted an attack on Zunguin, but the Zulus then fled to Hlobane, where Wood observed about 4,000 Zulu that afternoon. News of the defeat at Isandlwana thwarted his planned offensive against the abaQulusi Zulus, but Wood continued to deploy his mounted force under the command of Lieutenant-Colonel Buller to conduct patrols to burn down local kraals as well as raid cattle. For just over two months the mounted element of Wood's column patrolled approximately 160 square miles of surrounding country.[1] Apart from the almost constant patrolling, the mounted soldiers were also used to defend the camp at Khambula and conduct guard duties, vedettes and night pickets. Having first fallen back to Tinta's Kraal, Wood decided to move his column north-westwards to Khambula Hill, about 14 miles due west of Zunguin. When they arrived there on 31 January, Wood was met with a message from Chelmsford informing him that all orders were cancelled, that he was now on his own with no expectation of reinforcements and that he must be prepared to face the whole Zulu army.

Sitting in the fortified camp at Khambula, Robert Fell described the landscape as 'a boundless expanse of green grass, as far as the eye can reach, the Hlobane Mountain away to our front'. He complains about the rough diet he and his soldiers had to accept, although some relief came when a canteen wagon brought the officers tinned lobster, salmon and two bottles of champagne apiece. Fell's father had asked him what he thought of Natal's prospects and if it was worth buying land there. 'I think it will take a little time to recover; undoubtedly the presence of so many troops has brought in money and given it an impetus. The telegraph has been brought within 30 miles of Utrecht now, the railway will soon be completed to Maritzburg and I have no doubt will be continued to the coal deposits at Newcastle and Dundee. There is no doubt the country is full of coal and mineral, and said to be gold, and as soon as it is opened up by rail traffic will become valuable. An old farmer and hunter called Rathbone told me that from the day the British troops crossed the Blood River his farm near Luneberg trebled in value. Before they never were safe from threatened Zulu incursion. You can grow any fruit you like about a farm, the soil seems very rich, gum trees grow like smoke; the climate is very healthy. It wants railways, population, and capital to push it ahead.'²

February passed quietly, except for mounted patrols sent out daily to raid the kraals of Zulus harassing No. 5 Column across the eastern Transvaal border. At Khambula, Wood formed a hexagonal laager with tightly locked-together wagons, while a separate kraal for the cattle was constructed on the edge of the southern face of the ridge. Trenches and earth parapets surrounded both and a stone-built redoubt was built on a rise just north of the kraal. A palisade blocked the 100 yards between the kraal and redoubt and four 7-pounders were positioned between the redoubt and the laager to cover the northern approaches. Two more guns in the redoubt covered the north-east.

By the middle of March 1879, Wood had his column strengthened by more mounted troops, comprising both mounted infantry and volunteers. The mounted infantry were Lieutenant-Colonel Russell's 1st Squadron, which originally had been attached to the Centre Column, but had been withdrawn back to Natal after the defeat at Isandlwana. The volunteers consisted of newly formed units of which the Frontier Light Horse were the largest contingent. They differed from the Natal Volunteers as they had been recruited from all over South Africa and required a longer service. Many of these volunteers, however, were known for their disorderly and undisciplined attitude. Lieutenant W. H. Tomasson of Baker's Horse, one of the new units, called the majority of these men 'fearfully slovenly and the variest drunkards and winebibbers to ever take carbine to hand'. But he did commend Colonel Buller, whom he calls a 'masterful man', for his leadership and as someone who can 'bring these desperados into subjection'.³ Evidently these volunteers had an unprofessional approach to military matters, and many were merely attracted to the new units with an eye on the increased rate of pay.⁴ Unfortunately for Colonel Buller, this lack of discipline would cause problems for him in future offensives.

Wood had hoped to detach the Zulus in the area from their allegiance to Cetshwayo, particularly those of Uhamu, Cetshwayo's half-brother. Uhama had always been friendly towards the British and at odds with the Zulu king, and on 13 March, he entered the camp with about 700 followers. He asked for escorts to bring the rest of his people out of hiding from their caves near the headwaters of the Black Umfolozi, 50 miles to the east and only 40 miles from Ulundi. Wood considered that the advantages of the exercise made it worthwhile, and soon an escort of 360 British mounted troops and about 200 of Uhamu's warriors returned to Khambula with another 900 refugees.

Chelmsford's next important move was to effect the relief of Colonel Pearson and his men at Eshowe, and he instructed Colonel Wood to create a diversion on 28 March. Knowing that an impi was preparing to leave Ulundi and attack either Khambula or the British fort at Utrecht, Wood believed that by attacking Hlobane on 28 March he could drive cattle off the mountain, thereby prompting the Zulus to attack him in his established position at Khambula.

Wood's strategy was to attack from both east and west, with Lieutenant-Colonel Redvers Buller leading the main assault from the east while Russell would act as a diversion from the west; they would then regroup somewhere near the middle on the main plateau.

Hlobane Mountain consisted of two plateaux, the lower and smaller of which rose to a height of about 850 feet at the eastern end of the 4-mile-long nek connecting it to Zunguin to the south-west. At the eastern end of this lower plateau the ground rose very steeply for another 200 feet up a narrow, boulder-strewn way, forming a series of giant steps, known as Devil's Pass, to the higher plateau. On the top of this plateau were about 2,000 cattle and approximately 1,000 abaQulusi Zulu, and Wood's plan was for mounted troops led by Lieutenant-Colonel Redvers Buller, to scale the eastern track to the higher plateau, supported by rocket artillery and friendly Zulu to lift the cattle. A similar force, under Major R. A. Russell, would occupy the lower plateau.

The forces departed at dawn on 27 March, hampered by a thunderstorm and also Zulu sniping by the light of lightning flashes. Buller's mounted troops reached the summit by 6:00 a.m. the following day and his African infantry began herding the cattle westwards. During the route out, Colonel Weatherley and his Border Horse became separated from Buller's party and he was then instructed to rejoin Buller on the upper plateau as he was making his ascent. Both Buller's and Wood's men came under fire from caves, and five of Wood's escorts charged the caves, resulting in his staff officer Captain R. Campbell and his interpreter Llewellyn Lloyd being killed. Buller was already facing difficulty in ascending the mountain as the path was almost impassable to mounted men. To make life more difficult for them, a small number of Zulus fired down on his men from the top, causing casualties amongst both men and horses. Buller was eventually able to get the rest of his force on the plateau, but not before he had lost two officers in the ascent.[5]

Buller was hindered by lack of intelligence, but needed to find routes back down. He could either retreat back the way he had come, or head west towards the lower plateau. The latter routes were more treacherous than the ascending route had been, but were secure from flanking fire. After he had scouted the plateau, Buller ordered his second in command, Captain Barton, with a force of thirty men, to bury the two dead officers, and then instructed Barton to retrace their steps and regroup with Weatherley with the intention to return to Khambula via the south of the mountain. Moments later, however, a Zulu army of some 20,000 were seen approaching from the south-east – the main Zulu army, many of whom had seen action at Isandlwana. Realising that the southern route away from the mountain was now no longer an option, he sent two men to tell Barton to return via the 'right' side of the mountain (meaning the north). Barton received the warning as he was heading eastward, but due to the confusing message he mistakenly interpreted the right side of the mountain to be the south. And so, by going south Barton and Weatherley found themselves face to face with the main Zulu army and of course had very little chance of escape. They were struck a huge blow as Barton himself was killed along with eighteen men and Weatherley was also killed with forty-four of his men.[6]

Buller still had to get off the plateau and decided to move westward towards the lower plateau where he expected Russell to be. Russell, too, had problems with poor instructions. He had successfully reached the lower plateau but could not see Buller on the plateau above. He had seen the Zulu army approaching and thought it wise to begin to descend as quickly as possible, and then cover Buller's retreat from the base of the mountain. Before Buller was able to make his descent, Russell had received orders from Wood to move to the 'Zunguin Neck' and join up with Wood there. He was unsure of exactly where Wood meant but after consultation with his officers, quickly moved into a position where he thought Zunguin Nek was. Unfortunately for Russell, the position he was holding was a whole 6 miles west of the position Wood had in mind. For the remainder of the battle, Russell was unable to provide any support to cover the extraction of Buller's mounted force and natives, and returned back to the camp in the late afternoon. The error proved costly.

With the support Buller needed now absent, the retreat descent down the mountain was always going to be a nightmare. Buller began his descent on the lower plateau around 10 a.m. and it soon dawned on him that Russell had already retreated off the mountain. There would be no supporting fire from those quarters. Buller utilised the Frontier Light Horse as a rear guard to keep the Zulus at bay, but the firing quickly stopped when the men mistook the advancing Zulus as friendlies. This error was exploited by the Zulus, who began to fire on the men as they made their way down. Buller was not only picking up casualties from the Zulu fire, but the dangerous terrain also caused casualties among both men and horses. Eventually though, Buller's troops were able to get onto the lower plateau, but by that time he had lost an officer, sixteen men and the Boer commandant Piet Uys, a highly experienced fighter who had proved invaluable to Wood's column both as a guide and soldier.

Buller's force was now beginning to lose discipline, as many were dismounted having lost their horses in the descent. Fortunately for Buller the main Zulu army did not pursue his force; he was able to rally his men and conduct a more organised retreat back to Khambula. Although he was pursued by a small force of abaQulusi Zulu, he did not sustain any further casualties. He showed great bravery by continually riding back and forth to rescue any of his men who had either lost their horse or had been isolated by the Zulu. The Baker's Horse volunteer, Lieutenant Tomasson, afterwards described Buller's bravery as the 'only bright spot' of the battle.[7] Buller was in fact later awarded a Victoria Cross for rescuing these men.

It is true that circumstances were made very difficult by the treacherous route down the mountain, but there was no denying the lack of training and discipline of Buller's mounted men. The retreat was manoeuvred badly with very little covering fire. Earlier in the campaign, Buller had shown that a mounted fighting withdrawal was highly effective; at Hlobane, however, he failed to maintain control of the situation. His poor instructions to Barton and the evident lack of reconnaissance caused unnecessary casualties, while inadequate communications had also been a problem during the battle.

The Battle of Hlobane turned out to be the second major disaster of the war after Isandlwana. Fifteen officers and seventy-nine men were killed in the battle, with far more uncounted native deaths. Colonel Buller received the Victoria Cross for his conspicuous gallantry and leadership, as did Lieutenant Henry Lysons and Private Edmund Fowler for charging the caves that morning. Major William Leet and Lieutenant Edward Browne were awarded the VC for going back to save the lives of wounded men in the descent of Devil's Pass.[8]

Despite the acts of bravery for which the five Victoria Crosses and four Distinguished Conduct medals were awarded, the result was a failure. The event was a good example of mounted troops not being utilised correctly, and illustrated what a huge impact terrain can have on their performance. It also illustrated how misunderstanding and poor communication between officers affect a battle. Although Wood's column had been very active doing reconnaissance patrols in the early part of March, they failed to successfully scout the Hlobane Mountain. Had this been done properly, they would have noted that the routes up and down the mountain were almost impassable to mounted troops; also, the Zulus would have been discovered much earlier. Wood knew that the Zulu army was camped within 5 miles of his position.

Fortunately for Wood, there was the victory at Khambula the next day, which overshadowed the defeat at Hlobane Mountain.

The Illustrated London News of 31 May 1879 carried a report of the battle.

A private letter from Captain H Vaughan, Royal Artillery, written on 29 March, addressed to Mr. Morgan Williams of Neath, brother of their deceased Captain George Williams, gives an account of the event:

'An expedition started on the 27th, consisting of the Frontier Light Horse and two other volunteer corps of mounted men, with a few artillery and a number of friendly Kaffirs, all together 1000 men, under command of Colonel Redvers Buller, VC. Another column started about 6 hours later, under Colonel Russell, the whole being under the immediate command of Colonel Evelyn Wood, VC, CB. The object of this expedition was to storm the Inhlobane Mountain, a great Zulu stronghold, where they had collected all their cattle. I send a rough sketch of the place. Colonel Buller, with his men, had to go around to the back of the mountain coming up from Zululand, as this was the only accessible place for mounted men. On the site nearest the camp Colonel Russell had to go up and meet Colonel Buller on the top. On his arrival at a certain height it was found he could not go up the slope to the top, as it was full of immense boulders and stones, and there was a wall built across by the Kaffirs. Some of his men got up on foot, but came down again. Meanwhile Colonel Buller had reached the place he was to go up, and sent Lieutenant George Williams' troops to hold a small hillock on the left, to keep the fire down and cover his advance. The place was in the shape of a horseshoe, and there was a ridge running up the centre. The whole of this horseshoe space was filled with Kaffirs, under the cover of rocks, firing away. Colonel Buller and his force, by keeping on the left side of the ridge, were protected from the fire coming from the right of the horseshoe; but there was the fire from the left-hand side to be put down. So Lieutenant George Williams and his men were tolled off; and, while he was in the act of placing them, a bullet that nearly struck Colonel Buller hit Lieutenant George Williams in the head and knocked him over. His death must have been instantaneous; he could not have suffered any pain. His body for the time was left where it was; but afterwards Captain Barton, of the Coldstream Guards, with 25 men, went down to the spot, tied in the body on a spare horse, and was coming back to the camp, when they fell in with a large force of Kaffirs and were dispersed. Colonel Buller's force had by this time reached the top, captured the cattle, and we're coming back again when they encountered an immense number of the enemy, who came up the same way as they did, and there was a regular scramble to get down to where Colonel Russell should have been at the time. The place, however, was quite impracticable for horses. How any got down was a mystery, with the horses plunging madly, while the Kaffirs we're shooting and assegaing the poor fellows. It was a disastrous day.'[9]

The report added:

Another officer of the same surname, Lieutenant Charles Ellis Williams, of the 58th Regiment, was killed in this day's fighting on the Inhlobane Mountain. Lieutenant James Pool, who shared the fate of his superior officer, Colonel Weatherly, was a brother of Mr. John Pool of Newcastle upon Tyne, and had many friends in the north of England. 11 officers fell in this unlucky business, and there were some remarkable escapes. The bravery and generous self-devotion of Major W Knox Leet, of the 13th Light Infantry but, in saving the lives of his comrades in their retreat, it did not pass unnoticed. Brigadier-General Wood has recommended him for the Victoria Cross. The following letter from Lieutenant Metcalfe Smith, of the Frontier Light Horse (belongs to 5th West York Militia, serves as volunteer with the Colonial Corps of the FLH) relates this praiseworthy exploit:

'Khambula Camp, March 31.

I am most anxious to bring to notice that, in the retreat from the Inhlobane Mountain on the 28th instant, Major Leet, of the 13th Light Infantry, who was quite a stranger to me, saved my life, with almost the certainty of losing his own life by doing so. We were going along the top of the mountain, pursued by the Zulus, when Major Leet said to Colonel Buller that the best way to get the men down was by the right side; and the Colonel said it was, and called out so to the men. However, everyone but Major Leet, myself, and one other man, kept on to the front of the mountain; while we began to descend on the right side. Major Leet and the other man were on horseback, but I was on foot, my horse having been shot. When we had got down a little way, a great many Zulus rushed after us, and we're catching us up very quickly. The side of the mountain was dreadfully steep and rugged, and there was no pathway at all. They were firing and throwing their assegais at us while they rushed upon us. The third man, whose name is unknown to me, was killed about halfway down. While I was running by myself and trying to get away from the Zulus, who were rapidly catching me up, I turned round and shot one with my revolver. I was then quite exhausted and out of breath, and intended to sit down and to give up all chance of saving my life, as the Zulus were within a few yards of me; but Major Leet persisted in waiting for me, and called to me to catch hold of the pack saddle he was riding, which I did. Major Leet then, finding that I could not keep beside the horse, I was so done up and the hill so steep and rugged, insisted, though I told him it was of no use, on stopping and dragging me up behind him on the horse, which was also greatly exhausted. By the greatest good luck, he escaped from the bullets and assegais of the Zulus and got near the Colonel's men, coming down the end of the mountain. Had it not been for Major Leet nothing could have saved me, and I owe him the deepest gratitude, which I shall feel has long as I live.'

The unfortunate comrade of whom he speaks as having followed himself and Major Leet down the right side of the mountain, but who was overtaken by the Zulus and killed, was Lieutenant Duncombe, of Wood's Irregulars, but likewise of the Yorkshire militia.[10]

The report of Colonel Buller on the action of 28 March reads:

The Zulus pursued us in force, and with so many dismounted men we experienced a greater difficulty in descending the mountain, and but for the exertions of a few our retreat would have been a rout; as it was we got down with a loss of those men who were too badly wounded to be kept on horses. As especially distinguishing themselves in the retreat, I wish to mention Commandant Raaff, Transvaal Rangers, and Captain Gardner, my staff officer, both of whom were also conspicuous in the assault in the morning. Major Leet, 13th Light Infantry, as well as Captain Darcy, Frontier Light Horse, although himself dismounted, rallied the men, saving the lives of many footmen – Lieutenants Blaine and Smith, Frontier Light Horse; Lieutenant Wilson, Baker's Horse; Captain Loraine White and Adjutant Brecher, Wood's Irregulars, Sergeants Crampton and Ellis, Troopers Landsill, Whitecross, Duffy, Pietersen, Hewitt and Vinnicombe, Frontier Light Horse.[11]

15

KHAMBULA:
A TURNING POINT

After the disaster at the Battle of Hlobane on 28 March 1879, the forces of Colonel Evelyn Wood prepared to confront an attack by the entire Zulu impi, of which they had encountered only the leading sections. Soon after dawn of 29 March, the Transvaal Rangers rode out to locate the impi, the cattle were put out to graze and after some deliberation, two companies were despatched to collect firewood. By 11:00 a.m. the Rangers had returned with the news that the impi was on the move and was to attack Khambula at noon. Wood also received information that the impi was nearly 21,000 strong, consisting of regiments that had already defeated the British at the Battle of Isandlwana and other battles.[1]

Many of the Zulus were armed with rifles taken from the British dead at these battles. Shortly after this, the Zulu impi was sighted 5 miles away across the plain, coming on due westwards in five columns. The warriors of the impi had not eaten for three days. The woodcutters and cattle were brought back in. Confident that the defences could be manned within a minute and a half of an alarm being sounded, Wood ordered the men to have their dinners.[2]

Cetshwayo ordered the main Zulu army not to attack fortified positions but to lure the British troops into the open, even if it had to march on the Transvaal to accomplish this, but his orders were eventually ignored. Wood initially thought the army was advancing on the Transvaal, but it halted a few miles south of

Khambula and formed up for an attack. Wood's force consisted of 121 Royal Artillery and Royal Engineers, 1,238 infantry and 638 mounted men. With headquarters staff, it totalled 2,000 men, of whom 88 were sick in hospital.

The defences on Khambula appeared solid and consisted of a hexagonal laager formed with wagons that were tightly locked together, and a separate kraal for the cattle, constructed on the edge of the southern face of the ridge. Trenches and earth parapets surrounded both sections and a stone redoubt had been built on a rise just north of the kraal. A palisade also blocked the 100 yards between the kraal and redoubt, while four 7-pounder guns were positioned between the redoubt and the laager to cover the northern approaches. Two more guns in the redoubt covered the north-east. Two companies were positioned in the redoubt, another company occupied the cattle kraal and the remaining infantry manned the laager. The gunners had instructions that if the Zulus got in close, they were to abandon their guns and make for the laager.[3]

Around 12.45 p.m. the tents were struck, reserve ammunition was distributed, and the troops took up their battle stations. It would very soon become clear to Wood that the left and right horns would eventually move round and encircle the camp. When news arrived from his scouts that the left horn was getting bogged down and their advance had slowed, Wood seized the opportunity to send out Colonel Buller, acting as overall commander of the mounted troops, to take on the advancing right horn. Buller and his force of about ninety mounted men rode to within 100 yards of the Zulu right horn, dismounted and fired a few volleys into the Zulu flanks. As the Zulus began to charge the mounted men, they quickly remounted and galloped back to the safety of the camp.

As soon as the horsemen had reached Khambula and cleared the field of fire, the British infantry opened fire with support from their four 7-pounders firing shell, which had been firing over the heads of the horsemen and then when the Zulus got closer, engaging them with case (canister shot). The right horn (Nkobamakosi) continued their attack on the camp but was quickly forced to retreat in the face of very heavy fire from it. As the right horn made its withdrawal, the left horn and centre comprising the Umbonambi (uMbonambi), Nokene (uNokhenke) and the Umcityu advanced towards a ravine below the redoubt, then attacked from the ravine. The leading warriors fell to volley fire from the 13th Light Infantry in the south face of the laager and the shrapnel and case shot from the six British guns in the laager and the two in the redoubt. More and more Zulu got into the ravine, about 100 yards from the cattle kraal. About forty Zulu riflemen climbed to the lip of the ravine and two parties took over some huts to the east and the rubbish dump to the west, about 400 yards either side of the camp.

The fire of the Zulu riflemen from the three positions forced most of the infantry in the cattle kraal to retreat into the redoubt and the rest to shelter at the wagons to the rear. As the Zulu morale rose at the sight of the British retreat, the men in the ravine advanced on the cattle kraal. They were confronted only by fire from one side of the main laager and soon forced their way into the kraal, fighting hand-to-hand with men of the 1/13th Company. Most of the British troops managed to extricate themselves and pull back to the redoubt, but four were killed and seven wounded. Zulu riflemen now also opened fire from behind the walls of the kraal, providing covering fire for more Zulu to advance from the ravine.

At about this time the right horn came on again from the north-east and charged across the north face of the redoubt towards the guns and the eastern sides of the laager. Aware that to the south 5,000 Zulu could shelter in the cattle kraal only 50 yards away, Wood ordered two companies of the 90th Light Infantry to retake the cattle kraal with a bayonet charge. Led by Major Hackett, they shifted a wagon from the north-east corner of the laager and formed line with bayonets fixed. As they charged across the open ground, the Zulus were forced back over the rim of the ravine, and then, lining the crest, the troops opened volley fire into the mass of warriors.

However, Hackett's men suddenly found themselves under fire from their right, as Zulu marksmen in the huts and rubbish dump on the left opened fire. Wood ordered the recall and the men returned to the cover of the laager, losing a colour sergeant, a subaltern and Major Hackett receiving a blinding head wound. Forty-four men were killed or wounded. The Royal Artillery fought with their guns in the open and poured round after round directly into the right horn and bombarded the huts with explosive shell and shrapnel to suppress the Zulu riflemen. The rubbish dump on the other side of the laager was struck by volley fire, which stopped the Zulu reply.

During this period the Umcityu massed in dead ground beyond the ravine and another wagon was pushed aside for a company of the 13th Light Infantry to engage, but they were forced back by the Zulu. This encouraged the Zulus in the ravine to charge again, but the gunners bombarded the Zulu infantry with case shot, creating a killing zone in front of the laager. The Uncityu was repulsed but rallied as Zulu all round the perimeter attacked continuously. The Nkobamakosi (right horn) attacked the redoubt again but were repulsed by volley and artillery fire from behind the wagons and the redoubt.

Again and again the Zulus charged, but the head of each charge was shot away. More Zulu massed in the ravine but before their attack got going, two companies of the 13th Light Infantry rushed to the edge of the ravine and shot down the Zulu below. Once they realised that it was futile to carry on like that, that the British lines would not be broken, the Zulus began to withdraw from the camp. The call was now sounded for Buller and his mounted men to stand to their horses, and with the defeat at Hlobane the previous day still fresh in their memories, they chased down the Zulu warriors towards Zunguin Nek with a vengeance. Mounted men even picked up the assegais from fallen Zulus to use in the killing. The pursuit continued for some 7 miles and was only halted when darkness began to fall; also, many horses were fatigued from the action at Hlobane the day before

Captain Cecil D'Arcy of the Frontier Light Horse told his troopers to take no prisoners and told them, 'No quarter boys and remember yesterday!' referring to the action at Hlobane. The FLH singled out the abaQulusi, chasing them as far as Hlobane. D'Arcy recalled that they 'butchered the brutes [Zulus] all over the place' while Buller was 'like a tiger drunk with blood'. Following in the wake of the cavalry, the British infantry and African auxiliaries combed the field killing any wounded or hiding Zulus.

Khambula was the decisive battle of the war. In four hours the British fired 138,000 rounds and 1,077 shells.[4] It demonstrated that shield and assegai were no match for an entrenched force with artillery and the Martini-Henry rifle. The Zulu commander,

Mnyamana, tried to get the regiments to return to Ulundi but many warriors simply went home. The Zulu fought another battle at Ulundi but without a belief in victory. A total of 785 Zulu dead were counted in the vicinity of the camp by burial parties two days after the battle, but their total losses were significantly higher. Frances Colenso in 1880 wrote of 1,000 dead.[5] Many more warriors retreating from the battle were overtaken and killed by British mounted troops and, furthermore, many wounded warriors died before they could reach home and help; the following day 157 bodies were counted along the line of retreat with reports of more in the distance. The official British estimate in the War Office narrative put the total Zulu losses of dead and wounded at 'nearly 2,000'. On the British side, eighteen soldiers were killed, eight officers and fifty-seven men wounded, eleven of whom later died.

At Khambula, for the first time in the war, mounted troops had successfully pursued and probably put the fear of the devil into fleeing Zulus. Wood's mounted troops also proved their worth in battling with the Zulu right horn. This was also the first time they had been used successfully in an offensive role and were able to force the Zulu into making an attack. Some questioned the necessity of the bloody pursuit, but it was clear that it had a major impact on the war. It broke the morale of the Zulu army, and after the battle many Zulu soldiers simply returned home broken, resigned to the fact that it was becoming unlikely they would win the war in the field. Also, it laid down the format of subsequent battles, and pursuing the fleeing enemy became the norm and continued to be used effectively after Khambula.

The British forces badly needed a victory to restore morale, and it finally came here at Khambula on 29 March 1879. Private Joseph Banks wrote to his parents describing the pursuit of the routed Zulus that followed: 'When the enemy were in full retreat the mounted men followed them, and accounted for all followers that lagged behind, and did some execution.'[6] The pursuit after Khambula was particularly ferocious, and the correspondence of Private John Snook, in particular a letter to his pub landlord written on 3 April, caused great controversy when it was reprinted in the newspapers: 'Then we let our mounted men out of the laager wagons, and I can tell you some murdering went on ... On March

30th, about eight miles from camp, we found about 500 wounded, most of them mortally, and begging us for mercy's sake not to kill them; but they got no chance after what they had done to our comrades at Isandlwana.'[7]

The Aborigines' Protection Society protested to the War Office concerning the actions described in Snook's letter and Evelyn Wood published an official rebuttal. His case was not helped by the existence of a number of other letters detailing the aftermath of Khambula. An anonymous infantryman recalled the events of the battle: 'The cavalry ... followed them up for about eight miles, killing every one they could lay hands upon.'[8] Captain Cecil D'Arcy of the Frontier Light Horse described in a letter printed in the *Eastern Star* how he took part in the pursuit himself: 'We killed a little over 2,300, and when once they retired all the horsemen in camp followed them for eight miles, butchering the brutes all over the place. I told the men, "No quarter, boys, and remember yesterday", and we did knock them about, killing them all over the place.'[9]

The account of Commandant Frederick Schermbrücker, the leader of the group of German colonial volunteers, of his part in the pursuit as described in *The Friend* of the Free State and *Bloemfontein Gazette*, would have equally upset the Aborigines' Protection Society: 'I took the extreme right,' he said, 'Colonel Buller led the centre, and Colonel Russell with mounted infantry took the left. For fully seven miles I chased two columns of the enemy. They fairly ran like bucks, but I was after them like the whirlwind and shooting incessantly into the thick column, which could have not been less than 5,000 strong. They became exhausted and shooting them down would have taken too much time; so we took the assegais from the dead men, and rushed among the living ones, stabbing them right and left with fearful revenge for the misfortunes of the 28th [i.e., at Hlobane]. No quarter was given.'[10]

Buller he saw enraged 'and, no doubt, the vivid recollection of the cruel manner in which the Zulus destroyed part of his forces on the 28th increased his war fury'. Schermbrücker believed that Khambula 'finished the Zulu war, and I am proud of the part my men have taken in it'.[11]

An officer of Wood's Swazi Irregulars added further proof of the vulnerability of the Zulus in retreat. 'Towards the end of the pursuit,' he wrote, 'they were so tired and exhausted that they couldn't move out of a walk, some scarcely looked round and seemed to wish to die without seeing the shot fired. Some turned round and walked to meet their death without offering resistance, some threw themselves down on their faces and waited for their despatch by assegai or bullet, some got into antbear holes, reeds or long grass and tried to evade detection, but very few succeeded in this. It was indeed a slaughter.'[12] The infantrymen saw nothing of all this, but they were jubilant at the crushing effect of their shot and shell. As one of the defenders told his sister, the Zulus 'did me out of my dinner, but we did a good many of them out of their tea'.[13]

16

THE PRINCE
IMPERIAL TRAGEDY

One of the most tragic incidents of the Zulu War was the death of Napoleon Eugene Louis Jean Joseph, the Prince Imperial of France. The death of the twenty-three-year-old coincided with the early stage of Lord Chelmsford's second invasion of Zululand, and reverberated around Britain, its colonies and Europe.

He was born at the Tuileries, Paris, on 16 March 1856, to Empress Eugenie and Napoleon III (1808–73), Emperor of France and third son of Louis Bonaparte. His mother was Eugenie Marie de Guzman, the beautiful younger daughter of the Spanish Count de Montijo and his Scottish wife, Donna Maria Kirkpatrick. They were married in the Cathedral of Notre Dame on 30 January 1853, before the Archbishop of Paris and many other important dignitaries. Almost endless deputations came daily to the palace from near and far to congratulate the sovereign and his consort. Every legitimate child born in France on the same day received a present and was accorded the honour of having the Emperor and Empress as godparents. The young prince was privately baptised at the palace on 17 March 1856, and the public baptism was held at Notre Dame on 15 June. Pope Pius IX agreed to be the prince's godfather and the many cardinals, bishops, princes, ministers, noblemen and women added further colourful splendour to the occasion.[1]

The prince's education began at the age of seven, and as both his parents spoke English well and his devoted nurse, Miss Shaw, was English, the prince in due course acquired a good knowledge of English. Latin, history and literature. When he was fourteen, the Franco-Prussian War broke out. The war did not last long and, in a brief letter, Napoleon III surrendered to the King of Prussia, spelling the end of the French Empire. Napoleon was taken as a prisoner of war and the young prince joined his mother at the Marine Hotel in Hastings, England, where she had arrived a few days earlier. Towards the end of September, 1870, the Empress and the prince took up their residence at Camden House, an estate in the district of Chislehurst, Kent. Soon afterwards, the Emperor also arrived after his release by the Prussians. Napoleon III and his family found refuge in England and were befriended by Queen Victoria.[2]

The prince became a military cadet at the Royal Military Academy, Woolwich, in 1872, and was attached to the Royal Horse Artillery at Aldershot. During his stay at Woolwich, his father died on 9 January 1873, and he became head of the Bonapartist Party in France. At graduation in 1875, Louis achieved first place in riding and fencing. Political circumstances prevented his taking a commission in the British Army but by permission of Queen Victoria, he was attached to 'A' Battery, Royal Artillery, with the privilege of wearing the uniform of a Royal Artillery lieutenant.[3]

In the Army he made friends with Captains Woodhouse, Slade and Arthur John Bigge. Woodhouse and Slade were to become generals, while Bigge was private secretary to Queen Victoria for many years and was created Baron Stamfordham in 1911. Slade and Bigge fought at Khambula and later returned to South Africa with Colonel Wood and the party which escorted Eugenie on her pilgrimage to South Africa in 1880. The prince's name was romantically linked with many famous women, including Queen Victoria's daughter, Princess Beatrice. When the Zulu War broke out, Louis asked to be allowed to go but Prime Minister Disraeli disapproved. After the news of Isandlwana, and further appeals, he was given permission to go out in his private capacity as a 'spectator' in the role of additional aide-de-camp to Lord Chelmsford.

In his will drafted on 27 February 1879, he directed that if he were killed, he should be buried beside his father until such time as their bodies could be buried in France. A further request stated that the last uniform he had worn should be bequeathed to his mother. He sailed on the *Danube* from Southampton on 28 February

1879, and on 26 March the ship docked in Cape Town. Here he was entertained by Sir Bartle Frere and Lady Frere, before his ship sailed for Durban the next day, where it arrived on 31 March. In Durban he bought a horse from the managing director of Randles, Brother and Hudson and named it Percy. Shortly afterwards, he purchased another, which he named Fate.

At this time, Lord Chelmsford was preparing for the second invasion of Zululand and on 17 April, he moved his headquarters from Durban to Pietermaritzburg. Louis, who accompanied him, was one of the earliest patrons of the Oaks Hotel and the Imperial Hotel boasts the hitching rail that the prince used. Chelmsford then moved up country and the prince later caught up with him at Dundee. They made their way to Khambula where Louis met his great friends, Arthur Bigge and Frederick Slade, who had served the guns in the open during the attack on the Khambula camp on 29 March. They travelled on via Conference Hill and Balte Spruit to Utrecht where Chelmsford set up his headquarters on 8 May. Louis was now attached to the staff of Colonel Richard Harrison, Royal Engineers, acting Quarter-Master General.[4]

On 16 May, Louis was sent out on his first patrol into Zululand from Koppie Alleen under Colonel Harrison, a day patrol only. The second occurred when Commandant Bettington with sixty mounted men under his command penetrated into Zululand as far as the headwaters of the Nordwent River. On Sunday 1 June, the Second Division moved towards its new camp just north of the Itelezi Hill (Fort Warwick). A patrol had to proceed about 10 miles south-east to select a suitable site for the advancing Second Division, and Louis volunteered to lead this patrol. Since he was not officially an officer, however, he could not command the patrol.

At this stage, Lieutenant Jaheel Brenton Carey asked permission to join the patrol to verify some observations and at 9.15 a.m., they left the Koppie Alleen camp. In addition to Louis and Carey, the patrol also consisted of six Bettington troopers: Corporal Grubb, a Natal farmer and Royal Artillery veteran; Le Tocq, a French-speaking Channel Islander; and Troopers Abel, Rogers, Cochrane and Willis. A Zulu guide was riding Louis' horse Fate, while Louis himself was on Percy. Louis' little fox terrier also ran with them. Colonel Harrison rode with them for about an hour, and noticing the absence of Commandant Bettington, assumed that Carey was replacing him.

They rode down the valley to the west and reached the end of the ridge where they halted while Louis made a sketch of the countryside. About 230 yards further on they reached a deserted kraal where they off-saddled and knee-haltered their horses. As the area appeared clear of the enemy, they didn't post a lookout. However, about 4 p.m., their Zulu guide reported that some Zulus had been seen in the vicinity. They were ordered to mount but then a volley burst from the tall grass nearby and some forty screaming Zulus charged out of the grass. The prince made desperate efforts to mount his horse but was impeded by the animal's terrified rearing and plunging.

With the Zulus closing in, he decided to run with the horse, holding the stirrup leather, but it broke free and the prince found himself alone with his sword and revolver. He fired three shots with his left hand as his right hand had been trampled by his horse as it fled. Despite being hit by an assegai, Louis momentarily held the Zulus back, defending himself with the weapon that had hit him. But he never stood a chance against overwhelming numbers, and it was over in a few moments. When the first shots were fired, Rogers' horse also bolted and he was last seen trying to load his rifle. Trooper Abel managed to mount his horse but was shot in the back as he rode off, and throwing up his hands fell from the saddle.[5]

What became clear from Zulus' evidence is that a party of between thirty and sixty Zulus were scouting in the region of the Tshotshosi River to monitor the advancing British. From the Mhlungwane Hill overlooking the valley from the south-east, they saw the British patrol descend from the hill to the north-west of the river where they had been resting, and then off-saddle at Sobhuza's abandoned kraal. Realising they had superior numbers, the Zulus decided to attack, and under cover moved in close to the patrol. However, they were scarcely in place when the patrol's Zulu guide spotted some of them and the order was given to mount their horses. The Zulus waited for them to be drawn up ready to mount before they fired a volley and charged at the soldiers. 'The horse broke away from the Prince at the donga,' Langalibalele recalled,

I was about 50 yards behind. Klabanga (Zabanga) [a member of the uMbonambi who was later killed at Ulundi] was in front of me. I came up as Zabanga, hiding himself in the grass, threw an assegai at the Prince. When the Prince first saw Zabanga he rushed at him. When he saw us surrounding him he stood up and fought us. He fought like a lion, we did not dare close on him, until he sank down on his hips. The Prince fired two shots, I think at Zabanga, but no one was hurt. I threw an assegai which I thought, and said at the time, had hit him, but I always allowed Zabanga's claims to having struck him first.

Zabanga's assegai was the first to hit the Prince. It was thrown when close to him, and struck either the chest or inside the left shoulder. Zabanga then hit him again, then Gwabakana. Just then the Prince put his left foot in a hole, and ... he was then wielding an assegai I had thrown ... When he fell my assegai was in one hand, the pistol in the other, I cannot remember which. [Nyadana and Mphlazi both recalled, however, that the Prince had a pistol in his left hand and an assegai in his right, and that he tried to change the pistol from left hand to right as he fell.] When the Prince sank down on his hips we all rushed on him and Zabanga stabbed him, and he fell on his back, after which I stabbed him. I think Zabanga and Gwabakana each stabbed him three times altogether. I saw another Zulu stab him near the eye when he was on his back.[6]

As soon as the prince was dead, Klabawathunga ritually stripped him. Dabayane held his clothes while Klabawathunga made the ritual incision in the prince's abdomen to prevent the killer from swelling up. Nine of the Zulus interviewed affirmed that they left the prince's necklace around his neck, a custom observed to leave ornaments on the slain as a sign of admiration if they had fought bravely.[7]

There was even a suggestion that the young prince did not have time to escape because he had busied himself with a Zulu woman at the kraal and had literally been caught with his pants down, but that has never been substantiated.[8]

On 2 June, Lord Chelmsford wrote from his camp near Thelezi Mountain to the Secretary of State for War: 'Prince Imperial acting under orders of the Assistant Quarter Master General reconnoitered on 1st June road to camping ground of 2nd June accompanied by

Lieutenant Carey 90th Reg. D.A. Quarter Master General and his six white men and friendly Zulus all mounted. Party halted and offsaddled the road about 10 miles from this camp, but as the Prince gave the order to mount a volley was fired from the long grass around the Kraals. The Prince Imperial and two troopers are reported missing by Lieut Carey who escaped and reached the camp after dark. From the evidence taken there can be no doubt of the Prince being killed ... I send this off at once hoping to catch mail.'[9]

The next morning, search parties were sent out from Wood's camp, as well as from the camp of the Second Division. They first found the body of Trooper Abel, badly mangled and naked, about a hundred yards from the kraal. Nearby lay Rogers, also naked with his belly ripped open, and at this spot lay the body of the prince also. He too was naked except for a thin gold chain with a medal and his great-uncle's seal about his neck. His body was riddled with seventeen separate wounds, all in front. The ground about the body was bloody and trampled, and nearby lay the speared remains of his terrier. As mentioned above, seven Zulus who were captured at Ulundi later testified that the prince had 'fought like a lion'.[10]

The prince's body was placed on a blanket, carried to a nearby ambulance and taken to the camp on Itelezi Hill. Here the viscera were removed and buried in a biscuit box while the body was crudely embalmed by the surgeons as well as possible with the materials – mainly salt – available. The body was sent back to Natal and was accompanied by an escort of the Natal Carbineers. Travelling via Koppie Alleen, Vegkop, Landman's Drift, Dundee and on to Pietermaritzburg, they arrived on Sunday 8 June. Here there were impressive ceremonies and the body lay during the night in the Catholic Church in Loop Street (which is now St Mary's, School Lane). By 11 June the cortege had reached Durban where the whole town turned out to pay their last respects to the prince. The coffin was taken aboard HMS *Boadicea* and conveyed to Cape Town where it was transferred to HMS *Orontes*, which arrived in Plymouth on 10 July.[11]

The casket was opened in the chapel at Woolwich for formal identification by the prince's doctor, Dr Conneau, and an American dentist, Dr Evans. The obsequies in the chapel at Chislehurst were conducted by Cardinal Manning, with over 40,000 people attending the funeral, including Queen Victoria and her daughter, Beatrice. The pall-bearers were the Prince of Wales, the Duke of Edinburgh, the Duke of Connaught, Crown Prince Gustave of Sweden and two Frenchmen.[12]

> The death of the Prince Imperial has made great sensation in France and created among the Bonapartists real dismay,' reported *The Witney Express*. 'They were always opposed to his expedition to the Cape through fear of both the climate and of the possibility of something critical in France in his absence, and the credit for the courage he acquired by the step did not reconcile them to these dangers. Of late they have entertained serious uneasiness as to his health, though their organs angrily denied all reports of any serious illness ... The *Times* correspondent at Berlin states that the news created there also a profound sensation, and elicited feelings of sincere sympathy ... Now that the Empress has got over the bewildering stupor that overwhelmed her in the first hours of her grief, she is bearing herself with a noble Christian selfpossession. She is still physically very weak and excessively low in spirits, but is gradually coming round to the mood of resignation.[13]

Lieutenant Carey, who had survived the attack to tell the tale, was openly blamed by his fellow officers for abandoning the prince to his fate. In mitigation, Lord Chelmsford later said that he 'lost his head'. Carey requested an official inquiry and he was tried by general court martial on 12 June at the British camp on the Phoko River and found guilty of 'misbehaviour before the enemy' in that he galloped away without having attempted to rally the escort. He was duly suspended and shipped home.[14]

An insensitive person sent the dead prince's mother a box containing the blood-stained and muddy remains of his uniform. His remains, together with those of his father, were reinterred in the crypt of Farnborough Abbey, Hampshire, in 1888.

In 1880, his mother Eugenie visited South Africa, and accompanied by Sir Evelyn and Lady Wood, Bigge and Slade, visited Durban, Pietermaritzburg, Seven Oaks, Greytown and Utrecht. On 16 May they lunched on the Khambula battlefield and five days later erected a stone cross on Campbell's grave on Eastern Hlobane. They crossed Hlobane, descended via the Devil's Pass where Buller won his VC and also visited Piet Uys' grave at the foot of the pass. Then, on 1 June 1880, on the anniversary of Louis' death, Eugenie spent the night in prayer at the very spot where he was killed. Towards dawn, a very strange thing happened. 'Although there was not a breath of air,' she says, 'the flames of the candles were suddenly deflected, as if someone wished to extinguish them, and I said to him. "Is it indeed you beside me? Do you wish me to go away?"' She rose slowly in the early light and walked to her tent, her pilgrimage completed.[15]

Today, a 20-foot Maltese cross stands on the common at Chislehurst in Kent. The inscription on the base reads: 'I shall die with a sentiment of the deepest gratitude to Her Majesty the Queen of England, to all the Royal Family and to the country where, for eight years, I have received such cordial hospitality.' And also: 'In memory of the Prince Imperial and in sorrow at his death, this cross is erected by the residents of Chislehurst 1880.'

The Prince Imperial wrote the first sentence as the sixth clause of his will the day before he sailed for South Africa.

The Prince Imperial's Prayer
It is written in his own hand and was found in his prayer book. The English translation reads:

My God I give Thee my heart, but Thou, give me faith. Without faith there can be no ardent prayer, and prayer is one of my soul's needs.

I pray to Thee, not that Thou shouldst remove the obstacles that stand in my way, but that Thou shouldst allow me to overcome them.

I pray to Thee, not to disarm my foes, but that Thou shouldst aid me to conquer myself and deign, O God, to hear my prayer.

Preserve to my affection those who are dear to me. Grant them lives of happiness. If Thou wilt shed upon this earth only a certain sum of joy, O God, take my share from me.

Distribute it among those most worthy, and let the worthiest be my friends. If Thou wouldst make reprisals upon me strike me.

Misfortune is turned to joy by the sweet thought that those whom one loves are happy.

Fortune is poisoned by this bitter thought: I am glad and those whom I love a thousandfold more than myself are suffering. Let there be no more good fortune, O God, for me. I flee from it. Take it from my path.

Joy I may not find save in forgetting the past. If I forget those who are no more, I shall be forgotten in my turn, and how sad is the thought which makes one say 'Time wipes out everything'.

O my God, show me always where my duty lies; give me strength always to do it.

When I have come to the end of my life, I shall turn my eyes towards the past without fear. Its memory will not be for me a long remorse. Then shall I be happy. Instil deeper into my heart, O God, that the conviction that those whom I love and who have died are the witnesses of all my actions. My life will be worthy for them to see, and my inmost thoughts will never cause me to blush.[16]

The Battlefield of Isandlwana, with a cairn marking one of the many British mass graves at the site.

The Battle of Isandlwana, from a painting by Charles Edwin Fripp (1854–1906).

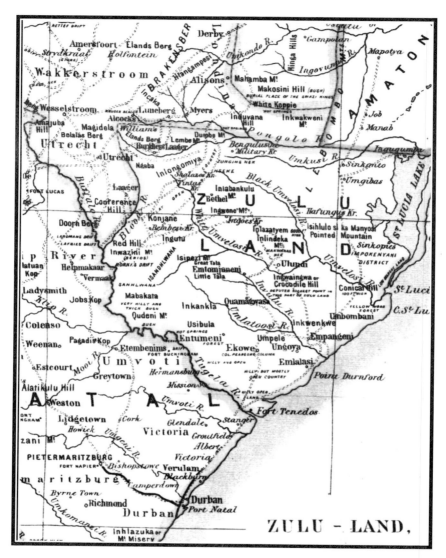

Military map of Zululand/Natal, 1879.

The Heroic Defence of Rorke's Drift, from a painting by Lady Butler, 1880.

The men of the 24th of Foot after the Battle of Rorke's Drift.

The Zulu leader Dabulamanzi. (*Illustrated London News*)

Zulu warriors, Battle of Gingindlovu, 2 April 1879. (*britishbattles.com*)

Royal Navy Gatling gun team, Gingindlovu, 2 April 1879. (*britishbattles.com*)

Officers of the Flying Column in the field. Sitting: Lt Lysons, Brig Gen Wood, Lt Col Buller. Standing: Capt Beresford (2nd from left), Major Clery (2nd from right), Capt Woodgate. (*The Illustrated Guide to the Zulu War*)

Above left: Lord Chelmsford.

Above right: Lieut Gonville Bromhead, Rorke's Drift hero. (*britishbattles.com*)

Fort Pearson, situated above where the British crossed the Tugela River to invade Zululand. (*The Historical Monuments of S.A.*)

The Ulundi Battlefield monument. (*KwaZulu Natal Province*)

Above: Cetshwayo on the bastion at his prison in Cape Town.

Left: A plaque marks the place where Cetshwayo stayed at 18 Melbury Road in London in 1882. (Courtesy of Simon Harriyott under Creative Commons 2.0)

17

ULUNDI: THE FINAL CONQUEST

After the decisive Zulu victory at Isandlwana on 22 January over Chelmsford's main column and the consequent defeat of the first invasion of Zululand, the British prepared to launch a new invasion of Zululand, and despite decisive victories at Khambula and Gingindlovu, were back where they started. In response to Isandlwana a flood of reinforcements arrived in Natal with which Chelmsford prepared the second invasion of Zululand. He was aware by mid-June that Sir Garnet Wolseley had superseded his command of the British forces, having been ordered by the British Government to 'submit and subordinate your plans to his control'.[1] Chelmsford ignored instruction, as well as various peace offers from the Zulu king Cetshwayo, determined to strike while the Zulus were still licking their wounds and regain his reputation before Wolseley could remove him from command of the army.[2]

For his second offensive Chelmsford's overall strength was increased to 25,000, but the very size of this force overwhelmed the supply and transport capacity of Natal and Chelmsford would have to utilize a number of troops that could be sustained in the field. So, for his main column, he fielded two cavalry regiments, five batteries of artillery and twelve infantry battalions, amounting to 1,000 regular cavalry, 9,000 regular infantry and a further 7,000 men with twenty-four guns, including a first ever British Army Gatling gun battery. The supply train consisted of 600 wagons, 8,000 oxen and 1,000 mules. The force's structure was also reorganised, with

Colonel Evelyn Wood's No. 4 Column becoming the flying column, Major General Henry Crealock taking over command from Colonel Charles Pearson with his No. 1 Column becoming the 1st Division, and Major General Newdigate given command of the new 2nd Division, and accompanied by Lord Chelmsford himself.

Lieutenant Willie Lloyd of the 2/24th was among the officers with Chelmsford's half-column on the fateful day of Isandlwana, but afterwards he spent the next few months bottled up 'in this cursed hole' at Helpmekaar. On 6 May he wrote:

> The difficulties of this country are something enormous. The transport is all oxen, to drive them you must employ Kaffirs, and we have just heard that Wood's foreloopers [leader boys] and drivers have run away. New ones will have to be got from the old colony (British Kaffraria), as the ones here can't be trusted, so that's another delay. The roads are fearful. Food there is none, and the great danger now is the grass which is about 8 or 9 feet high, and in a strong wind the grass burns at the rate of about 6 or 7 miles an hour … I have had a little shooting here, snipe, partridge, dikkop, buck of all sorts, rock rabbits, pigeons, etc. To give you some idea of the changes that come round in 24 hours, in the middle of the day a thermometer would be 115 or 120 in the sun, and when you turn out at reveille there is often a thick white frost. The cold has been something fearful here. We are on a high ridge and the wind whistles over it sometimes enough to take the skin off even a Kaffir. I have never been so cold at home but it's mostly dry, the only damp is the mists and clouds that come roaring up a high kloof near the camp.[3]

Officer Horace Smith-Dorrien recorded in his memoirs: 'My fate was Helpmakaar,' wrote Smith-Dorrien. 'There the Commandant constructed a fort with a huge ditch, revetting the parapet with sacks full of mealies. The wet season came on, the grain went rotten, and the ditch filled up with putrid water, the smell of which was appalling, and out of thirty-two officers all but one were down within a couple of months with fever, mostly typhoid. I got it, and was carted in a mule-wagon via Dundee down to Ladysmith some seventy miles, where a General Hospital had been formed in the Dutch Church. Hospital comforts were conspicuous by their absence in those days. Straw on the stone floor formed our beds, and there I lay for two months, hovering between life and death. The hospital was full, as far as I recollect, almost all typhoid cases, and dead were carried out every day.'[4]

A special correspondent with General Crealock's column complained about the want of pure water and the diseases plaguing them, stating that the soldiers had the idea that the country itself was unhealthy, whereas the illness had to do almost entirely with the water. 'Private soldiers are much the same as children; they have to be taken almost the same care of,' he lamented. 'It is a common thing to punish a soldier for doing something which is wrong because it is highly injurious to his own health. Officers are constantly reprimanding their men for going about in the midday sun with their hats off, though slight sunstrokes are common amongst them. They have sometimes to be threatened with punishment if they drink certain water which they are told is positively poisonous. But then they are just the same as the British public; sanitation has to be forced upon them...At Gingindlovu, for instance, where the water was like pea soup, if a soldier was thirsty he drank it. No other water was in his way, so he was bound to drink it. There can be little doubt that blame is to be attached to the home authorities, who omitted to equip the forces in South Africa with proper means for tapping the earth of fresh water, especially now that appliances for the work are so simple.'[5]

All through April and May there was much manoeuvring, particularly with supply and transport, but eventually on 3 June, the main thrust of the second invasion began its slow advance on Ulundi. The 1st Division was to advance along the coastal belt supporting the 2nd Division, which with Wood's flying column was to march on Ulundi from Rorke's Drift and Khambula. As Cetshwayo was still hoping for an end to hostilities, he refrained from attacking the long and vulnerable supply lines, meaning that the British advance was unopposed. While the force advanced, Cetshwayo sent envoys from Ulundi to the British, which reached Chelmsford on 4 June with the message that Cetshwayo wished to know what terms would be acceptable to cease hostilities. Chelmsford then sent a Zulu-speaking Dutch trader back with their terms in writing.

During its slow advance towards Ulundi, all the old fears were revived by the killing of the Prince Imperial on 1 June, particularly among the newly arrived battalions containing many young, half-trained soldiers in their ranks. Nerves were stretched to breaking point, illustrated by a series of panic situations where the troops fired by mistake at their comrades. First among the victims of this folly were 5 Field Company, Royal Engineers, then attached to Wood's Flying Column. On 5 June, Wood's advance guard engaged with Zulus at the Ipoko River, and suffered casualties, and as he wished to camp there to wait for supplies to come up, he decided to fight. He detached the Engineers and sent them back to Newdigate's column, which was in laager with hundreds of wagons about 13 miles to the rear. When the sappers arrived at 18.30 on 6 June, they pitched their tents on site and began work, well outside Newdigate's laager. About 22.00 they were awakened by shots and dived into the protection of the walls, not even a metre high. Outlying picquets retreated to the shelter within the walls, and at once they all came under heavy fire from Newdigate's laager.

Corporal Howe recalled the frightening incident: '"Good heavens, they are taking us for the enemy. Under cover at once!" cried Chard, the hero of Rorke's Drift. It was not safe to move. The buglers sounded the cease fire. Our men got over the wall to rush on the laager when they, taking us for a rush of Zulus, poured another volley into us. Back we had to go helter-skelter over the wall. Men jumped on to one another and were lying huddled in hopeless confusion, whilst shot was pouring into us like hail. Before it ceased, five Engineers (including a sergeant and two corporals) had been wounded. Next morning we found the stones on the wall covered with lead and bullet marks. The artillery told us they were just going to fire when they heard our bugle sound. If they had, not one of us would have escaped.'[6]

So Fort Newdigate, known to the troops as Fort Funk, started off on a somewhat disastrous note. Similar false alarms ruffled the columns as they continued their slow advance, and the artillery did in fact fire in one of the worse incidents just before Ulundi. Lapses of soldierly conduct were dealt with by flogging offenders, encouraged by Chelmsford, and over 500 floggings were administered during the campaign. This at a time when it was otherwise little used as an army punishment, and indeed it was abolished in 1881.[7]

Despite much difficulty in securing wagons, teams and drivers, the second invasion of Zululand began on 11 June. By 16 June, the slow advance picked up speed with the news that Wolseley was on his way to Natal to take command of the forces.[8] On the 17th, a depot named 'Fort Marshall' was established – not far from Isandlwana. Eleven days later, Chelmsford's column was only 17 miles away from Ulundi and had they established the supply depots of 'Fort Newdigate', 'Fort Napoleon' and 'Port Durnford' when Sir Garnet Wolseley arrived in Cape Town.

Once the advance had begun on 31 May, the Zulus were subjected to severe destructive action, particularly in the path of Wood's and Newdigate's columns. The spotlight of publicity on the Prince Imperial's death probably diverted attention from what was in effect indirect warfare on a civilian population. As they went along, they systematically burnt kraals, destroyed crops and stored mealies, and drove away cattle. Amongst the mounted volunteers serving with Wood was Baker's Horse, raised in Port Elizabeth and district and known as the 'Canaries' because of their yellow facing and, also as 'Baker's Boozers' for other self-explanatory reasons. One of its troopers took part in a raid on three military kraals in late June. It involved all the mounted troops of both Wood's and Newdigate's commands, 600 strong, but the Zulus opposing them were scared off by the big guns, and with Khambula still fresh in their minds did not fight. Instead, according to the trooper, 'the expedition returned having succeeded in destroying three kraals, and over 3,000 huts must have been consumed that day, with large quantities of grain stored in the different kraals'.

As early as 6 June, Corporal Howe of the Engineers wrote: 'We are burning all the kraals we come to,' and just after Ulundi, he was complaining of the winter cold, adding 'How the Zulus will manage I don't know, we burnt about 20,000 huts. I feel for the poor women and children.'[9]

Wolseley had cabled Chelmsford ordering him not to undertake any serious actions on the 23rd but the message was only received through a galloper on the 23rd itself. Chelmsford had no intention of letting Wolseley stop him from making a last effort to restore his reputation, and did not bother to reply. Wolseley sent a second message on 30 June reading: 'Concentrate your force immediately and keep it concentrated. Undertake no serious operations with detached bodies of troops. Acknowledge receipt of this message at once and flash back your latest moves. I am astonished at not hearing from you.'

In his effort to assert command over Chelmsford, Wolseley tried to join the 1st Division, which was lagging along the coast behind the main advance. He sent a final message to Chelmsford explaining that he would be joining 1st Division, and that their location was where Chelmsford should retreat if he was compelled. To make things worse for Wolseley, high seas prevented him from landing at Port Durnford and he had to travel by road. At the very time Wolseley was riding north from Durban, Chelmsford was already preparing to engage the enemy, so Wolseley's efforts to reach the front would be in vain.[10]

Cetshwayo's representatives again appeared on 23 June. A previous reply to Chelmsford's demands had apparently not reached the British force, but now these envoys bore some of what the British commander had demanded – oxen, a promise of guns and a gift of elephant tusks. But as the terms had not been fully met in Chelmsford's view, the peace offer was rejected and he turned the envoys away without accepting the elephant tusks. He also told them that the advance would only be delayed one day to allow the Zulus to surrender one regiment of their army. By now the British were visible from the Royal Kraal with Cetshwayo desperate to end the hostilities. With the invading British in sight, he knew that no Zulu regiment would surrender so he sent a further 100 white oxen from his own herd along with Prince Napoleon's sword (which the Zulus had taken on 1 June when the prince was killed).

The Zulu umCijo regiment was guarding the approaches to the White Umfolozi River where the British were camped, and they now refused to let the oxen through, arguing that it was a futile gesture as it was impossible to meet all Chelmsford's demands, and that fighting was inevitable.[11] Wolseley's telegram of 30 June now reached Chelmsford, and with only 5 miles between him and Ulundi and redemption, there was no way he was going to sit back. So Wolseley's request was simply ignored.

On 3 July, Colonel Buller led a cavalry force across the river to scout the land beyond. They saw a party of Zulus herding goats near the Mbilane stream and troopers moved to round them up. Buller shouted for them to stop and prepare to fire from the saddle, and the next moment 3,000 Zulus rose from the long grass and fired a fusillade, before charging forth, having killed three troopers. Buller ordered his men to retire and as they rushed back to the river, Baker's Horse, which had been scouting further across, gave covering fire for the river crossing. The Transvaal Rangers on the opposite bank, in turn, covered their crossing. Chelmsford was under no illusion that the Zulus wanted to fight and replied to Wolseley's third message, saying that he would indeed retreat to 1st Division if the need arose, and that he would be attacking the Zulus the next day, 4 July.

With Isandlwana in the back of his mind, Chelmsford would not chance facing the Zulu army in the open with their normal line of battle. Their advance would begin at first light, prior to forming his infantry into a large hollow square, with mounted troops covering the sides and rear.[12] Neither wagon laagers nor trenches would be used, to convince both the Zulus and critics that a British square could 'beat them fairly in the open'.[13]

At 6 o'clock in the morning on the 4th, Buller led out an advance guard of mounted troops and South African irregulars, and when they had secured an upper drift were followed by the men of the infantry, led by the experienced Flying Column battalions. An hour and a half later, the column had cleared the rough ground on the other side of the riverbank and formed their rectangular square. At 8.45, the Zulu engaged the cavalry on the right and left, which slowly retired and passed into the square.[14]

The leading face of the square was made up of five companies of the 80th Regiment in four ranks, with two Gatling guns in the centres, two 9-pounders on the left flank and two 7-pounders on the right. The left face was made up of the 90th Light Infantry with four companies of the 94th Regiment, with two more 7-pounders. On the right face the 1st Battalion of the 13th Light Infantry and four companies of the 58th Regiment were positioned, with two 7-pounders and two 9-pounders. The rear face consisted of two companies of the 94th Regiment and two companies of the 2nd Battalion of the 21st Regiment (Royal Scots Fusiliers). Within the square were headquarters staff, No. 5 Company of the Royal Engineers led by Lieutenant John Chard, the 2nd Native Natal

Contingent, fifty wagons and carts with reserve ammunition and hospital wagons. Buller's horsemen covered the front and both flanks of the square, while a rearguard of two squadrons of the 17th Lancers and a troop of Natal Native Horse followed.

Amidst unfurled regimental colours and the 13th Light Infantry band's music, the mobile square of 5,317 men began its spectacular advance across the plain. By 8 a.m. no Zulus in any numbers had yet been sighted, and consequently the Frontier Light Horse were sent out to stir the enemy. As they crossed the Mbilane stream, the entire Zulu inGobamkhosi rose out of the tall grass in front of them, followed by regiment after regiment rising up all around them. The Zulu Army, around 12,000 to 15,000 strong and under the command of umNtwana Ziwedu kaMpande, now stood in a horseshoe shape encircling the north, east and southern sides of the British square. A Zulu reserve force was also at the ready to complete the circle. The Zulu forces were made up of both veterans and novices with varying degrees of experience. They stood stomping the ground with their feet and drumming their shields with their assegais, which would have made for an awesome spectacle.[15]

The mounted troops by the stream opened fire from the saddle in an attempt to trigger a premature charge, and then wheeled back through gaps made in the infantry lines for them. As the cavalry cleared their front, the four ranks of the infantry opened fire at 2,000 yards into the advancing Zulu ranks. With the range gradually closing between the British lines and the enemy, the Zulu troops faced concentrated fire. They had to charge forward directly into massed rifle fire, non-stop fire from the Gatling guns and the artillery firing canister shot at close and then point-blank range. Charge after charge was made by the Zulus, trying to get within close range, but they could not prevail against the British fire. In spite of a number of casualties within the square, the British firing did not allow any warrior to get within 30 yards of the British ranks.

The Zulu reserve force now rose and charged against the south-west corner of the square, but the 9-pounder guns tore huge holes in this force while the infantry opened fire. Despite the speed of the charge, the Zulu reserves could not get close enough to engage in hand-to-hand combat. Chelmsford ordered the cavalry to mount, and the 17th Lancers, 1st King's Dragoon Guards, colonial cavalry, Native Horse and 2nd Natal Native Contingent charged after the now fleeing Zulus. The Zulus fled towards the high ground with the cavalry at their heels and shells falling ahead of them. The Lancers were checked at the Mbilane stream by rifle fire from of a hidden party of Zulus, which several casualties to their ranks, but they overcame the resistance and continued the pursuit. In the end, not a live Zulu remained on the Mahlabatini Plain, with members of the Natal Native Horse, Natal Native Contingent and Wood's Irregulars slaughtering the Zulu wounded, taking revenge for the bloodbath at Isandlwana.[16]

After half an hour of concentrated fire from the artillery, the Gatling guns and thousands of British rifles, Zulu military power was broken. British casualties were ten killed and eighty-seven wounded, while nearly 500 Zulu dead were counted around the square;[17] another 1,000 or more were wounded. Chelmsford ordered the Royal Kraal of Ulundi to be burnt, and it burned for days. He relinquished command to Wolseley on 15 July at the fort at St Paul's, and left for home two days later on 17th. While he had partially salvaged his reputation and received a Knight Grand Cross of Bath, mainly because of Ulundi, he was severely criticised by the Horse Guards' investigation and he would never serve in the field again.[18]

Despite their failure to close with the British formations at Khambula and Gingindlovu the Zulu army attack developed along familiar lines once more. Major F. W. Grenfell, 60th Regiment, serving on Chelmsford's staff, was in the square at Ulundi. 'The Zulus now appeared in great numbers on all sides of us and soon came into collision with our mounted men who, after firing a few volleys, retired rapidly into the square ... It was a dramatic sight, the small square of under four thousand men with the Zulus closing in on it ... the Zulu army manoeuvring in different regiments ... closing on to the square, their skirmishers firing wildly from every sort of weapon. ... The Zulus fought in their old way, advancing in a horn-shaped formation, continually feeding their flanks, till the square was entirely enveloped. Their fire ceased and they came boldly on with their stabbing assegais, and sought to close with the British Force.'

Captain J. E. L. Jervis, 7th Hussars, attached to 17th Lancers and shortly to become the 4th Viscount St Vincent, was also surprised by the Zulu strategy. 'As soon as we reach the centre of the plain our enemy's tactics begin to develop. On the hills on our right and left the Zulus were lining the crests, and closing in on our fronts and rear [they] advance in beautiful order, covered by skirmishers, apparently in one long continuous line about four deep, with intervals between the different regiments – not in the dense irregular crowds we had been led to expect. It is evidently their object to surround us, with their largest force in our rear to cut off our retreat; it was a grand sight.'[19]

Four days after the battle, Private Ellis Edwards wrote to his family from Ulundi:

I wish to express my opinion of the great battle which we had on the 4th day of July whilst taking the capital of Zululand. The scene was horrible. The fight lasted for one hour and ten minutes and was extremely hard. The strengh of the enemy was 25,000 whilst our strengh was only 4,500. After hard fighting we repulsed the enemy with the loss of 3000 killed and 500 wounded; our loss was 10 killed and 40 wounded. I can assure you that the Zulus are a lot of fearless men. They poured upon us like a number of lions. The burning of Ulundi – their main support – was the greatest fire I ever saw. It continued burning for four days. I am very much pleased to tell you that I really think the war is close at an end now. We captured 800 head of cattle.

I am very sorry to tell you that it is rumoured in this camp that we are going to India after this affair is settled. At the same time I hope it is wrong as we have had plenty of foreign climates. I can assure you that the hardships which I have gone through are beyond measure. I have got to wash all my clothes and bake the bread which we eat. We have to march fourteen miles a day and, after arriving in a strange camp, we have to dig trenches before we get any food. If this regiment does not go to India I shall be at home by Christmas ... I am very sorry to tell you of the sad misfortune which befell the young Prince Napoleon whilst scouting out in the wilds of Zululand. After the Zulus had killed him they stabbed him in fourteen different places. I was one of the men who removed his body in the van in order to send it home to England ...

It is very hard to get any paper or stamps in this part of the world. I have been forced to steal out of the way every time I want to write because we haven't got one moment as we can call our own ... Wood is very scarce here at present. We cook our food with dried cow dung ... [20]

Private Edward Hughes of E Company, 1/24th Regiment, 2nd Division, wrote to his parents from the Upoko River camp after the battle:

We have had a very hard time of it but we are now enjoying a few days' ease. We have been up as far as the King's Kraal, Ulundi on the White Umvolosi and after burning all the kraals we came across and knocking the Zulus out of time, have returned to this camp to wait the issue of affairs.

We arrived, after a very hard and tedious march, at the King's Kraal, encamping opposite it on the 1st of July. Nothing of any importance occurred until the 3rd when the Zulus surprised us by opening a smart fire on some of our men who were down at the river getting water. The fire was quickly returned by our men down there on duty. The light cavalry were immediately got ready; 4 nine-pounders were got into position; and it was determined to shift the Zulus out of the place, for as long as they were allowed to remain there, it was evident that we could not get any water without great danger. A couple of shells were, therefore, thrown across the river. This had the effect of making the Zulus scamper off to their kraals at full speed. But our horsemen were waiting for them and chased the enemy as far as their kraals. Our men were obliged, however, to retire for the enemy were reinforced by some thousands. Our loss was slight; that of the enemy considerable. The same night the Zulus kept us awake for nearly two hours singing and shouting in a terrible manner.

Next morning, the 4th, we were all quietly awakened at a very early hour. No bugles sounded and everything was done as quietly as possible. Our men crossed the river and made for the open plain. This movement was quite unexpected by the Zulus, for at seven o'clock about 15,000 of them were seen making for our side of the river; but just at this critical moment our column had reached the open. They were then seen by the enemy who imagined that they had a very easy thing of it. But they calculated wrongly for they were greeted by a tremendous fire from our men as they advanced. Forty-five minutes passed after the first shot, when the Zulus wavered; our men cheered heartily; away went the Zulus as hard as they could run, closely followed by the 17th Lancers who mowed them down like grass.

So ended the battle of Ulundi and with it Cetywayo's power over his people.

Our loss, as near as I can ascertain, was ten men killed and about fifty wounded ... [21]

Major C. W. Robinson, Rifle Brigade, a 2nd Division staff officer, recalled: 'When the cavalry were in, the guns opened with shell, but the Zulus were too much in skirmishing order for them to do much damage at first. They gradually came down in the long grass, running round to try and surround us. There were no dense bodies such as I have read of ... The formation was rather like our loose file advance ... covered by skirmishers. Our men's infantry fire did not check this at all at first, and the corner of the square between the 21st and 58th, where I stood principally, the Zulus came on steadily in spite of it working round at a sort of half run (fired at by case and musketry) in the most determined way ... It surprised one enormously though to see them come on thus in the face of a withering fire and 7 rounds of case (from Trench's 2 guns) up to less than 100 yards from us.[22]

Guy Dawnay, who earlier fought at Gingindlovu, recalled: 'After about twenty minutes came the event of the attack, a large dense black mass of Zulus, the only really thick mass I ever saw attacking, appeared opposite our corner about 130 yards off, the ground favouring their getting so far, and made a rush. Our fire didn't check them the least; nearer they came – 100 yards – 80 yards – still rushing on, a thick black mass. Lord Chelmsford came galloping up, telling the 58th and 21st to fire faster; Newdigate pulled out his revolver. The nine-pounder crashed through them again and again; but at that short distance the canister did not burst. Everyone thought it would be hand to hand in another minute, when at 60 yards the mass faltered, wavered, and withered away.'[23] Philip Robinson, the correspondent of the *Daily Telegraph*, noting the strength of the British firepower, felt, 'It was impossible for any force long to face the deadly storms of lead poured in among them at such short distance.'[24]

The common experience of both Khambula and Ulundi had been a vengeful pursuit of the beaten Zulu warriors. At Ulundi, where Cetshwayo's army was finally destroyed, it was again a matter of no quarter given. An anonymous correspondent of the 17th Lancers, in a letter to his brother, described how the infantry 'kept up a fire like one continual blaze, but notwithstanding this the Zulus got to within fifty or sixty yards of us, and I could see them on one side breaking their assegais short for a final rush, so you can form some sort of idea as to the sort of metal they are ... They tried lying down to escape, but it was no use, we had them anyhow, no mercy or quarter from the "Old Tots".'[25]

An account in the *Cape Journal* described another such example of 'no quarter': 'It was a singular time, and a dangerous spot, in which to interview a man, especially a wounded man, but the questioner went to work seriously, and got all the news of the week ... on being assured that there was no more information to be had, he quietly shot the man, mounted his horse, and joined again in the chase.'[26]

At the end of the campaign, the British soldiers that fought the Zulu army during the Zululand invasions were nevertheless full of admiration for their opponents. They had entered the war with overconfidence and a condescending attitude through all ranks, but events like Isandlwana, Hlobane and even Ulundi changed their views. The Zulu army displayed great courage and skill in battle, and had earned their respect. Rather than purely relying on their superiority of numbers in mass attacks, the Zulus had generally launched well-controlled attacks and used tactics not unrecognisable to a European army: a main body approaching in strength, then sending out 'horns' to outflank the enemy, and extensively using skirmishers to shield the advance.

18

HEALERS AND HOSPITALS

Army Medical Department (A.M.D.)
When the invasion of Zululand took place, Surgeon-General John Andrews Woolfryes was still Principal Medical Officer at the Cape. He then had under his command an average strength of sixty-nine officers of the A.M.D and eight officers of orderlies, with a number of civil surgeons also employed. At the commencement of the war the strength of the Army Hospital Corps (A.H.C.) was 124, and these were supplemented by drafts amounting to 310 during the campaign. The regulation field hospital of 200 beds was divided into eight separate units for convenience in dealing with small bodies of troops. Each of these units was allotted two M.O.'s, two A.H.C., a cook and a wagon orderly. The transport consisted of an ambulance wagon, a store wagon, a water cart and two packhorses. Unfortunately the authorised transport personnel was never supplied, and the service suffered from using civilian or native drivers.

The most advanced field hospital was usually made up of two of these units, but the medical officers were not increased. For every batch of ten patients after the first, a regimental orderly had to be demanded. The ambulance wagons were either the unwieldy country wagons used in the late campaign, fitted with a spring floor, or converted store wagons. Later on, thirty regulation ambulances were sent from Britain. Regimental units had a M.O. attached, with two stretcher-bearers per company. To facilitate wound treatment on the battlefield, each soldier was supposed to carry a piece of lint and a bandage in his left-hand trousers pocket as a first field dressing.[1]

Base hospitals were formed at Durban, Pietermaritzburg, Ladysmith, Newcastle and Utrecht, and auxiliary hospitals and convalescent depots were subsequently added. Except where station hospitals already existed, these base hospitals usually seem to have been stationary field hospitals. The equipment of a stationary and a movable field hospital only differed in that the stationary hospitals had twice as much clothing.

When Lord Chelmsford's force crossed into Zululand around 6 January 1879, in four columns, each column had a bearer party of eight A.H.C. and forty native carriers with eight Ashanti cots attached, additional to its field hospital establishment. At Rorke's Drift a store depot was established, and a hospital of forty beds, with Surgeon James Henry Reynolds in charge.

During the disaster at Isandlwana, some 12 miles away, on 22 January, Surgeon-Major P. Shepherd, Lieutenant and Acting-Surgeon Boue of the native contingent, Lieutenant of Orderlies A. Hall and eight men of the A.H.C. were among the killed. Six ambulance wagons and all the medical equipment were also lost. Then on the same day the epic defence of Rorke's Drift followed, where Surgeon-Major Reynolds not only played a major part in the defence, but was also awarded the Victoria Cross for his bravery.

His own account of the fight read:

At 1.30 a large body of natives marched over the slope of Isandlana in our direction, their purpose evidently being to examine ravines and ruined kraals for hiding fugitives. These men we took to be our native contingent. Soon afterwards appeared four horsemen on the Natal side of the river galloping in the direction of our post, one of them was a regular soldier, and feeling they might possibly be messengers for additional medical assistance, I hurried down to the hospital as they rode up. They looked awfully scared, and I was at once startled to find one of them was riding Surgeon-Major Shepherd's pony. They shouted frantically, 'The camp at Isandlana has been taken by the enemy and all our men in it massacred, that no power could stand against the enormous number of the Zulus, and the only chance for us all was by immediate flight.' Lieutenant Bromhead, Acting-Commissary Dalton, and myself, forthwith consulted together, Lieutenant Chard not having as yet joined us from the pontoon, and we quickly decided that with barricades well placed around our present position a stand could best be made where we were. Just at this period Mr. Dalton's energies were invaluable. Without the smallest delay, he called upon his men to carry the mealie sacks here and there for defences. Lieutenant Chard [R.E.] arrived as this work was in progress, and gave many useful orders as regards the lines of defence. He approved also of the hospital being taken in, and between the hospital orderlies, convalescent patients (eight or ten) and myself, we loop-holed the building and made a continuation of the commissariat defences round it. The hospital, however, occupied a wretched position, having a garden and shrubbery close by, which afterwards proved so favourable to the enemy; but, comparing our prospects with that of the Isandlana affair, we felt that the mealie barriers might afford us a moderately fair chance.

At about 3.30 the enemy made their first appearance in a large crowd on the hospital side of our post, coming on in skirmishing order at a slow slinging run. We opened fire on them from the hospital at 600 yards, and although the bullets ploughed through their midst and knocked over many, there was no check or alteration made in their approach. As they got nearer they became more scattered, but the bulk of them rushed for the hospital and the garden in front of it. We found ourselves quickly surrounded by the enemy with their strong force holding the garden and shrubbery. From all sides, but especially the latter places, they poured on us a continuous fire, to which our men replied as quickly as they could reload their rifles. Again and again the Zulus pressed forward and retreated, until at last they forced themselves so daringly, and in such numbers, as to climb over the mealie sacks in front of the hospital, and drove the defenders from there behind an entrenchment of biscuit boxes, hastily formed with much judgment and forethought by Lieutenant Chard.

A heavy fire from behind it was resumed with renewed confidence, and with little confusion or delay, checking successfully the natives, and permitting a semi-flank fire from another part of the laagar to play on them destructively. At this time, too, the loopholes in the hospital were made great use of. It was, however, only temporary, as, after a short respite, they came on again with renewed vigour. Some of them gained the hospital verandah, and there got hand to hand with our men defending the doors. Once they were driven back from here, but others soon pressed forward in their stead, and, having occupied the verandah in larger numbers than before, pushed their way right into the hospital, where confusion on our side naturally followed. Everyone tried to escape as best they could, and, owing to the rooms not communicating with one another, the difficulties were insurmountable. Private Rook, 2/24th Regiment, who was acting as hospital cook, and Private Conolly, 2/24th Regiment, a patient in hospital, made their way into the open at the back of the hospital by breaking a hole in the wall. Most of the patients escaped through a small window looking into what may be styled the neutral ground. Those who madly tried to get off by leaving the front of the hospital were all killed with the exception of Gunner Roward. The only men actually killed in the hospital were three, excluding a Kafir under treatment for compound fracture of femur. Their names were Sergeant Maxfield, Private Jenkins, both unable to assist in their escape, being debilitated by fever, and Private Adams, who was well able to move about, but could not be persuaded to leave his temporary refuge in a small room.

The engagement continued more or less until about 7 o'clock p.m., and then, when we were beginning to consider our situation rather hopeless, the fire from our opponents appreciably slackened, giving us some time for reflection. Lieutenant Chard here, again, shined in resource. Anticipating the Zulus making one more united dash for the fort, and possibly gaining entrance, he converted an immense stack of mealies standing in the middle of our enclosure, and originally cone fashioned, into a comparatively safe place for a last retreat. Just as it was completed, smoke from the hospital appeared and shortly burst into flames. During the whole night following, desultory firing was carried on by the enemy, and several feigned attacks were made, but nothing of a continued or determined effort was again attempted by them. About 6 o'clock a.m., we found, after careful reconnoitering, that all the Zulus with the exception of a couple of stragglers had left our immediate vicinity, and soon afterwards a large body of men were seen at a distance marching towards us. I do not think it possible that men could have behaved better than did the 2/24th and the Army Hospital Corps (three), who were particularly forward during the whole attack.

In his narrative, Reynolds omits the fact that during the most critical part of the struggle round the hospital, he crossed and recrossed the space between the building and the store to bring a fresh supply of ammunition under heavy fire.

In March, Wood's column did some hard fighting. His medical staff consisted of the usual field hospital detachments, with Surgeon-Major Reilly as S.M.O., and a party of native bearers. As mentioned earlier, on 28 March a force of mounted troops and irregulars under command of Lieutenant-Colonel Buller were surrounded, and nearly cut off on the Hlobane Mountain. During the stampede back to camp, and during which many casualties occurred, civil surgeons Jolly and Conolly were the last in the retirement, pursued by several thousand Zulus, and frequently dismounted to assist the wounded. In the attack on the Khambula camp the next day, the whole medical staff and their orderlies won the admiration of the column commander. During the hottest part of the fight, and in a very exposed part of the camp, Brown and Thornton, two regular surgeons, successfully amputated an arm.[2]

During May, the troops were concentrated in two divisions under Generals Crealock and Newdigate, and a flying column under Brigadier-General Evelyn Wood. The first division troops, with Surgeon-Major Tarrant as S.M.O., were concentrated round Gingindlovu, and remained stationary in the unhealthy, low-lying country near the coast till late in June.

Malaria, dysentery and enteric fever were prevalent, and the medical staff and A.H.C. had a difficult time. The hospitals at Fort Chelmsford and Fort Pearson were evacuated by road to Durban, with the last 15 miles done by train. For this purpose, ten English ambulance wagons were employed, and rest stations in the charge of A.H.C. non-commissioned officers were established along the road. After the advance, the sea route from Port Durnford was available.

The 2nd Division, which with the flying column did most of the fighting during the second invasion, had less problems as they were operating in the healthy upland country of central Zululand, and where Surgeon-Major Giraud was the S.M.O. On 20 May, Wood's flying column joined the column at Inceni Mountain, and the combined force advanced eastward. Then on 4 July, Lord Chelmsford defeated the Zulus at Ulundi. During the action, casualties were attended to at the field hospital in the left rear of the square. The evacuation of wounded and sick from the force during its advance was to Koppie Alleen by sick convoy, from where the more serious cases proceeded to Ladysmith and the remainder to Utrecht.[3]

The Nurses

The Crimean War of 1853 to 1856 highlighted the need for the improved care of the wounded and sick near the fields of battle, and it also introduced to Victorian England a new heroine in the nurse Florence Nightingale. The British Army, however, remained unconvinced of the need for nurses other than in static hospitals and they were not seen as having a place on the battlefield. Partly due to the interest of Queen Victoria, who remained in close personal contact with Florence Nightingale, the British Army Nursing Service was established in 1861. However, the British Army was slow to reform nursing services, and between 1861 and 1882, there were only twelve women employed in the Army Nursing Service and these were stationed at the military hospitals at Netley and Woolwich. By 1895 the number had increased to just seventy-two, and it was only during and especially after the South African War (1899–1902) that the Army enrolled women as nurses in significant numbers. Until then, the work of nursing the sick and wounded in the British Army had been done chiefly by male orderlies.

During the Anglo-Zulu War, while the Army still saw the nurses' role mostly as being appropriate for static hospitals in Britain, the first overseas deployment of the service was seen, with the Service's Netley Superintendent, Mrs Jane Cecilia Deeble, and six nurses deploying to South Africa, which proved that such a move would work. Ms Deeble was insistent that if circumstances required it, her nurses would rough it under canvas. She and her small party sailed for Cape Town on 19 June 1879, but more about this later.

In Natal, in the absence of British Army nurses, the Army called on the services of other trained nurses, such as those in the Community of St Michael and All Angels in Bloemfontein. In early April 1879, a few months before the arrival of Ms Deeble and her nurses in South Africa, the principal medical officer of British troops in Natal requested that sisters be sent from the Community of St Michael and All Angels to nurse sick and wounded soldiers in the military hospital at Ladysmith. Consequently, Mother Emma, Sister Louisa and two associates, Misses Potts and Langlands, left Bloemfontein for Natal later that month.[4]

The Community of St Michael and All Angels

The Community was an Anglican religious community of women, established in Bloemfontein, Orange Free State, in April 1874. Between that date and 1914, fifty women were professed sisters of St Michael and All Angels. The sisterhood was established firstly in the context of the mid-nineteenth-century Catholic revival within Anglicanism, and secondly in the context of changing roles for women, which saw their increased engagement in public philanthropy.[5] Arguably the best known member of the St Michael and All Angels community was Henrietta Stockdale, who was instrumental in the 1891 Act of the Cape Parliament, which provided for state registration of nurses, and so laid the foundations of nursing as a profession for women in South Africa.[6] Other sisters of the community also played a pioneering role as nurses, particularly in the 1879 Anglo-Zulu War, and subsequently during the 1880–1881 1st Transvaal War of Independence and the South African War of 1899–1902.

The initiative for the foundation of the community came from Bishop Allan Webb, himself influenced by the Catholic revival in the Church of England. After an initial visit to his diocese, he saw the need for women workers to undertake nursing, visiting and teaching, and decided that a community of sisters who would provide continuity was the best way of achieving this. Webb also wanted a community established in southern Africa, and the

Sisterhood of St Thomas the Martyr in Oxford offered to lend Sister Emma as the first superior for five years. In the end, she remained with the community in Bloemfontein until her death in 1887. She was the daughter of a naval officer and well educated, with experience in home visiting, nursing and teaching, and her Oxford community told Bishop Webb 'we are giving to South Africa one of our best'. All the other sisters of the community were professed in South Africa, so they were aware of conditions under which they would live their lives, with no expectation of a permanent return to England.[7]

The sisterhoods carried the domestic work considered suitable for women into public life, through running hospitals and elevating nursing to a profession, and through establishing schools and securing higher education for women. They took on these responsibilities without receiving remuneration. The bishop and the sisters were loyal and patriotic, and to them British colonial rule was just and beneficial. In 1876, when they began work among indigenous people, they noted that 'neither Dutch nor English colonists as a rule sympathised with work among Coloured people, thinking it waste of time and misguided sentiment'.[8] War in southern Africa provided occasions for the sisters to express their political opinions more forcefully than they did at other times.

British propaganda created the impression of the Zulu king Cetshwayo as a warmonger disrupting the subcontinent, and that he was responsible for the outbreak of war here, there and everywhere. The sisters supported this view unreservedly, Mother Emma writing in May 1879: 'I hope you do not believe what the papers are saying about this being an unjust war. If ever there was a just war, this is one. Until Cetewayo's power is broken, there will be no peace in South Africa. He has been at the bottom of all the disturbances of last year, and every colonist out here knows that his own life and the lives of those dear to him are not safe, [as long] as Cetewayo is a free king.'[9]

The general feeling among the sisters was that the British cause was just and that Cetshwayo ought to be punished. A letter in the *Quarterly Paper* of 1879 from the community published for English consumption in August 1879 summed up their views: 'I do hope there will be no nonsense about a patched up peace. It will only make Cetewayo believe himself invincible or rather confirm him in that opinion and make Natal unsafe, wasting utterly all those streams of brave and noble blood which have flowed through South Africa during the last eighteen months.'[10]

The sisters were no advocates of peace and war was seen as an imperial duty. Mother Emma wrote: 'We fear so much that the Government will make peace too easily, the result of which would be that directly the troops are withdrawn, the Zulus will break out again. It would be the easiest thing in the world for them to devastate and lay waste to this colony from end to end ... I fear that our soldiers are rather afraid of the Zulus; one of the hospital orderlies said last Tuesday evening, "You see, it is not as if they were ordinary men, but it seems as if they had ten lives."'[11]

The sisters caring for the sick and wounded at Ladysmith were no novices. Sister Louisa Olden, a cheerful woman, had already trained as a nurse in Ireland. She came to South Africa as an associate of the community and arrived in Bloemfontein in February 1876. She took charge of the hospital in Kimberley in the same year, and remained there until March 1879, while the more famous Sister Henrietta was training as a midwife. Miss Langlands came out as a 'lady worker' offering three years' service to the community and was sent to Kimberley in 1877, where she and Miss Potts were among the six women first trained as nurses under the scheme set up by Sister Henrietta Stockdale.[12]

Ladysmith during those days was a small place where the British had built a fort in 1860 to protect the villagers from possible Zulu attacks. Having arrived there, the sisters found that the military hospital had been set up in the old Dutch Reformed Church, then a thatched-roof building, and augmented by four large tents. It was occupied by eighty soldiers suffering from fever and dysentery and was staffed by a sergeant, four orderlies and a doctor, 'all overworked'. The beds were made of three planks raised 15 cm above the floor, and each soldier had his kit, bread rations and medicine next to his bed. The sisters' first step was to reorganise the sick room so that the kit was stored in the pulpit and medicine was dispensed by the nurses instead of the sick being responsible for taking their own.[13]

Here in Ladysmith the sisters lived in the church rectory of Revd Hermanus Theodorus Kriel, minister from 1878 to 1883. They were so far from the war front that they were never really in danger, although there was one false alarm in May when information suggested that the town might be attacked by a large Zulu force. According to the sisters' accounts of this alarm they were getting ready for bed but without fear, even though they had been warned that they might be called into a laager at short notice.[14] Because of the Zulu War, there was very little activity in the Ladysmith Dutch Reformed congregation during 1879/80.[15]

The sisters were very aware of complaints that war nursing was inappropriate for women, and were determined to disprove those who regarded women as a liability. Fortunately, Sister Louisa knew several of the doctors who served at Ladysmith through family connections, which helped them be accepted in their roles.[16]

Military Orderlies

Doctors saw great difficulties in integrating women into the army, because as ladies they could supervise ward work, but in the Army they would have to accept subordination to male officers, and orderlies would find it difficult to accept orders from a woman who was not an officer. But in Ladysmith the sisters had an excellent relationship with the military orderlies. Mother Emma wrote: 'time and paper would fail me if I tried to write all the little attentions and kindnesses of these goodhearted orderlies. Best of all, six or seven of them may now be seen every Sunday night at Church.'[17] This was significant, because the relationship between orderlies and military nurses was controversial in the South African War, when orderlies often refused to recognise the authority of military nurses. The sisters reported that there were hospital sergeants and hospital orderlies trained in the military hospitals in England, 'so the work is not hard' and 'they all work under us'.[18] One reason for this harmonious state of affairs is that the orderlies responded to the sisters with deference, following the attitude of their senior officers; being religious might have heightened this respect. They would also have felt less threatened because of the fact that the number of nurses was relatively small and that they were obviously only working in a temporary capacity.[19]

In the military hospital at Ladysmith, their patients were mostly cases of dysentery and enteric fever, with relatively few injuries until early July, when the wounded from the battle of Ulundi arrived at the hospital. At the end of August, military nurses from the Royal Military Hospital at Netley in England arrived, and the sisters from the Community of St Michael and All Angels felt 'less wanted' and left early in September.[20]

Their relationship with the Army was strained and they felt uneasy about officials' attitudes towards their service. A letter from the medical officer at the Base Field Hospital in May 1879 told Bishop Webb that the doctors and patients valued 'the kind and thoughtful services of the ladies'[21] – and is an indication of the condescending tone towards these trained women. Another letter from a senior medical officer, however, stated his appreciation for their work: 'Having heard that you were informed that the Sisters attending on the sick and wounded at the Base Hospital, Ladismith, were of little use, and not appreciated either by the patients, or the authorities there, ... I consider they were most useful in carrying out the orders of the Medical Officers, more especially in giving the patients their food and medicine regularly, looking after the cleanliness of the sick and wounded ... and preparing for them many little articles of diet ... Altogether I am of opinion they are not only most useful, but skilful nurses, and were of considerable assistance to me.'[22]

The sisters spoke of the extreme ferocity of the Zulu and the fact that among the British sick soldiers had been 'many cases of heart disease brought on by excitement, and there have been cases of men losing their minds and their speech'.[23] They not only cared for their own soldiers, but also for some Zulu casualties. Following the Battle of Ulundi, two Zulu prisoners were brought to the hospital at Ladysmith: '"Pashongo" had his leg amputated but died soon afterwards, though not before he had taught our soldiers many lessons in patience. One never heard a cross word pass his lips, and he was so grateful to his nurse for her kindness. The other, "Dick" (I never could pronounce his Zulu name), was very sulky at first, but kindness was in his heart. One night that "Pashongo" was very wakeful, and asking for water, he crawled out of bed to hand the drink, so as to save the orderly, who awoke, and so discovered his thoughtful conduct.'[24]

After the Zulu War, the nurses of the Community of St Michael and All Angels still saw service during the 1st Transvaal War of Indepence when the Transvaal burghers resorted to arms in December 1880, aiming to besiege British garrisons in the Transvaal. In this instance their quarters were part of the military camp, they seldom saw other women, and regularly faced the possibility of a military attack.

Stafford House Committee Nurses

The Stafford House Committee was established following a meeting in 1879 at Stafford House, St James, the home of George Granville William Sutherland-Leveson-Gower (1828-92), 3rd Duke of Sutherland, and chaired by the duke himself. The objects of the organisation were 'to furnish trained nurses and hospital comforts and to supplement arrangements for promoting the convalescence of the sick and wounded in South Africa'. This venture was similar to the scheme that had been established for the assistance of troops in the Russo-Turkish War of 1877–78. The Committee expressed the hope that 'subscriptions will be raised to do for our own soldiers what was so well and generously done for others during the Carlist, Franco-German, Servian, and Russo-Turkish wars'.[25]

The Stafford House Committee party that was sent out was comprised of Surgeon-General J. T. C. Ross and Dr George Stoker, brother of Bram Stoker (author of *Dracula*), and seven trained nurses. The *Burnley Express* of 14 June 1879 reported that Surgeon-General Ross and Dr Stoker, with seven nurses and a quantity of surgical stores and appliances, had left Dartmouth at noon that day in Sir Donald Currie's mail steamer, the *Dublin Castle*, for Natal.[26]

According to a report from Dr Ross, the party arrived at Durban on 14 July. Dr Ross wrote: 'The supplies of poultry, etc., that we brought with us are very valuable here. There are between about 200 and 300 hundred sick, and about 250 expected. Two of our nurses go to the auxiliary base hospital near the sea coast, and two more to the base hospital itself, which is in charge of the principal medical officer. These latter will have sole care of 13 tents, holding 140 patients, and I am sure that they will do good work. They are delighted at the prospect.' The newspaper carrying his report also said: 'Dr Ross speaks in the highest praise of the energy and sound sense which has been displayed by Lady Frere in preparing everything for his arrival and Dr Ross was much astonished at the successful efforts which the colonists have already made in aiding the sick and wounded, and which appear not to be sufficiently known at home. Dr W. H. Russell, a member of the committee, wrote from Fort Durnford on 13 July: "There will only be too many cases for the Stafford House South African Aid Fund. So press it, do."[27]

Dr Ross and the nurses had to wait until the 14th for the heavy sea swell to calm down before they could be taken to the shore. Once they landed, the nurses were split into pairs, with the exception of Sister Janet, who was sent to the border settlement of Utrecht, where the hospital supporting Sir Evelyn Wood's column was located. Sisters Ruth and Elizabeth remained in Durban, Sisters Mary and Annette went to Pietermaritzburg, and Sisters Emma and Edith went to Ladysmith.[28] Their deployment involved long journeys over rough country and sometimes severe weather, ranging from freezing days to scorching heat.

On 29 August 1879, a letter from Lady Frere was published in *The Morning Post*, dated 29 July 1879. It read: 'All accounts which I hear from Natal speak of the energy of Dr. Ross and the value of the trained nurses' work. I think the selection of him as your agent, and his appointment as commissioner to act, was an excellent arrangement. As willing as I should be to do anything I could to help, it could have been impossible for me, from this distance, to accomplish all he has by being on the spot. I fear the hospital work must continue for some time, although I hope we may say the sick are doing well.'[29]

Of all these nurses, the experiences of Sister Janet have by far been best recorded. In 1878, she served as a volunteer nurse during the Russo-Turkish war. Now, in 1879, having arrived at Utrecht, she found the makeshift hospital well established and in good condition. It was protected by an outer barricade in the event of a Zulu attack. The hospital consisted of a substantial wooden single-storey structure situated just inside the main defensive laager of marquee and bell tents. At the time, the total civilian population was just under 300, consisting mostly of Dutch Boers. The Battle of Ulundi left the hospital full of soldiers suffering from wounds and also general sickness. Many had been in the hospital for a considerable period.[30]

To familiarise Sister Janet, Surgeon-Major Fitzmaurice gave her a document to read, entitled 'Report on the climate and diseases of Natal and Zululand', issued by the Army Medical Department. More serious medical cases that involved hospitalisation included scarlet fever, measles, diptheria, typhus, pneumonia, dysentery, polio and syphilis. The Army hospital at Gingindlovu recorded that in April 1879, they treated out of seventy-six officers: fever one, sunstroke one, diarrhea four, dysentery four, other diseases four. Out of 2,000 other ranks: fever 180, rheumatism twenty-nine, diarrhoea forty, dysentery twenty-nine, bronchitis two, boils eleven, other diseases and accidental wounds forty-four. Personal hygiene was still to be properly applied; latrines and urine pits were dug near the tents and filled in every morning.[31]

After a period in northern Zululand Sister Janet was sent to the garrison at Rorke's Drift where the legendary defence of the post took place on 22 January. Within a few days of arriving at the Rorke's Drift, she had examined all of the thirty-five British soldiers still stationed at the Drift. Most were in rude health, though the majority were suffering from abrasions and sores, with the ever-present stomach problem still prevalent. She then had the water collected upstream and boiled and the camp's cooking utensils and cutlery properly sterilised after every meal. She set up a laundry to wash the soldiers' bed linen and their clothing. She also confined eight sick men suffering from fever to two tents outside the fort to prevent infection from spreading further.[32] In looking after her patients, she did not take sides and treated all of them equally, including Zulus and even the imprisoned Chief Cetshwayo himself.

Chief Petty Officer Henry Eason from HMS *Shah* spent some time in the military hospital in Durban, where he met Sisters Ruth and Elizabeth. 'About a fortnight before I came out of hospital, the Stafford House Committee sent two female nurses to our hospital, and they soon became very popular as they made themselves very agreeable and did everything they could for us,' he wrote. 'They had a large stock of goods at their disposal, consisting of jams, jellies, cocoa and milk, and many other things which they distributed very liberally indeed. They were called Sisters Ruth and Elizabeth, and their dress when on duty was a serge one, white apron and cap, and a band on one arm with the letters SHC on it.'[33]

Both commissioners of the Stafford House Committee gave brief accounts of the party's services in their reports, while a number of testimonials in their appendices attest to the appreciation with which their work was received. The Senior Medical Officer at Ladysmith, Thomas Babington, reported in a memorandum: 'I could not testify too highly to the excellent services rendered by these ladies [Sisters Edith King and Emma Durham] to the sick and wounded officers and men of Her Majesty's army who were treated at Ladismsith.'

Lieutenant Colonel R. J. C. Marter of the 1st King's Dragoon Guards, who was in charge at the capture of Cetshwayo in August 1879, recorded that on 25, 26 and 27 December he was 'very ill on these days, and don't know much about them. There were no hospital diets to be had, only the ordinary ration of "trek" ox, and my soldier servant could in no way make this into an acceptable broth, nor was there anything to be bought in place.' Marter sunk very low, and when so weak he could hardly speak in an audible whisper, a 'Stafford House' Sister arrived and borrowed one of his horses, and rode around native kraals and returned with an egg which she beat up with some whiskey and gave it to him. This was the turning point, the Sister was equal even to trek ox beef, and produced soup and other things, which enabled him to gain his strength. There were several doctors in the camp, each about as inefficient and indifferent to the welfare of his patients as the other. The real or imaginary grievances of their Department seemed to be the only matters they could fully attend to, and they were never weary of discussing them. Marter found they had plenty of champagne amongst the 'medical comforts', but although he needed it badly enough, they refused to allow him any until he threatened to report them to the Secretary of State for War. They had made their own minds up that the case was hopeless, and demurred at wasting the wine.[34]

Her Majesty's Army Nursing Service

As mentioned, the British Army was slow to reform nursing services, and between 1861 and 1882 only twelve women were employed in the Army Nursing Service, all of them based at the military hospitals at Netley and Woolwich. Until the South African War (1899–1902), the work of nursing the sick and wounded soldiers of the British Army had been done mainly by male orderlies.

However, at least during the Anglo-Zulu War, even though the Army still regarded the nurses' role mostly as being suitable for the hospitals in Britain, for the first time Her Majesty's Army Nursing Service nurses were deployed overseas when the Service's Netley Superintendent, Mrs Jane Cecilia Deeble, and six nurses were sent to South Africa to assist in the military hospitals over there. *The Graphic* reported in August that six nurses from Her Majesty's Army Nursing Service, with their headquarters at Royal Victoria Hospital Netley and led by Lady Superintendent Ms Jane Cecilia Deebles, sailed from Southampton in the Union Company's SS *Pretoria* on 19 June 1879 to tend the sick and wounded soldiers at the Military Hospital in Durban. They duly arrived in Cape Town harbour in July and immediately started for Durban.[35]

Jane Cecilia Deeble was the widow of Surgeon-Major William Deeble, who died in the Abyssinian Campaign of 1867. She entered the military establishment on 1 November 1869, having previously been a probationer in Florence Nightingale's training school at St Thomas' Hospital. On taking up this appointment, she became Superintendent of the Staff of Nursing Sisters at the Royal Victoria Hospital at Netley and in 1870 was appointed as Lady Superintendent of the Army Nursing Service, a post she continued to occupy until 1889 – a record span of office. She was immensely popular as a 'homely' type of woman. Her initial appointment sprung from an interview with Florence Nightingale in November 1869, but after Miss Nightingale's report to one Dr Sutherland it is quite surprising that she found a job in nursing at all. 'She is brave, sincere, courageous – but she has no observation – she is quite incapable of understanding far less of making a Regulation or an organisation,' Nightingale wrote. 'Any officer may turn her round his finger. She will be engaged in planning a nice tea for the Nurses, while she lets the Nursing go to ruin ... I have not approached the subject of the Regulations yet with Mrs. Deeble. I doubt whether she has seen them. I doubt whether she is able to understand them. I doubt whether she has a glimmer of the fact that she is to have a personal relation with and report to the War Office.'[36]

Notwithstanding the negative nature of the report, Mrs Deeble was accepted. She had strong views on the type of woman suitable for such employment. As late as 1887 she was busy observing that many nurses were not ladies but rather offspring from 'the shop girl class'. She was also very eager that her nurses should prove themselves tough enough for military campaigning. To that end she fought rigorously for their employment in South Africa during the Anglo-Zulu War and at length gained approval to set out with a small team of six Netley nurses, albeit in the wake of seven women from the Stafford House Committee mentioned above. These nurses were Ann Clark, Lucy Emm, Jane Kennedy, Jessie Lenox, Rebecca Strong and Lucy Wheldon. Before 1869 nurses would wear a uniform of a starched apron worn over a brown dress; Mrs Deeble introduced the grey ward dress with short scarlet cape that are now worn by QA officers.

They went aboard the ship the *Dublin Castle* from London to Cape Town along with reinforcements to the Anglo-Zulu War. The *Dublin Castle* would then return to Britain with wounded and sick who would then be taken to Netley Hospital. Mrs Deeble and her six nurses had made themselves ready for Zululand in less than a week's notice. In a week's time substitutes to take their place at Netley were found, and all their own preparations were made; stores, drugs, appliances were all got together and packed, but no finery, no toys, no useless encumbrances of any kind were included. All was strict, business-like and purposeful, and the work that they did was as satisfactory, as were the workers. They were away for eleven months, working cheerfully and well all the time.

Sister Emma Durham, a Stafford House nurse stationed at Ladysmith, recalled that in order to assist Mrs Deeble's party, she had prepared rooms for them, but Mrs Deeble 'stoically decline[d] a roof over their heads and insist[ed] that they too would live under canvas. Brave Mrs. Deeble; her nurses were unused to erecting tents and all offers of help were refused by the stern matron ... Meanwhile, unnoticed by Mrs. Deeble, the daily thunderstorm gathered menacingly over Ladysmith. With the nurses' tents in the process of being haphazardly pitched, and with their luggage still in the open wagon, the rain squall and high winds suddenly arrived. Within seconds a heavy, noisy and very severe thunderstorm flattened their tents, which terrified and drenched the startled nurses ... After just this single experience, which was no worse than any thunderstorm at that time of year,

Mrs. Deeble announced that the entire Netley team would return to civilized Durban. They departed the following morning where they thereafter staffed the main hospital from their safe and comfortable quarters.'[37]

The pay of these nurses were small, beginning at £30 per annum and ending at the maximum of £50 by a rise of £2 yearly. In addition, they had food and washing found, and were given £4 7s yearly for uniform. After twenty years' service they were pensioned off, but they received a pension if they had been disabled in the service after five years' work. There were some among them who thought their pay should be increased by £5 a year; the greater the remuneration offered, the better would be the class of woman secured to the service. But the just scale of class payment was one of those contentious issues.[38]

Mrs Deeble was later awarded the Royal Red Cross medal, the tenth to be awarded it following the inception of the award in 1883. Of the previous nine issues, eight had been bestowed on ladies of royal or similar connections and the other on Florence Nightingale. Therefore, Mrs Deeble's R. R. C must be considered the second to be awarded to a lady for nursing services. Approximately fifteen medals were awarded to nurses during the Anglo-Zulu War.[39]

19

THE LAST YEARS OF CETSHWAYO

Since 3 July 1879, the day before the decisive Battle of Ulundi, the Zulu king Cetshwayo had been sheltered in a village and fled upon hearing of the defeat. The British forces were dispersed around Zululand in the hunt for Cetshwayo, and they burnt numerous kraals in an attempt to get his Zulu subjects to give him up. He was finally captured on 28 August by soldiers under Wolseley's command at a kraal in the middle of the Ngome Forest.

Cetshwayo was brought to Cape Town where he was held captive in the historic old castle from the Dutch East India Company days. On 1 November, he was interviewed by some British officers at the Cape Town Castle before their departure back to England. A newspaper report of the interview read:

He said that he had known in his head that his army would be beaten by the English, and he did all he could to prevent a war, but was driven to it by the young men of the army; that after Isandlwana and Khambula, where his regiments lost very many men, more than he could count, they had only half hearts in the fights, and that it was only with the greatest difficulty that he could get the men together again; that very few of the things taken at Isandlwana were ever brought to him, and when he asked about them his men said they had got nothing, but he knew that they had, and he supposed they had hidden them away at their kraals. The two guns were brought to him by his order a week after Isandlwana, during which time they had been left on the battlefield; one was caught his side of the hill, the other ours. He had never heard anything of the lost colors, and did not know what they were, and did not think it likely that we should hear of them again … He was exceedingly angry with the army for killing the officers at Isandlwana, and had given his men strict orders to bring all the officers to him alive; his men had said that they could not tell the officers from the men, and so killed them all.[1]

After the war, Sir Garnet Wolseley divided the country into thirteen districts, each under a chief, who swore: (1) not to allow arms of any kind; (2) not to establish any military system; (3) to allow marriage; (4) to abolish witchcraft and 'smelling out'. All disputes were to be settled by the British Resident, who should be subsequently appointed. This arrangement did not last long, as disputes arose that ended in bloodshed in several instances, with the consequence that the country, except for John Dunn's territory, lapsed into anarchy and confusion.

Not too long after the war, Cetshwayo was portrayed as 'treacherous, even to his friends, preferring a crooked to a straightforward policy. He is petulant, sour tempered, and revengeful in the last degree. He will promise anything to get back to power, and his promise is not to be depended upon, even if he could keep it. His whole career has been one of bloodshed, deceit, and crime. Experience has shown that he has broken faith with us [Britain] on more than one occasion. The only condition on which he could be restored to power would be – to take such measures as would render him powerless to do any further mischief. This could only be done by the permanent occupation of the country by a body of troops, and virtually keeping him a prisoner, which would be a great expense to the British taxpayer.'[2]

The author Captain (later Colonel) W. R. Ludlow of the First Battalion, Royal Warwickshire Regiment, was concerned that 'some people in England now seriously propose to send back the king, who will most surely form the centre round which all the discontented and idle will rally. That there is a party in Zululand, headed by the late prime minister – Umnyamana and the relations of the ex-king, who are anxious for the return of Cetewayo, is a fact; but who are they? They do not represent the bulk of the nation but are a number of men who were "Indunas" under Cetewayo, and were passed over by Sir Garnet Wolseley when he partitioned out the country ... Should Cetewayo return, these men would be joined by hundreds of others ready for any fiendish work, provided they had the prospect, however distant, of getting a beast for their reward.'[3]

When the Anglo-Zulu War broke out on 11 January 1879, there were certain individuals in Britain and the colonies who believed that Frere's invasion of Zululand was a blatant contradiction of the British 'civilizing mission' in Africa, and therefore morally indefensible. They were part of the growing humanitarian movement in nineteenth-century Britain, while in southern Africa, missionaries and agents of the Church Missionary Society and the Aborigines Protection Society had long been active in reprimanding both the British government and officials and white settlers for having forsaken their moral Christian duty to Britain's civilizing mission, when they advanced policies that dispossessed Africans of their land.[4]

The Anglo-Zulu War brought about a head-on collision between the imperialist advocates of the war and their liberal humanitarian opponents over the moral justification for it, and over the conduct of people like Frere and Shepstone in instigating it. The man responsible for debunking the negative stereotypes of Cetshwayo was Bishop John W. Colenso, the leading humanitarian and intellectual figure of Natal. He dealt with the Zulu people with compassion and sensitivity, and concluded that the war was a 'mistake, a sad mistake'.[5] The bishop extended great sympathy toward Cetshwayo and lamented his exile: 'While the King, who, if the war was unjust and unnecessary, is assuredly a most innocent and injured man, is a prisoner, cut off from all friends, all help, without being allowed to speak a word in his defence.'[6] Along with his daughters Harriette and Frances, Bishop Colenso portayed a much more humane image of Cetshwayo, whom they believed had been grievously wronged by British imperial policy. The Colenso family wrote and published a number of substantial and detailed books that laid the full blame for the Anglo-Zulu War and its aftermath squarely on the shoulders of the imperialists Sir Bartle Frere, Sir Theophilus Shepstone and Sir Garnet Wolseley.

Despite fears such as those expressed by Captain Ludlow and others, and the fervent protests of Natal's Legislature and grave pronouncements of other officials, Cetshwayo was formally granted permission to visit London. In September 1881, Lord Kimberley granted permission for Cetshwayo to visit England and plead his case.[7] The Zulu king took every opportunity in his correspondence with Kimberley to persuade him of the wishes of the majority of the Zulu to have him reinstated. He also made an appeal to British liberal sentiment: 'I have great hopes of obtaining what the English people value – justice … the Zulu nation would rejoice to see me back. I hope that I am not going to England for nothing.'[8]

Cetshwayo and his party arrived on Thursday 3 August 1882, and travelled by special train to Kensington. On his arrival, No. 18 Melbury Road, one of a pair of semi-detached houses dated 1877, was made more appropriate to his needs and those of his chiefs. The beds, for instance, were reduced to floor level. On waking on 5 August, he found that a huge crowd of people had gathered outside. *The Times* described how 'at times the ex-king would appear for a moment at one of the windows, and he was invariably greeted with cheers'. By the close of his visit, he had become something of a celebrity.

During his stay in London, he was regularly interviewed by British reporters, eager to spread information on the Zulu king to their readership. The *Illustrated London News* described the king as 'a fine burly man, with a pleasant good-humoured face, though almost black; his manners are frank and jovial, but still dignified, and he wears European dress'.[9]

The initial news coverage of Cetshwayo's visit specifically worked to play up the monarch's 'civilized' and fitting royal behaviour, in contrast to the press depictions of the previous years, which emphasised his barbarism. He was rendered as a gracious and friendly king, whose royal demeanour challenged the legitimacy of the British conquest of his kingdom. Cetshwayo was aware of the power of the press and its ability to shape imperial discourse and reports reveal that he focused on particular questions that were likely to enhance his cause.

He 'declared in emphatic tones that there never ought to have been any war, and ascribes the conflict to "the little grey-headed man" (Sir Bartle Frere) and the newspapers, against the majority

of which he is deeply prejudiced. His people he says, want him.'
While Cetshwayo demonstrated an understanding of the press
as a means of pursuing his own claims, not all reporters were as
sympathetic. In the same issue of the *Leeds Mercury* that lauded
Cetshwayo's arrival, another reporter sniffed at the entire affair,
writing:

> Cetywayo has duly reached England, and already we hear that
> the usual deplorable but seemingly inevitable lionising has
> begun ... the ex-King was besieged by the notoriety hunters
> of the town ... It would be well if 'the little grey-headed man',
> as Cetywayo designates Sir Bartle Frere, were to make the
> public of England acquainted with some facts regarding the
> life and habits of the King when he was supreme in Zululand
> with which the students of the South African Blue Books are
> familiar, but of which it is to be hoped the female admirers of
> the gentle monarch are ignorant.[10]

After a series of interviews with Lord Kimberley, it was agreed
that he was to be restored as King of Zululand, though he would
be under the supervision of a British Resident. He also reluctantly
accepted Kimberley's conditions that Chief Zibhebhu of the
Mandlakazi, his most deadly rival, be given a separate autonomous
district in the north and that a Reserve Territory be carved out of
the southern part of Zululand for chiefs who did not wish to live
under Cetshwayo and the Usuthu.[11]

The Return to Zululand

The move for Cetshwayo's reinstatement as King of Zululand
developed from three quarters: Cetshwayo himself, anxious to
return to his former kingdom; the king's brothers, Ndabuko,
Dabulamanzi and Ziwedu-Mnyamana, and the loyal Usuthu
faction; and lastly, the humanitarian lobby comprising the Colensos,
Lady Florence Dixie[12] and prominent members of the Society for
the Propagation of Gospel, the Aborigines Protection Society, and
Liberal Party parliamentarians. Cetshwayo was returned in secret
to Zululand in January 1883.[13]

Several months after his return, Cetshwayo and the Usuthu became inevitably locked in a life or death struggle with their deadliest enemies, Chief Hamu of the Ngenetsheni section and the Mandlakazi section under the leadership of Chief Zibhebhu. On 30 March 1883, Zibhebhu's Mandlakazi inflicted a severe defeat on the Usuthu in the Msebe Valley. The king returned to Ulundi where on the morning of 21 July, Zibhebhu launched a surprise attack on the Usuthu kraals and decimated the Usuthu leadership. King Cetshwayo suffered two assegai wounds in his thigh during his flight after the battle. He was forced to seek refuge with the British Resident in the Reserve, and it was here that he died on 8 February 1884 – officially from a heart attack, though some suspected poisoning. Then, two months later, Dinizulu[14] as Cetshwayo's only surviving son was proclaimed king.[15]

In 2006, a plaque was erected by English Heritage at 18 Melbury Road, Holland Park, London, W14 8LT, Royal Borough of Kensington and Chelsea, with the inscription: 'CETSHWAYO c.1832-1884 King of the Zulus stayed here in 1882'. Cetshwayo's plaque at No. 18 Melbury Road rests immediately above that of the English painter William Holman Hunt,[16] thus forming a rare 'double blue'.

APPENDICES

*THE ROLL OF THOSE PRESENT AT RORKE'S DRIFT
22/23 JANUARY 1879*

The roll is compiled from research undertaken by Julian Whybra and Norman Holme and is largely based on the Chard and Bourne Rolls. Biographical notes on the soldiers of the 24th Foot who were present at Isandlwana and Rorke's Drift, 22/23 January 1879, are contained in both *The Roll Call for Isandlwana and Rorke's Drift* by Julian Whybra, published by Roberts Medals Publications, and *The Noble 24th* by Norman Holme, published in 1999.

General's Staff
Mabin, G. W. Colour-Sergeant.

Royal Artillery N Battery 5th Brigade
Cantwell, John. Gunner 2076, awarded Distinguished Conduct Medal
Evans, Abraham. Gunner 1643
Howard, Arthur. Gunner 2077
Lewis, Thomas. Bombardier. 458

Royal Engineers 5th Company
Chard, John Rouse Merriott, Lieutenant, awarded Victoria Cross
Robson, Charles John, Driver. 12046 (Chard's Batman)

2nd Battalion, 3rd (East Kent) Regiment of Foot (The Buffs)
Milne, Frederick. Sergeant. 2260

1st Battalion, 24th (2nd Warwickshire) Regiment of Foot

Beckett, William. Private. 25B/135, died of wounds 23 January 1879
Desmond, Patrick. Private. 25B/568
Horrigan, William. Private. 1-24/1861, killed in action 22 January 1879
Jenkins, David. Private. 25B/295
Jenkins, James. Private. 25B/841, killed in action 22 January 1879
Nicholas, Edward. Private. 25B/625, killed in action 22 January 1879
Payton, Thomas. Private. 25B/372
Roy, William. Private. 1-24/1542, awarded Distinguished Conduct Medal
Turner, Henry. Private. 25B/l04
Waters, John. Private. 1-24/447
Wilson, Edward. Sergeant. 25B/56

2nd Battalion, 24th Regiment (2nd Warwickshire)

Adams, Robert. Private. 25B/987 D Company, killed in action 22 January 1879
Allen, William Wilson. Corporal. 2-24/1240, B Company, awarded Victoria Cross
Ashton, James. Private. 2-24/913, B Company
Barry, Thomas. Private. 25B/1381, B Company
Bennett, William Private. 25B/918, B Company
Bessell, William. Lance-Corporal. 25B/l287, B Company
Bly, John. Private. 2-24/2427, B Company
Bourne, Frank. Colour-Sergeant. 2-24/2459, B Company, awarded Distinguished Conduct Medal
Bromhead, Gonville. Lieutenant, B Company, awarded Victoria Cross
Bromwich, Joseph. Private. 25B/1524, B Company
Buckley, Thomas. Private. 25B/1184, B Company
Burke, Thomas. Private. 25B/1220, B Company
Bushe, James. Private. 2-24/2350, B Company
Camp, William Henry. Private. 25B/1181, B Company
Chester, Thomas. Private. 25B/1241, B Company
Chick, James. Private. 25B/1335 D Company, killed in action 22 January 1879
Clayton, Thomas. Private. 25B/755, B Company
Cole, Robert. Private. 25B/1459, F Company

Cole, Thomas. Private. 25B/801 B Company, killed in action 22 January 1879

Collins, Thomas. Private.25B/1396, B Company

Connolly, John. Private. 25B/906, C Company

Connors, Anthony. Private. 2-24/2310, B Company

Connors, Timothy. Private. 2-24/1323, B Company

Cooper, William. Private. 2-24/2453, F Company

Davies, George. Private. 25B/470, B Company

Davis, William Henry. Private. 25B/1363, B Company

Daw, Thomas. Private. 25B/1178, B Company

Deacon, George. Private. 25B/1467, B Company, alias George D Power

Deane, Michael. Private. 25B/1357, B Company

Dick, James. Private. 2-24/1697, B Company

Dicks, William. Private. 2-24/1634, B Company

Driscoll, Thomas. Private. 25B/971, B Company

Dunbar, James. Private. 25B/1421, B Company

Edwards, George. Private. 25B/922, B Company, alias George Edward Orchard

Evans, Frederick. Private. 25B/953, H Company

Fagan, John. Private. 25B/969 B Company, killed in action 22 January 1879

French, George. Corporal. 2-24/582, B Company

Galgey, Patrick. Drummer 2-24/1713, D Company

Gallagher, Henry. Sergeant. 25B/81, B Company

Gee, Edward. Private. 2-24/2429, B Company

Hagan, James. Private. 25B/978, B Company

Halley, William. Lance-Corporal. 25B/l282, B Company

Harris, John. Private. 25B/1062, B Company

Hayden, Garret. Private. 2-24/1769 D Company, killed in action 22 January 1879

Hayes, Patrick. Drummer 2-24/2067, B Company

Hitch, Frederick. Private. 25B/1362, B Company, awarded Victoria Cross

Hook, Alfred Henry. Private. 25B/1373, B Company, awarded Victoria Cross

Jobbins, John. Private. 25B/1061, B Company

Jones, Evan. Private. 25B/1428, B Company, alias Patrick Cosgrove

Jones, John. Private. 25B/1179, B Company

Jones, John. Private. 25B/970, B Company

Jones, Robert. Private. 258/716, B Company, awarded Victoria Cross

Jones, William. Private. 2-24/593, B Company, awarded Victoria Cross
Judge, Peter. Private. 2-24/2437, B Company
Kears, Patrick. Private. 25B/972, B Company
Keefe, James. Drummer 2-24/2381, B Company
Key, John. Corporal. 2-24/2389, B Company
Kiley, Michael. Private. 25B/1386, B Company
Lewis, David. Private. 25B/963, B Company, alias James Owen
Lines, Henry. Private. 2-24/1528, B Company
Lloyd, David. Private. 25B/1409, B Company
Lockhart, Thomas. Private. 25B/1176, B Company
Lodge, Joshua. Private. 25B/1304, B Company
Lynch, Thomas Michael. Private. 25B/942, B Company
Lyons, John. Corporal. 25B/1112, B Company
Lyons. John. Private. 2-24/1441, A Company
Manley, John. Private. 2-24/1731, A Company
Marshall, James. Private. 25B/964, B Company
Martin, Henry. Private. 25B/756, B Company
Mason, Charles. Private. 25B/1284, B Company
Maxfield, Robert. Sergeant. 25B/623 G Company, killed in action
    22 January 1879
Meehan, John. Drummer 2-24/2383, A Company
Minehan, Michael. Private. 2-24/1527, B Company
Moffatt, Thomas. Private. 25B/968, B Company
Morris, Augustus. Private. 25B/1342, B Company
Morris, Frederick. Private. 25B/525, B Company
Morrison, Thomas. Private. 25B/1371, B Company
Murphy, John. Private. 25B/662, B Company
Neville, William. Private. 25B/1279, B Company
Norris, Robert. Private. 25B/1257, B Company
Osborne, William. Private. 25B/1480, B Company
Parry, Samuel. Private. 25B/1399, B Company
Partridge, William. Private. 25B/1410, G Company
Pitt, Samuel. Private. 25B/1186, B Company
Robinson, Edward. Private. 25B/1286, B Company
Ruck, James. Private. 25B/1065, B Company
Savage, Edward. Private. 25B/1185, B Company
Saxty, Alfred. Corporal. 25B/849, B Company
Scanlon, John. Private. 25B/1051 A Company, killed in action 22
    January 1879
Sears, Arthur. Private. 2-24/2404, A Company

Shearman, George. Private. 2-24/1618, B Company
Shergold, John. Private. 2-24/914, B Company
Smith, George. Sergeant. 2-24/1387, B Company
Smith, John. Private. 25B/1005, B Company
Stevens, Thomas. Private. 25B/777, B Company
Tasker, William. Private. 2-24/1812, B Company
Taylor, Frederick. Private. 25B/973, B Company
Taylor, James. Lance-Sgt. 25B/82, E Company
Taylor, Thomas Edward. Private. 25B/889, B Company
Thomas, John. Private. 25B/1280, B Company, alias Peter Sawyer
Thompson, John. Private. 25B/1394, B Company
Tobin, Michael. Private. 25B/879, B Company
Tobin, Patrick. Private. 25B/641, B Company
Todd, William John. Private. 25B/1281, B Company
Tongue, Robert. Private. 25B/1315, B Company
Wall, John. Private. 25B/1497, B Company
Whetton, Alfred. Private. 2-24/977, B Company
Wilcox, William. Private. 25B/1187, B Company
Williams, John. Private. 25B/1395, B Company, awarded Victoria
    Cross, alias John Fielding
Williams, John. Private. 25B/934, E Company
Williams, Joseph. Private. 25B/1398 B Company, killed in action
    22 January 1879
Williams, Thomas. Lance-Sergeant. 25B/1328, died of wounds 23
    January 1879
Windridge, Joseph. Sergeant. 2-24/735, B Company
Wood, Caleb. Private. 25B/1316, B Company

90th Light Infantry
Graham, James. Corporal. 1123, alias Daniel Sheehan

Army Service Corps
Attwood, Francis. Second Corporal. 24692, awarded Distinguished
    Conduct Medal

Army Commissariat and Transport Department
Byrne, Louis Alexander. Acting Storekeeper, (civilian attachment),
    killed in action 22 January 1879
Dalton, James Langley. Acting Assistant Commissary, awarded
    Victoria Cross
Dunne, Walter Alphonsus. Assistant. Commissary

Army Medical Department and Army Hospital Corps
Reynolds, James Henry. Surgeon. BA MB ChB, awarded Victoria
   Cross
Pearse, Mr., Surg. Reynolds's servant
Luddington, Thomas. Private.
McMahon, Michael. Private. 3359, awarded Distinguished
   Conduct Medal
Miller, Robert. Corporal.

1st Battalion, 3rd Regiment Natal Native Contingent
Adendorff, James. Lieutenant
Mayer, Jessy H. Corporal.
A native of Mkungo's tribe, killed in action 22 January 1879

2nd Battalion, 3rd Regiment Natal Native Contingent
Anderson, Michael. Corporal, killed whilst deserting 22 January
   1879
Doughty, William. Corporal.
Scammell, Carl. Corporal.
Schiess, Ferdnand Christian. Corporal, awarded Victoria Cross
Wilson, John. Corporal

Natal Mounted Police
Green, Robert S. Trooper.
Hunter, Sydney H. Trooper., killed in action 22 January 1879
Lugg, Henry. Trooper.

Acting Chaplain to the Volunteers
Smith, George. The Reverend
The Rev Smith's native servant

Daniels, Mr
Not included in these figures are those who did not remain to
assist in the defence, viz. Stevenson's Natal Native Contingent
detachment, Henderson's fugitive Natal Native Horse from
Isandlwana, Otto Witt and his native companion, Lieutenant
Thomas Purvis 1st Battalion, 3rd Regiment, Natal Native
Contingent – a hospital patient – who accompanied Witt to safety,
Chard's native voorlooper, Chard's native wagon driver who hid
in a cave on the Oskarberg throughout the attack, and all those
fugitives from Isandlwana who stopped to give a warning and rode
on. Of all these only Adendorff remained to assist in the defence

and is thus the only man to have fought in both the Isandlwana and Rorke's Drift actions.

NATALIA vol. 5 pp. 15–28 (Natal Society Foundation)

The Defence of Ekowe by LIEUT. W. N. LLOYD, R.H.A.

On New Year's Day, 1879, No. 1 Column, under the command of Colonel C. K. Pearson, was encamped at Thring's Post, 24 miles from the Lower Tugela drift, better known as Fort Pearson. At this time all hope of King Cetewayo complying with our conditions had been set aside, and our column was under orders to march to the Lower Tugela drift on 3rd January; should no signs of compliance on the part of the King be visible by 11th January, we were to cross the river into Zululand. On 12th January, at daybreak, the passage of the river commenced, but it was not till the 16th that the whole column was encamped in the enemy's country. On Saturday, 18th, at 5 a.m., our column commenced its forward march, the troops being in excellent spirits and eager for the fight which we well knew was at hand. Everything progressed in the most satisfactory manner until the 22nd, for although we had, up to this time, observed the Zulu scouts watching our movements from the hills in front, yet we apprehended no imminent danger. However, on that morning we marched as usual at daybreak and all went on quietly until 8 o'clock, at which hour we were ordered to halt for breakfast. The 'Buffs' and Naval Brigade had just 'piled arms', and the gunners were on the point of 'unhooking', when we were startled by the rattle of musketry in the bush about 50 yds. to our front, where our native scouts had been posted. We lost no time in taking up position on a knoll which lay to our left, from the top of which we could overlook the bush in our rear and right and left, but which was commanded by hills in front; from this point we saw the Zulus swarming down our right flank, in what appeared to me to resemble echelon of companies. The infantry and Jack Tars swarmed up the side with all speed, and, with the assistance of some of the latter men the guns soon gained the summit, so that in a few minutes from the time the first shot was heard we were firing shrapnel into a cloud of Zulus. The tactics of the enemy were now apparent; they evidently intended to engage us in front, while large numbers swept round our flanks. However, the plan of attack, fortunately for us, was ill-timed, for the movement round our right flank was executed with marvellous rapidity, but that round our left we were happily enabled to check by sending round some mounted men and natives before it had funy developed itself. For the first hour the Zulus fought most stubbornly; havin~ taken to the bush they directed most of their fire on our force on the knoll, and although we plied them with shell, rockets, and Martini bullets, yet it was fully an hour-and-ahalf before they commenced to retreat from the bush on our right flank. The 2nd division of the column, which had extended itself from the bottom of the knoll down the line of wagons, now brought its right shoulder forward and skirmished prettily through the bush. Having cleared the enemy from this part we were enabled to bring the fire of both guns to bear on the hill in front, to which the enemy still clung. It was now suggested to Colonel Pearson by Commander Campbell of the Active, that it would be advisable to drive them from the heights. The Naval Brigade and a company of the 'Buffs' were ordered to carry out the operation under cover of the guns. The Jack Tars seemed mad for blood, for they charged up the hiLl in any formation, banging away right and left, driving the Zulus before them. The company of the 'Buffs' did their best to keep up with the sailors, but were not equal to the occasion, as they had been 'doubled' up from the rear in order to take part in the attack. One of the Zulu prisoners taken in this action informed me that they considered they were getting the best of the action until 'those horrible men in white trowsers rushed up and showered lead on them'. These were, of course, the Tar's in their ducks. The enemy now fled precipitately, throwing away their shields and assegais. The ground was strewn with dead bodies, some lying in heaps where shells had burst among them. The Zulu loss was estimated at 600 killed and wounded, while 7000 attacked us; on our side 13 killed and 17 wounded, while Col. Pearson and Col. Parnell of the Buffs both had their chargers shot under them. Such, in brief, was the action of the Inyezane, and without further comment I may say we were thankful for having come out of it as we did. rhe artillery fired 65 rounds of shell; at the commencement of the action the practice with the shrapnel was excellent, but the want of a more perfect time fuze was sorely felt. Some splendid chances were lost through loss of time in boring and fixing. It is impossible to suppose that in the heat of action a time fuze can ·be bored with any degree of accuracy. A man may be possessed of great nerve, yet I defy him to have a perfectly steady hand on such occasions. Undoubtedly, one's first impulse is to discard the time fuze in action and use the percussion fuze altogether. When the enemy took to the bush the common shell and percussion fuze acted extremely well – we did not notice a single case of 'blind' shell, although 40 rounds of this nature were fired. The rockets, as I expected, proved of little value; so much had been said of their moral effect on savages, but, to my mind, the Zulus displayed the utmost contempt for them. The enormous 24-pr. Hale's war rocket fired from tubes by the Naval Brigade seemed to cause as much anxiety to our own men as to the enemy. The column now pursued its route with delay, and bivouacked for the night on a ridge about three miles from the battle field. We started again at daybreak on the following morning and arrived at Ekowe mission station about noon. This Norwegian mission station is built on a high range of hills overlooking the sea; in the distance were large rugged mountains, over which lay our path to Ulundi. The station itself consisted of a small church. the parsonage, school, and a few out-houses, built of brick with thatched roofs. all being hidden away among plantations, orange groves and gum trees – it was a most picturesque spot. The approach to the station was across fairly level meadow-land, with clumps of magnificent trees and patches of bush here and there; while close to the church was a lovely little bubbling stream shaded by forest trees. It seemed such a pity to destroy a beautiful, peaceful-looking little spot of this sort. The site was well adapted for a mission station but was by no means a position on which to build a fort. It was commanded on three sides by rising ground within rifle range, while on the fourth side a ravine covered with bush ran up within a few yards of it; but, of course, the church and out-houses were invaluable as a hospitaL and storehouses, so that this site was chosen in preference to others which were better suited for defence. Our orders were to form an advanced depot at Ekowe, to construct a fort there, and, having completed our work, to move forward on Ulundi, leaving a sufficient garrison behind us. We were naturally in high spirits; our column had so far progressed admirably. We had encountered and defeated the enemy, and were fully convinced that with good honest work we ought to be on our way to Ulundi within two weeks' time. Having, therefore, pitched our camp round the mission station, with the parsonage as Head-Quarters, we commenced to clear away everything which could afford cover to an enemy; the magnificent trees gradually disappeared. the gardens and orange groves were cut away, and out-houses, too far distant for use, were blown up. When this clearance was completed, ground was broken and the fort itself commenced. It was now 28th January, but such a miserable system of inter-communication between the different columns existed that at this date we were in total ignorance of the disastrous battle of Isandlwana, which had been fought on the same day and at the same hour as the action of the Inyezaneso much so, that we actually sent down our empty wagons (50 in number) to the Tugela, to bring up supplies, under escort of two companies of infantry! Easily then can an idea be formed of the sensation in camp caused by the arrival of the following despatch: 'From Lord Chelmsford to Colonel Pearson – Consider all my orders cancelled, you may expect the whole Zulu army down on you; do, therefore, what you may think best for the safety of your column.' As may be supposed, the news came like a thunder-bolt among us; it was, however, no time for arguing or conjecturing; a meeting of commanding officers was at once summoned. The momentous Ljuestion now put to us was, whether to retire at once to the Tugela or to hold our position against overwhelming odds for an indefinite period? This question was certainly a difficult one to decide. On the one hand by retiring we should lose the ground already gained; we should, moreover, have not a single column left in Zulu territory, since t.he others must, as we knew, be forced to retire; in addition, the mere fact of our beating such a hasty retreat on all sides would have a most disastrous effect on the minds of the Natal Kaflirs. These Kaffirs would otherwise say (Lord Chelmsford afterwards informed us they did say) 'Oh! no, the English are not yet beaten; why, there is still a column in the heart of Zululand.' On the other hand, by holding our position we overcame these difficulties and, moreover, held a check on the Zulus should they contemplate an invasion of British territory, for they could scarcely attempt such an enterprise with such a large force in their rear. An argument more forcible than these was, that a convoy of two months' provisions was within seven miles of our camp at that very moment. It was decided, then, to hold the fort at all hazards. The mounted men, together with the two battalions of native contingent, were ordered to retire at once, as we had not sufficient corn for the horses of the former, and no room for the latter in the fort. We kept merely a sufficient number of mounted men and natives for vedette duty. Our cavalry ought, no doubt, to have been kept at any risk; even if corn failed, there was an abundance of grass in the vicinity of the fort. We felt their loss greatly – we were able to gain literally no information of the movements of ihe enemy without them. Major Barrow, who was in command of them, was ordered to tell Colonel Ely, the officer in charge of the convoy. to hasten on with all speed, and to leave any wagon behini which could not keep pace with him. On that evening, to our delight, the convoy made its appearance, but it had been found necessary to abandon eight wagons, containing flour. biscuit, lime juice. coffee, and sugar – how we grudged their loss afterwards! On the following day all the troops came inside the entrenchment, for as yet it had not assumed the dimensions of a fort. Tents were discarded, and the officers and men slept under wagons, which had been placed inside, round the parapet. Now the defence of Ekowe commenced in reality. The garrison was as follows: Combatants – Staff 7; The 'Buffs' (6 companies) 609; 99th Regt. (4 companies) 380; Naval Brigade 174; Royal Artillery 26; Royal Engineers 96; Natal Pioneers 50; Native Contingent 15. Non-Combatants - Commissariat and Transport 12; Army Medical Dept. 20; Conductors 15; Wagon leaders and drivers 270; Native servants 20; Total, 1,339 whites, 355 blacks. Armament – 1 gatling, with 127,000 rounds; 2 rocket tubes; 83 rockets; 1 rocket trough; 25 rockets; 4 7-pr. M.L.R. guns, 150 rounds per gun. For the next few days every available man was at work on the entrenchments, while the country round was cleared as much as possible, and although clusters of Zulus might be observed watching our movements, yet we were not interfered with. Occasionally we fired a shell at them, but as soon as they saw the smoke from the gun they would either lie flat down, or, bending themselves nearly double, would run like madmen. In the space of a week we made our position practically safe; the ditch and parapet were now a respectable size, and it was merely a matter of improving and strengthening our work by degrees. The fort was in shape an oblong, the north and south sides being 120 and 180 yds. respectively, the east and west sides 300 yds. each. The ditch was 12 ft. wide and 7 ft. deep. The church was used as a hospital, while the schoolroom and parsonage acted as storehouses, and as I said before, the officers and men made shelters for themselves under the wagons, and by allowing the tarpaulin (with which every wagon is supplied) to fall over, the sides, they managed to make themselves fairly comfortable. It took some time before one became accustomed to sleeping under these wagons without doing daily damage to one's head, for on the command going round at night to 'stand to your arms' (which took place when the alarm was given) one naturally jumped up imagining oneself in a tent, but the real situation was promptly suggested to one by a violrent contact of head and wagon. After some time, when I got accustomed to my quarters, I found myself rolling out from under: the wagon on the alarm being given, having been taught on several occasions the folly of jumping up. I can safely say that for the first fortnight of our imprisonment at Ekowe there was a scare every night, during the rest of our stay there they occurred at intervals. As a rule the cry was false alarm. One night for instance I remember hearing a rifle shot, followed quickly by two or three more; in an instant the gunners were at their posts on the guns and the infantry lining the parapet, for we all slept in our clothes. These shots were quickly followed by a rattle of musketry along one face of the fort; so sure were we (the gunners) that the Zulus had made an attack that we produced the case shot. However, in a few seconds the firing ceased, and the cause of the alarm inquired into. The answer was, 'Please sir the sentry distinctly saw a Zulu loitering about round that bush outside'. The real cause of the scare being a pair of sailor's ducks which were hanging up to dry on a bush, having been blown about by the wind. Next morning we discovered those articles riddled with bullet holes, which at least spoke well for the shooting! Reveille sounded at daybreak, and we then commenced to work at the entrenchments, while 'last post' sounded at 8 p.m., at which hour lights were at once extinguished. Our rations at first consisted of flour, biscuit, tea, sugar, and meat. The two excellent officers of the 'Buffs' (my messmates) and I divided our rations as follows. At breakfast toasted biscuit and tea, at mid-day meal the same, and at dinner our meat and anything our soldiercook could make out of the flour. At first his cakes were most indigestible, as we had no baking powder, but he improved as time went on. Occasionally, when our troops made a raid on the Zulu mealie fields, a large supply was brought into camp, we then had an entree of roast mealies, while we made the green tops into an excellent vegetable. The 2000 head of cattle in our charge were a source of great trouble and inconvenience. During the day they were driven to the grazing ground under escort of two companies of infantry, while at dusk they were drawn in close round and under fire of the fort. A large number were placed in a wagon laager, the sides of which were enfiladed from the parapet, and the remainder tied down to their yokes. The horses and the mules were at first picketed outside, but as we soon became aware of their immense vallue we constructed a stable in the ditch, and had them driven there at night, by means of a ramp cut in the counter scarp. The stench at night then may be easier imagined than described, thus surrounded by cattle on the outside, and packed like herrings within. But in the daytime the men were encouraged to keep outside the fort as much as possible in their leisure hours, while the blacks were positively forbidden to enter the fort till nightfall, and were driven out at daybreak; our sanitary arrangements being exceedingly well managed, and the greatest attention was given to them by all hands. As regards ammunition there was a plentiful supply so we now felt perfectly secure. Every means of procuring oover had been taken; traverses were constructed at intervals along the parapet, the guns placed on platforms, and protected by blinded batteries. As the weary days wore on, trous-de-loups, wire entanglements, caponiers in the ditch, and finally a drawbridge made their appearance. What we felt sorely was the want of medicine. We searched through the kits of the mounted men who had retired with Major Barrow and discovered a fair supply of 'Eno's fruit salt', and 'Cockle's pills', also some private stores, which were afterwards sold by auction. It may be interesting to mention that some of these articles fetched the following prices: Bottle of pickles, 25s.; curry powder, 23s.; Worcester sauce, 25s. (per bottle); tin of lobster, 18s.; box of sardines 12s.; and a ham, £7 10s.! Tobacco fetched 20s. per lb. I recollect talking to a group of officers in the fort some few days after this sale about the reported surrender of Oham, brother of

King Cetewayo. We were standing outside the wagon of the officer who had purchased the ham for £7 10s. He was amongst us in a moment, and said 'What is that about another ham? Quite ready to give another £7 10s.' He was ever afterwards called 'Old Ham!' Although there was a fair supply of gun ammunition, yet we discovered that the quantity of case shot was not sufficient, as this projectile would be most necessary in case of attack. Fortunately the idea struck me that one of Morton's jam pots might be made into a projectile of this description. It exactly fitted the bore. This important intelligence was conveyed to General Pearson, who issued orders for all the jam tins in camp to be left at the residence (under a wagon) of the O.C.R.A. Needless to say, the order was readily complied with, for I discovered the outside of my 'chateau' littered with every conceivable description of tin, from those which contained butter (in shape like a forage cap) to the most diminutive potted meat tin. Having selected those required, we constructed, with the assistance of a tin-smith of the 'Buffs', 25 excellent rounds of case shot. One of these articles may be seen in the R.A. Institution. We tested three rounds against dummies, and found they acted admirably. On 7th February we received in a despatch an account of the disaster at Isandlwana, which cast a gloom over the fort, for among the names down as killed we found many old and valued friends – many of them our companions in arms in the late Kaffir war. In this despatch Lord Chelmsford said: 'Should like to see Naval Brigade garrisoning forts of Lower Tugela; you and your staff should be there also. Endeavour to arrange for the holding of an entrenchment requiring a smaller garrison. Your best field officers should remain in command. Bring back only what baggage is absolutely necessary – sick and wounded in empty wagons.' At a council of war at once summoned it was unanimously agreed that it would be impossible to carry out Lord Chelmsford's wishes. In the first place we knew that a force of about 15000 Zulus lay between us and the Tugela. How then could half our garrison, encumbered with wagons and with sick and wounded, hope to cope with such numbers. Again, we could not attempt to break through under cover of night, as we could not by any possibility cover the distance (32 miles) in the time. Moreover we could not carry out Lord Chelmsford's plan of 'arranging to hold an entrenchment requiring a smaller garrison'. For, should half our garrison be sent away, the remainder would be insufficient to man the parapet of our fort in case of attack. To this despatch, Colonel Pearson therefore replied, that these reasons in support of his remaining where he was were so strong, that he determined to communicate them to him (Lord Chelmsford) before taking further action in the matter; and that he hoped Lord Chelmsford would reconsider the words of his despatch. We waited anxiously for a reply from Lord Chelmsford, but the 'runner' who took this despatch shared the fate of many others; so our garrison remained at Ekowe. Some of the Kaffirs, composing our Native Contingent in the fort, would volunteer to run through the Zulus at night for a sovereign! Many were the letters I sent home, but I have since discovered that only three arrived safely, so conclude our poor 'runners' seldom escaped the vigilance of the enemy. We had now been 20 days shut up; the monotony of the situation was becoming dreadful; we were of course unable to walk or ride out of sight of the fort, so we found difficulty in passing the time. The impertinence of the Zulus was becoming laughable. They would shout out 'come out of that hole you old women; we always thought the English would fight, and not burrow under the ground!' Having in the meantime looted the wagons of the convoy abandoned by Colonel Ely, they frequently informed us that our coffee and sugar, &c., was excellent, and that they hoped soon to come and share ours with us! This war of words was carried on between our cattle boys and the Zulus posted on the neighbouring hills. On the 22nd February the enemy made a faint-hearted attack on our cattle, but were repulsed with loss by two companies of infantry, and the mounted men. Beyond this attack, and few successful raids made by our troops on their mealie fields, nothing important occurred until 1st March. We intended on that day to make a sortie against Dabulamanzi's military haal, which was situated about eight miles from the fort, and from which parties of Zulus frequently appeared for the purpose of harassing our cattle guard. Our plan of operation was to start about midnight, or a little after, and to arrive at the kraal if possible about daybreak. It was, however, 2 a.m. before all arrangements were complete, and our force started off. It was composed of the following troops: 400 infantry, some native pioneers, about 30 mounted men, and one gun R.A. The night was luckily clear, for we struck a path straight across country, under the guidance of one of our Zulu allies. It was the most silent march I ever took part in, and will be long remembered. All orders were given in whispers, we seemed to glide along, and yet the gun-wheels creaked outrageously, or rather one seemed to imagine so. Our progress was not rapid, as halts were called continually in order either to overcome obstacles, or to allow our guide to inspect the country. When within half-a-mile of the kraal the day began to break, and here an incident worthy of mention happened. About 500 yds., on a hill to our left, I noticed in the dim light some kraals, and perceived a Zulu strolling leisurely out of on:e of them. For a few seconds he had his back to us, but quickly turning round no doubt espied our little force wending its way along below. He fled like a hare. The circumstance was at once reported to Col. Pearson, who sent four mounted men to try and cut him off. It was, however, too late, and I feel sure that the man upset our plans, for on arriving in sight of the military kraal some few minutes after, we saw to our disgust the whole Zulu impi streaming out of it wit:h all their goods and chattels in their arms. We could hear the loud voice of the chief giving orders, and the cattle being driven away. We were unfortunately unable to bring our gun into action on them as they moved down a hill out of sight, but we sent our mounted men forward to take and burn the kraal. They found it evacuated. The rest of our force moved forward as rapidly as possible, and soon came in sight of the retreating Zulus, who were aLready some 1 500 yds. distant, streaming up a hilI opposite. We fired two or three rounds of shrapnel at them, killing and wounding about ten, but owing to the thick cover the fire was not very effective. The Zulus soon crowned the hill opposite, which overlooked the private kraal of Dabulamanzi, but Col. Pearson considered we should lose too many in attempting to burn it, so we had to content ourselves with having destroyed the military kraal. We therefore retired ignominiously. Dabulamanzi afterwards informed me that the Zulus considered that we had received a decided reverse in this little expedition. They showed us indeed 'at the time that they thought so, for our retreat was closely followed. They appeared on the crests of hills soon after we vacated them; took advantage of every patch of bush to our right and left by keeping up a hot fire on us. We divided our mounted men into a front and rear guard, and thus kept the enemy from closing in on us, but were forced to halt at intervals and silence them with a volley. It was really a pleasure to watch the manner in which these Zulus skirmished. No crowding, no delay, as soon as they were driven from one cover they would hasten rapidly to the next awkward bit of country through which our column would have to pass. Luckily for us their shooting was inferior, or we should have suffered severely. We arrived safely at the fort about midday. So ended the exciting but most unsatisfactory expedition to Dabulamanzi's kraal. It was on 2nd March that one of our vedettes reported that glasses were being flashed from the Lower Tugela. Sure enough, there was flashing going on as distinctly as possible. Our signallers were at once summoned, and were not long in reading the following message: 'Look out for 1 000 men on 13th; be prepared to sally out when you are aware of my presence.' This message was repeated for the next two or three days, as we were unable to convey to them that we understood. However, by 5th March we had fixed our glass sufficiently well to inform them we had taken in the message, and they commenced to forward further information. I cannot tell you how delighted we were on the receipt of this news. The spirits of the whole of the troops seemed to improve, even the poor sick men in hospital – some on the point of death – seemed to be cheered up with the happy intelligence. For some days the weather was cloudy, so signalling was impossible. Nothing worthy of mention occurred in the meantime except that a runner made his appearance in camp, bearing a despatch a fortnight old; this aroused our suspicions, more especially when we noticed that he wore an overcoat with the badge of 24th Regt. on it. Our Kaffirs, moreover, informed us that he could not have come from the Tugela by any possibility, as he was 'oiled' and his legs bore no marks of having been in the bush. In fact, he was no other than a Zulu spy. He was at once put in irons, and remained so till we were relieved. What became of the wretched man, I know not. When with us he was continually informed that his ultimate fate would be the gallows. Just at this time one of our vedettes was killed and another wounded by Zulus, who surprised them by creeping up through the long grass which surrounded their posts. The latter vedette escaped miraculously; while sitting on his horse, evidently half asleep, with his carbine slung across his shoulder (contrary to orders), he was suddenly surprised by about a dozen Zulus. By his own account they rushed in on him, one of them actually laying hold of his horse's bridle. By dint of spur he cleared himself. The Zulus then fired a volley at him, but to his delight his horse went on, although he felt himself wounded. This man arrived safely in camp, although he had been shot through both thighs, two fingers shot off (or had to' be cut off from effects of the wound), and his horse assegaied. We found, in addition, a bullet hole in the pommel of his saddle, and the splash where a bullet had hit the lock of his carbine. Curiously enough, this very man was afterwards brought before my brother, a resident magistrate in Ireland, for having assaulted an old man and stolen his hat, for which joke the Ekowe hero, I am sorry to say, paid the penalty. We had now thoroughly established communication with the Tugela by means of our primitive heliograph which in reality was nothing more than an eighteen-penny bedroom looking glass, which can be seen at any time in the United Service Institution. By degrees we became acquainted with the events of the past two months, of which we had hitherto been in total ignorance. As each message was flashed, the excitement was intense; the men crowding round and straining their ears to hear each letter as the signallers pronounced it. As each word was spelt it was communicated to the crowd, whose pleasure it was to anticipate the meaning of the whole message. I recollect, on one occasion, sitting next to General Pearson when the following message was spelt out: 'Mrs. Pearson is–' then a dead silence all round; the sun had gone in and, as yet, we were unable to tell what the next word would be; would it be dead. or alive, or what? I shall never forget my general's face when the sun having again shone out we read the letter 'W', and he at once knew the word would be 'Well'. His look was that of intense relief. At the end of each day the 'Latest Telegrams' were posted on a board in the fort, and eagerly devoured by the men. As we now fully expected relief on 13th March, we made every effort to repair the road for the advance of the relieving column. This operation was carried out under considerable difficulty, for so sure as the troops were marched down to their work, so certain were the Zulus to collect from the neighbouring kraals and open fire on them. We were obliged to take out the guns and an escort every morning to cover the road party. As a rule the Zulus opened their fire from long ranges and did no damage; however, they succeeded in wounding poor Lewis, of the 'Buffs', very badly in the head; he was directing the men of his company, which was posted just below the guns, when I saw him fall, he was instantly picked up by two of his men: on arriving on the spot, I saw his face covered with blood and found that the bullet had passed through the peak of his helmet and hit his forehead just above the eye – a very lucky escape. We were now receiving three-fourths our proper rations of everything except meat. We had killed all the 'fatted' oxen and were living on the trek or draft bullocks. Hard was no name for the meat; it was simply impossible to get one's teeth through it unless it was stewed down to ribbons. However, we were quite happy as we hoped to see the relief column on 13th. Our utter dismay and disappointment may then be easily imagined when we received the following flash-signal on 12th March: 'The relief column will not march till the end of the month, as Lord Chelmsford considers it advisable to await the arrival of reinforcements.' Our hopes, buoyed up for the past 10 days, were now dashed to the ground; we were to return to monotony and imprisonment. It was heartbreaking to be forced to impart this news to the sick, some of whom had, seemingly, taken a new lease of life at the idea of relief being so dose at hand. Poor Captain Williams of the 'Buffs' died on this very evening, and young Coker of the Active, the midshipman who was so popular amongst us all, died of dysentery. He was a fine young fellow, beloved by his men, and only eighteen years old. His burial was the most affecting sight I ever witnessed in my short life; there were very few dry eyes. Out of our small force there were 150 men in the hospital!, where there was overcrowding and a deficiency of medicine; the doctors worked manfully, and did all in their power to – alleviate the suffering of their patients. The majority of the sick suffered from fever, which in most cases turned to delirium. The moaning of these poor men 'throughout the night was painful to hear, especially as one was certain to be informed in the morning that another death had occurred. On the 11th and 12th of March we had observed from our 'lookout' hill large numbers of Zulus trekking towards the Tugela, evidently sent to oppose the relief column. So good was their 'Intelligence Department', that they discovered the relief had been temporarily postponed, and on the 14th we saw the impi marching back. We estimated this force at 35000 men, so that had the relief marched up as originally intended they would have fared badly. Three days and nights of rain now followed; it came down in torrents. The fort presented a miserable appearance. The mud in some places being about six inches deep, and everything and everybody soaked through and through! The poor sentries and vedettes suffered greatly. the remainder of the troops huddled together under the wagons and endeavoured to keep dry. It was indeed a wretched spectacle. Nothing to do, nothing to amuse ourselves with, not a book, paper, or game of any sort. People at home seemed to imagine that it was principally on account of the scarcity of provisions that our existence was rendered so unbearable. But to our minds the monotony of the situation had a far more dispiriting effect than the small quantity and badness of the food. We were unable to take much exercise, our appetites therefore were poor. So long as the men had work on hand – in fact during the time the fort was being constructed – when an hands were engaged, their spirits were good and little sickness prevailed. But when work ceased, monotony set in, and there was time on hand to brood over the situation; then I noticed the sick roll increased alarmingly. On 20th March a 'runner' arrived in camp from the Tugela. He received quite an ovation, as he was the first 'runner' who had reached us in safety for 38 days. In the despatch brought by him we learnt that the relief column would march on 29th, and eagerly we looked forward to that day. On 23rd, two Zulus made their appearance, bearing a flag of truce. They asserted that they had been despatched by King Cetewayo to inform us that he would give us permission to retire to the Tugela unmolested, provided we did no harm to his crops or kraals. He, moreover, invited us to send officers to treat with his indunas or chiefs on the other side of the Umlalazi River, and guaranteed that not a hand should touch them. We were not blind to the fact that these men were simply spies, and our ideas were confirmed on the receipt of a flash-signal received that very day to the effect that Cetewayo was doing his utmost to draw us out with the intention of annihilating the whole force. These two wily Zulus were also placed in irons. On the following day we received a message from Lady Frere, saying 'Her best wishes to all; we were constantly in her thoughts, and all news of us she communicated to our friends'. This kind message was highly appreciated. Another message was received on 29th, from Lord Chelmsford, as follows: 'Come down with 500 fighting men when I am engaged. Four thousand men will leave the Tugela to-day or to-morrow, and arrive at Ekowe on 3rd April; expect to be hotly opposed.' Colonel Pearson replied that he could not spare the 500 men, for owing to the ravages of sickness we had only just sufficient men to hold the fort in case of attack. There were now three large Zulu armies reported to be in the vicinity of Ekowe, and their instructions were to 'eat up' the relieving column, and then to turn their attention to us. We were most anxions for them to attack us. Had they dared to do so they would truly have fared badly; for our position, to a force without artillery, was very strong, and they would have come under a withering fire from the fort. The cavalry scouts of the relief column were first seen on 31 st March; they were evidently some miles ahead of the column, and about 13 miles from the fort. However, on the following day, with the aid of field glasses, we made out the white hoods on the wagons of Lord Chelmsford's Column. Towards evening we saw them halt and form laager. But in the meantime Lord Chelmsford had informed us by flash-signal, that at daybreak on the day on which he intended to march into Ekowe he would fire two guns as a warning for us to be on the look out; and in case of his force getting the worst of an engagement with the enemy to be ready to render him any assistance in our power with such troops as could be spared. Accordingly the following troops were ordered to be under arms at daybreak on 1st April, ready to turn out at a moment's notice 6 Companies of Infantry (350 men) some Naval Brigade and Royal Engineers (50 men), Mounted Infantry and one gun Royal Artillery. The laager formed by Lord Chelmsford's column lay in the plain below the Ekowe heights, about 12 miles distant from the fort. The name of the spot was Gingilovo. The relief column had not advanced by the road originally selected by our column, but had used the coast (or John Dunn's) road in order to avoid the thick bush, through which they would otherwise have been obliged to pass. But by 31st March they had commenced to work gradually inland again, and the laager which they formed at Gingilovo on that day was within four miles of the Inyezane, the spot where our first battle was fought. We then made certain that the Zulus would allow Lord Chelmsford to break up his laager and advance until his force reached the Inyezane, and had commenced the ascent of the Ekowe hills. Here the bush was very thick, the ground uneven, and favourable to their method of fighting. At the same time we fancied that their attack would be delivered 'as far from Fort Ekowe as possible, consistent with their tactics, as they must be aware the danger of being suddenly taken in rear by our force. There was not much sleep that night in Fort Ekowe. What with the hope of relief and the expectation of a fierce battle on the morrow, talking was kept up till a late hour. Of the events which took place next day, the 2nd April, I shall tell my own story: At the dawn of day I crawled out as usual from under my wagon. The niggers who, as I before said, were generally driven out at daybreak were still inside the fort, some slumbering peacefully, some few other restless creatures like myself had left their resting places, but as yet there was little stir. I was looking over the parapet at the horses in the ditch below, when I heard quite distinctty, the 'boom' of a gun in the distance. I at once said to myself 'the column is about to' commence its march'. I ran towards the middle of the fort to inform Colonel Pearson, but he was already astir; in fact, the whole camp was alive as if by magic. We listened for the second gun; the clear sounding 'boom' again fell on our ears, but was quickly followed by a third report! The battle had commenced! It was no march! In no time we were running as hard as our legs could carry us to the nearest point whence we could see the laager in the plain below. This point was about 300 yards from the fort. On arriving there I saw the laager enveloped in smoke, and could distinctly hear a terrific rattle of musketry and the booming of guns, and could see the rockets flying in all directions. It was a lovely, still, dear morning with a slight mist at first rising from the plain, but this soon cleared off, and with the aid of glasses and telescopes we made out fairly well what was taking place. The Zulus seemed to have surrounded the laager and to have made a most desperate rush, for their fire was apparently close to the wagons. They were met by a perfect blaze of fire which checked them. The incessant roar of musketry went on for about twenty minutes, when the enemy appeared to be retreating slowly and the fire slackened. We did not for a moment doubt what the result of the battle would be; but at the same time our excitement was intense as we felt that on the issue depended our safety, and should anything unforeseen occur whereby the Zulus would gain the day we knew that the only hope was to try and cut our way back to the Tugela, for at this time we had only three more days provisions left.

There was a deep sense of relief amongst us when we observed the Zulus commence to waver. Those looking through the telescopes informed the remainder of the different movements observed. 'Now the cavalry are coming out from the laager,' I heard. We knew that victory rested with us. Sure enough the mounted men had emerged from the square and were charging the enemy. The Zulus were now retreating precipitately, keeping up a dropping fire. In a few minutes firing ceased altogether, and this short but decisive battle was over, having lasted only 40 minutes. The Zulu loss in this engagement was 700 killed. They fought with the greatest determination, many dead bodies being discovered within 30 yards of the trenches, while four were found within a few yards of the muzzle of the Gatling gun. The loss on our side was comparatively smaIJ, two officers and six men killed, two oflicers and 30 men wounded. The Zulu force engaged in this spilited attack was estimated at 12000 men, while the 'relief column' was composed of 4000 whites and 3000 blacks. We 'flashed'congratulations to Lord Chelmsford on his success, and were in turn informed that three regiments of infantry would march to our relief next day, and that Fort Ekowe was to be abandoned altogether as the General considered that the coast road was preferable. This latter piece of news was as disagreeable to us as the former was pleasant. It was too annoying to think that all our work had been done in vain, that we were to give up the splendid fort on which we had taken so much pains and time. On the following day we were hard at work making preparations for our retreat. At about 5 p.m. on this day. the special correspondent of the Standard made his appearance. The first arrival at Ekowe! He was greatly pleased with his having outstripped the other correspondents, and chuckled to himself when he informed us that the *Times* had stuck in a bog, and the *Daily Telegraph* had met with some similar fate. However, we shook him warmly by the hand. and overwhelmed him with various questions; the first strange face we had seen for 72 days. It was late in the evening before the infantry appeared. The 91st Highlanders brought up the rear, and marched past the fort at midnight, their pipes playing the lively strains of 'The Campbells are coming'. The defenders of Ekowe manned the parapet, and greeted them with ringing cheers which were well responded to by the 'relievers'. Many were the greetings and congratulations exchanged next morning. The relief column had marched up on the shortest possible rations. They therefore informed us that they had suffered much from the pangs of hunger, and felt they undoubtedly had come to the wrong place for assuaging their appetites. However, as luck would have it, much to their surprise, we managed to assist them, for we had carefully put aside three days full provisions, in case we should be forced at any time to cut our way back to British territory. These rations were produced, and our gallant 'relievers' enjoyed a hearty meal after their exertions of the past five days. But it was remarked that most of the newspaper correspondents reported that the garrison of Ekowe had suffered but little from the scarcity of food, that they found the place well stocked with provisions, one of them went so far as to say that he never enjoyed a better meal in his life than that supplied by the starved-out heroes of Ekowe. The real truth being that they were gloating over these three days' provisions which we had treasured for so many days, and had longed to 'be at' on so many occasions. During the defence we buried six officers and 35 men; and took away with us about 120 sick, while Captain Wynne of the Engineers, and Thirkill of the 88th both died shortly after our arrival at the Tugela. On the morning of 4th April, we commenced our retreat from Ekowe, accompanied by all our wagons, ambulances, &c., and covered by the force under Lord Chelmsford. The sense of being once more free was delightful; and our men, notwithstanding their long confinement, marched splendidly. We passed our old battle field at the Inyezane, skirted Gingilovo, and on 8th April reached the Tugela. So terminated the first phase of the Zulu campaign as experienced by No. 1 Column. In a few days the Ekowe garrison, now distributed among the 1st Division, was on the march, once more ready to commence its battles o'er again.

ENDNOTES

1 *The Zulu Kingdom*

1. Chris Schoeman, *Churchill's South Africa*, pp. 43–4
2. Ian Knight, *The Zulus*, pp. 3-5
3. Ibid
4. Donald Morris, *The Washing of the Spears*, pp. 45–8
5. Ian Knight, *The Zulus*, pp. 11–13
6. Captain Allen Francis Gardiner set up the first mission station in what was then Natal after his retirement from the British Royal Navy. Gardiner (born 1794, died Patagonia 1851) arrived at the fledging settlement of Port Natal in 1834 following the death of his beloved wife to establish a missionary station, particularly at Dingane's kraal, and to bring the Gospel to the Zulus. When his request to establish himself at Dingane's kraal was refused, he returned to Port Natal and at the request of the settlers established a mission on the ridge overlooking the bay of Port Natal.
7. S. B. Bourquin, 'The Zulu Military Organization...', *Military History Journal*; Arthur Bryant, *A History of the Zulu and Neighbouring Tribes*
8. S. B. Bourquin, 'The Zulu Military Organization...', *Military History Journal*
9. Ibid
10. Ibid
11. Ibid
12. Ibid
13. The Piet Retief Delegation massacre was the 1838 killing of 100 Voortrekkers by the Zulu king Dingane in what is now KwaZulu-Natal, South Africa. The Voortrekkers, led by Piet Retief, negotiated a land treaty in February 1838 with Dingane, but realising the ramifications of the imposed contract, Dingane had the delegation including Retief treacherously killed near his

kraal at a nearby ridge, kwaMatiwane, on 6 February 1838. The land treaty was later found in Retief's possession. It gave the Voortrekkers the land between the Tugela River and Port St Johns. This event eventually led to the Battle of Blood River and the defeat of Dingane.

14. Involved a three-day attack by the Zulus on the Voortrekkers' laager (13–15 February 1838). The actual site now lies beneath the Wagendrift Dam.

15. George Chadwick, 'The Battle of Blood River.' *Military History Journal*, May 1978

16. Donald Morris, *The Washing of the Spears*, pp. 106–8

17. John Robert Dunn (1834 – 1895) was a South African settler, hunter and diplomat of British descent. Born in Port Alfred in 1834, he spent his childhood in Port Natal/Durban and later lived near the Tugela River where his conversance with Zulu customs and language allowed him increasing influence among Zulu princes and opportunities for trade. Representing both colonial and Zulu interests, he rose to some influence and power when King Cetshwayo became the Zulu king. Dunn acted as Cetshwayo's secretary and diplomatic adviser and was rewarded with chieftainship, land and livestock.

18. S. B. Bourquin, 'The Zulu Military Organization...', *Military History Journal*

2 *Firearms in Zululand*

1. J. J. Guy, *A Note on Firearms*, pp. 562–3

2. Vijn, *Cetshwayo's Dutchman*, pp. 38–9

3. The Great Xhosa Suicide of 1857 came about after a Xhosa girl, one Nonqause, and her witchdoctor uncle, Umhlakaza, prophecied that ancestral spirits had told them that if the Xhosa nation killed all cattle and destroy their crops, they would enter a new utopia on a certain day (18 February 1857). Everything was destroyed and it led to massive famine during which thousands died, while some 30,000 crossed the colonial border in search of food and work.

4. Chris Schoeman, *Die Negende Grensoorlog*, pp. 22–25

5. Sarili ka Hintsa was born in 1818, and became the 5th chief of the Gcaleka sub-group of the Xhosa nation, and paramount chief of all the Xhosa, from 1835 until his death in 1892 at Sholora, Bomvanaland. He was also known as 'Kreli', and led the Gcaleka armies in a series of Eastern Frontier wars.

6. Chris Schoeman, *Die Negende Grensoorlog*, pp. 30–35

7. Colonel Charles Duncan Griffith, 1830–1906. He was born at Grahamstown and educated there and at Cape Town. Next featured as a fighter in all the Kaffir Wars of the period. He was a lieutenant in the Hottentot Levy, also in the Kaffir Police, and was a captain commanding the former in the Kaffir War of 1851–52. He was appointed Civil Commissioner and Resident Magistrate

of Albert in 1858, subsequently Queenstown, Grahamstown, and Albany, then in 1869 at King William's Town. In 1871 he was Governor's Agent and Chief Magistrate of British Basutoland, and six years later he commanded the Frontier Armed Mounted Police Force.

8. Chris Schoeman, *Die Negende Grensoorlog*, pp. 41-45
9. Arthur Cunynghame (1812–84). Cunynghame joined the Army in November 1830 after purchasing a commission as a Second Lieutenant in the King's Royal Rifle Corps, 60th Rifles. He served in various imperial campaigns and from 1873 to 1978, commanded the forces at the Cape of Good Hope, serving through the Xhosa Wars in 1877, when he was appointed Lieutenant-Governor of the Colony. In 1878, he was upgraded to Knight Grand Cross of the Order of the Bath (GCB). In February 1876, he left the 36th Regiment to become Colonel Commandant of the 60th Rifles, his former Corps. On 1 October 1877, he was promoted to general. He was placed on the retired list in 1881.
10. Philip Gon, 'The Last Frontier War', *Military History Journal;* Chris Schoeman, *Die Negende Grensoorlog*, pp. 45-48
11. Philip Gon, 'The Last Frontier War', *Military History Journal*
12. Mgolombane Sandile was born in 1820 and became a chief of the Ngqika and Paramount-Chief of the Rharhabe tribe – a sub-group of the Xhosa nation. A dynamic and charismatic chief, he led the Xhosa armies in several of the Cape-Xhosa Frontier Wars. He died in the Ninth Frontier War 1877–78
13. Philip Gon, 'The Last Frontier War', *Military History Journal*
14. Frederic Augustus Thesiger (1827–1905). He purchased a commission in the Rifle Brigade in 1844, served in Nova Scotia, the Crimea, in India, in Abyssinia, and was promoted to major general in March 1877, appointed to command the forces in South Africa with the local rank of lieutenant general in February 1878, and in October succeeded his father as 2nd Baron Chelmsford. He brought the Ninth Cape Frontier War to its completion in July 1878, and was made a Knight Commander of the Order of the Bath in November 1878. His experiences fighting against the Xhosa created a low opinion of the fighting capabilities of native African tribesmen, which would later lead to a disastrous consequence. An expeditionary British imperial military force under Chelmsford's command entered the Zulu Kingdom uninvited, and was in consequence attacked on 22 January 1879 by a large Zulu army at Isandlwana, during which the Zulus overran and destroyed the central column of Chelmsford's separated forces.
15. Philip Gon, 'The Last Frontier War', *Military History Journal*

3 On the Brink of War: The Ultimatum

1. See A Wilmot, *History of the Zulu War*, Chapter III pp. 34-39; also Henry Rider Haggard, *Cetywayo and his White Nighbours*, Chapter III, 'The Annexation.'; Chapter IV, 'The Transvaal Under British Rule.'

2. Donald Morris, *Washing of the Spears*, pp. 273-4

3. Frances Colenso, *History of the Zulu War and its Origin*, p. 196

4. (1837–1916), 9th Baronet, Chancellor of the Exchequer 1885–1886 and 1895–1902, Conservative leader in the House of Commons 1885–1886

5. Frances Colenso, *History of the Zulu War and its Origin*, pp. 260–2

6. Jeff Guy, *The Destruction of the Zulu Kingdom*, p. 49

7. Donald Morris, *Washing of the Spears*, pp. 285–7. Smith was a surveyor in the Colonial Engineers Department, and inspecting the road down to the Tugela near Fort Buckingham, accompanied by Mr. Deighton, a trader and resident at Fort Buckingham.

8. A senior member of the Swazi royal house living in exile in Zululand, who had made an armed incursion into the Transvaal in October 1878, killing about 50 of its African inhabitants and making off with their cattle.

9. See John Martineau, *The life and Correspondence of the Right Hon. Sir Bartle Frere*, Vol. II, chapter 19

10. J. J. Oberholster, *The Historical Monuments of South Africa*, pp. 260–1. Unfortunately a series of floods and a fire have since destroyed all traces of the original tree, but a graft was taken from it and planted and according to last reports was doing quite well.

11. Frances Colenso, *History of the Zulu War and its Origin*, pp. 237–8

4 British Confidence

1. John Laband, *Lord Chelmsford's Zululand Campaign, 1878–1879*, p. 5

2. Knight, *Go to your God Like a Soldier*, p. 214

3. Emery, *The Red Soldier*, p. 154; letter of 20 January 1879

4. Ibid, p. 65

5. 'The news from Cape Town', *The Pall Mall Gazette*, 11 February 1879

6. 'The letters of George Wardell and the battle of Isandlwana, 1879.' *History Ireland*, Issue 1 (January/February 2016), Volume 24.

7. Ibid. Three years later his brother, Captain John Charles Wardell, Royal Marine Light Infantry, was shot dead at the battle of Tel-El-Kebir in Egypt. Another brother, Warren, a veteran of the South African War (1899–1902), was killed in France in November 1914.

8. Emery, *The Red Soldier*, p. 63

9. Edward Spiers, *The Victorian Soldier in Africa*, p. 38

10. Knight, *Go to your God Like a Soldier*, p. 185

11. Emery, *The Red Soldier*, p. 101
12. Ibid, p. 189
13. John Laband, 'The War-readiness and military effectiveness of the Zulu forces in the 1979 Zulu War.' *Natalia* 39 (2009)
14. Ibid
15. Ibid
16. Emery, *The Red Soldier*, p. 144
17. Mathew Annis, 'Half Devil and Half Child: British Perceptions of Native Opponents in Southern Africa, 1878–1879.' https://www.anglozuluwar.com
18. Ibid

5 *The Imperial and Colonial Forces*

1. S Monick, 'Profile of an Army: the Colonial and Imperial Forces of the Zulu War', *Military History Journal*
2. Ibid
3. www.1879zuluwar.com: Natal Hussars
4. See C. T. Hurst, *Short History of the Volunteer Regiments of Natal and East Griqualand.*
5. S. Monick, 'Profile of an Army...'; John Laband, *Historical Dictionary of the Zulu Wars*
6. C. F. Goodfellow, *Great Britain and South African Confederation, 1870–1881*, p. 124
7. S Monick, 'Profile of an Army...'; John Laband, *Historical Dictionary of the Zulu Wars*
8. S Monick, 'Profile of an Army...'; John Laband, *Historical Dictionary of the Zulu Wars*
9. See Dr F K Mitchell, 'Troop Sergeant Major Simeon Khambula, DCM: Natal Native Horse.' *Interesting Reads*, https://www.battlefieldsregionguides.co.za 1 March 2018
10. S Monick, 'Profile of an Army...'; John Laband, *Historical Dictionary of the Zulu Wars*
11. Richard Hallowes Addison (1857–1921). Addison began his career in the Natal civil service and served during the Anglo-Zulu War in the Stanger Mounted Rifles, seeing action at Nyezane. Commissioned second in command of the Reserve Territory Carbineers in 1883, during the 3rd Zulu Civil War he was present at the Battle of the Nkandla Forest. In June 1887, he was appointed resident commissioner of the Ndwandwe District in the British Colony of Zululand. He was political adviser to the Natal forces during the Zulu Uprising of 1906 (Bhambatha Rebellion) and retired as Chief Native Commissioner for Natal and Zululand (1913–16).

12. Frederick Schermbrücker (1832–1904) was an influential parliamentarian of the Cape Colony. He was a strong pro-imperialist, a foremost supporter of Cecil Rhodes and an early leader of the Progressive Party of the Cape. Born in Schweinfurth, Bavaria, he volunteered and fought in the Crimean War as part of the German Legion. He moved to the Cape Colony in 1857, and settled in the Eastern Cape as a German teacher. He was elected to the Cape Parliament in 1868. In 1877/78 he led a mixed force of German and African levies in the Frontier War and later led the Kaffrarian Riflemen in the Anglo-Zulu War. He commanded at Luneberg and distinguished himself at Pemvani River. He was a member of the Legislative Council for the Eastern Cape from 1882 until 1888, and once again for the House of Assembly from 1889 until his death. He served as Commissioner of Crown Lands for the Upington Ministry (1884–86) and for Sprigg's second Ministry (1886–90)

13. S Monick, 'Profile of an Army...'; John Laband, *Historical Dictionary of the Zulu Wars*

14. J. B. Kirkwood, *The Regiments of Scotland*, pp. 37–8

15. S. Monick, *Profile of an Army*

16. Its first operation outside the British Isles had been a disastrous raid on Brest in 1694. In 1741, during the fever-ridden siege of Cartagena (the present Colombia) they lost twelve officers and 800 other ranks. Then, in 1756, it was one of the regiments that had to surrender when Admiral Byng failed to relieve Minorca. In 1777 the regiment had to capitulate once again with General John Burgoyne at Saratoga. At Talavera (1809), the 2nd Battalion had lost almost half its strength in assisting the Guards Brigade. In 1810 the 1st Battalion had embarked in five transports to attack Mauritius, but French warships had found the convoy. Two transports, containing the colonel and five companies, were captured after an all-day fight. The Colours and Regimental records were thrown overboard before the enemy boarded.

17. *The Graphic* report reads: 'At Chillianwallah on the 13th January, 1849, being badly supported by the Native Regiments of its brigade, the 24th had to bear the attack of four times its number. The men fought gallantly, contending the ground inch by inch, but they were then beaten as completely by the Sikhs as the Regiment has now been by the Zulus. Their loss was 300 rank and file and 14 officers, amongst whom was their gallant leader, Colonel Pennycuick and his two sons.'

    The Graphic also quotes a report relating to a further reverse that the 24th suffered during the Indian Mutiny: 'The Regiment met with another reverse during the Indian Mutiny, when a detachment of the Regiment under Colonel (now General Sir Charles Ellice), was moved rapidly down from Rawul Pindi to disarm the 14th Native Infantry at Jhelum ... though the 24th acted bravely they were driven off with heavy loss (their Colonel being dangerously wounded), abandoning a gun to the Mutineers, who during the night effected their escape unmolested.'

18. J. B. Kirkwood, *The Regiments of Scotland*, pp. 85–7
19. A further change was effected in 1880, when the department was divided into a superior section, recruited from combatant officers of the Regular Army and a subordinate section of commissioned officers with the rank of quartermaster, carrying the honorary rank of lieutenant or captain, according to service. In 1881 the title Army Service Corps was abolished in relation to the Ordnance Store Department, and the companies performing Ordnance Store duties were designated Ordnance Store Corps. Subsequently, the regiment's designation changed to Army Ordnance Corps and Royal Army Ordnance Corps.
20. Lt Col G. A. Kempthorne, 'Notes on the History of the Medical Staff Corps and Army Hospital Corps, 1854–1898.' *British Medical Journal*, October 1928
21. Ibid
22. S. Monick, 'Profile of an Army...'; John Laband, *Historical Dictionary of the Zulu Wars*

6 Waiting for War

1. 'Soldiers' Letter from the Zulu War', *Natalia* 8 (1978)
2. Ibid
3. Ibid
4. Ibid
5. Alan Conway, 'Welsh Soldiers in the Zulu War', *National Library of Wales Journal* Vol XI/1 Summer 1959
6. 'Soldiers' Letter from the Zulu War', *Natalia* 8 (1978)
7. The Gcaleka chieftain.
8. Alan Conway, 'Welsh Soldiers in the Zulu War.'
9. Ibid
10. *North Wales Express* of 7 March 1879
11. 'Soldiers' Letter from the Zulu War', *Natalia* 8 (1978)
12. Ibid

7 The Battle of Inyezane

1. 'Newmarch Letters and Diary from the Zulu War 1879,' www.adam-williams.net
2. Donald Morris, *The Washing of the Spears*, pp. 423
3. Formed on 11 July 1865, the Natal Hussars came into being for the protection of the districts of Greytown, York and Noodsberg in the

Natal Midlands. They were a smaller unit than their sister regiment, the Greytown Mounted Rifles, surviving a period between 1864 and 1872 when many of the smaller units of the Natal Volunteer Corps were disbanded due to austerity cuts. During this period the Hussars experienced a drop in numbers but remained an effective unit throughout. In 1868 they numbered seventy but had reduced to sixty-five the following year despite an amalgamation with the soon to be defunct Greytown Mounted Rifles. The unit was mobilised on 25 November 1878 with thirty-five men under Captain Norton marching out from Greytown on 3 December to Potspruit near Kranskop where they were joined by the Durban Mounted Rifles. During the first week of January 1879 these two colonial regiments were joined by the 3rd Regiment (The Buffs) and marched to Thrings Post where they fell under the orders of Captain Barrow, who commanded all troops at the Lower Tugela. The Hussars reached Fort Pearson on 10 January and were brigaded with the Alexandra Mounted Rifles, the Durban Mounted Rifles, the Stanger Mounted Rifles and the Victoria Mounted Rifles.

4. Donald Morris, *The Washing of the Spears*, pp. 423–4
5. Ian Knight, *Great Zulu Battles 1838–1906*, p.80–4
6. Ibid, p.89
7. Newmarch Letters and Diary from the Zulu War 1879,' www.adam-williams.net
8. Ian Knight, *Great Zulu Battles 1838–1906*, pp. 95–7
9. Quoted in www.1879zuluwar.com. 'Colonel W. N. Lloyd, Royal Horse Artillery.'

8 Disaster at Isandlwana

1. Frances Colenso, *History of the Zulu War and Its Origin*, pp. 263–6
2. Ron Lock, *Zulu Victory: The Epic of Isandlwana and the Cover-up*, p. 82
3. Ibid, p.86
4. Ibid, pp. 87, 129–30
5. George Paton, *Historical Records of the 24th Regiment*, pp. 230–1
6. Frances Colenso, *History of the Zulu War and Its Origin*, pp. 294; 264–6, 273–5
7. Ian Knight, *Great Zulu Battles 1838–1906*, p.104
8. Ibid, p.105
9. Ibid, pp. 106–8
10. Ibid, pp.108–109
11. 'The Zulu War', *The Advertiser*, 8 March 1879
12. Ian Knight, *Great Zulu Battles 1838–1906*, pp. 110–1
13. Ibid, pp. 111–3

14. Frances Colenso, *History of the Zulu War and Its Origin*, p. 292. The officer states it was 3.00 p.m.
15. Bertrand Mitford, *Through the Zulu Country*, p. 95.
16. 'The Dead at Isandhlwana', *Belfast Evening Telegraph*, 9 September 1879.
17. Ibid
18. 'A Late Account of Isandhlwana', *The Nottingham Evening Post*, 28 February 1879, p. 4
19. 'The Zulu War', *The Illustrated London News*, 29 March 1879, p. 290
20. 'The war in Zululand. My escape from the battle of Isandlwana', *The Cheltenham Looker-on*, 13 December 1879, p. 796
21. Sir Horace Smith-Dorrien, *Memories of Forty-Eight Years' Service*; see also 'The Zulu War.' *The Norfolk News*, 15 March 1879, p.2; 'Escaped from the Zulus.' *The Weekly Telegraph*, 17 July 1907, p. 27
22. 'Saving the Queen's Colour.' *Natalia* 8 (1978)
23. Sir Horace Smith-Dorrien, *Illustrated London News*, 29 March 1879
24. Sir Horace Smith-Dorrien, *Memories of Forty-Eight Years' Service*, p. 16. Nevill Coghill was born in 1852, the eldest son of Sir John Joscelyn Coghill and Katherine Frances Plunkett. The family lived first in Dublin and later in Castle Townshend, County Cork. Educated at Haileybury College, he showed an early interest in sport. He was a prolific letter writer and diarist and much information can be found from his writings and a short biographical memoir published in 1968 by his nephew, Sir Patrick Coghill. On 26 February, 1873, he was gazetted sub-lieutenant, and posted to the 24th Regiment of Foot. His first posting was Gibraltar and three years later he first sailed for the Cape with his regiment. Teignmouth Melvill was the son of Philip Melvill of the East India Company. He was born in London in 1842, and received an excellent education at Harrow and Cambridge. His was gazetted to the 24th Regiment in 1868, and he sailed for the Cape with the 1/24th in 1875. He served as adjutant to the 1/24th from 1878 until his death in Zululand. Coghill was a bachelor, Melvill, a married man with two children.
25. 'Saving the Queen's Colour.' *Natalia* 8 (1978)
26. 'Saving the Queen's Colour.' *Natalia* 8 (1978). Born in India, Harford came from an eminent family and was well known to his colleagues for his intense interest in nature. His childhood was spent largely exploring and hunting both in England and then in Natal, His childhood friends in South Africa included Cecil Rhodes, Robert and Frank Colenso, and John Dunn. As a youth he learned to speak fluent Zulu and when serving in England he offered his services to the War Office, and soon found himself back in Natal in time for the Anglo-Zulu War. After service in Zululand, Harford remained in the British Army and served variously in the UK, Bahamas and India. Harford

participated in a number of important actions during the Zulu War and was at Rorke's Drift where he witnessed and recorded the fortification of the Mission Station prior to the invasion of Zululand. He accompanied Lord Chelmsford on his ill-fated reconnaissance from Isandlwana and recorded the chaos leading to the Zulu destruction of the main camp. He witnessed the aftermath of both the destruction of Isandlwana and the Zulu attack at Rorke's Drift, where he supervised the disbandment of the Natal Native Contingent. Following the Zulu defeat on 4 July 1879, Harford was part of the force that searched for Cetshwayo, who after his capture was given into the custody of Harford until his exile to Cape Town. He married late in life but lost his new young wife to fever in India. He was left with an infant daughter, Sweetie, and never remarried. He died at the age of eighty-six.

27. Luke Driver, *Perceptions versus reality? Newspaper coverage on the Anglo-Zulu War of 1879*, pp. 19–20

28. Saving the Queen's Colour.' *Natalia* 8 (1978).

29. 'The Lost Flag of Isandhlwana.' *Manchester Evening News*, 8 October 1894

30. Felix Machanick, 'Firepower and Firearms in the Zulu War of 1879', *Military History Journal*

31. Ibid

32. Ibid

33. Ibid; see also Ian Knight, *Great Zulu Battles 1838–1906*, pp. 122–3

34. Ian Castle, 'Brave Men Indeed', Anglozuluwar.com

35. Ibid

36. Ibid

37. 'The Zulu War.' *Thames Advertiser*, Volume XII, Issue 3326, 27 May 1879

38. 'The Killed at Isandhlwana', *The Shetland Times*, 29 March 1879.

39. Alan Conway, 'Welsh Soldiers in the Zulu War.'

40. Ibid

41. Ibid

42. Ibid

43. J. J. Guy, 'A Note on Firearms in the Zulu Kingdom...' *The Journal of African History*

44. Pat Rundgren, 'The "Little Drummer Boys" at Isandhlwana.' https://www.battlefieldsroute.co.za

45. Regimental number, names and age:
    2003 Drummer William Adams, aged 19.
    267 Drummer Charles Andrews. Aged 23.
    1786 Drummer George Dibden. Aged 22.
    1226 Drummer Charles Osmond. Aged 31.
    2 Drummer John Frederick Orlopp. Aged 19.

1/24 – 1 Drummer Thomas Perkins. Aged 36.

501 Drummer Timothy Reardon. Aged 18.

114 Drummer Michael Stansfield. Aged 22.

1787 Drummer John Thompson. Aged 21.

2004 Drummer Alfred Wolfendale. Aged 19.

1399 Drummer James Wolfendale. Aged 26.

Norman Holme in his "The Noble 24th" adds another two names:

1387 Boy Joseph McEwan. Aged 16.

1491 Boy Damiel Gordon. Aged 15.

D.R. Forsyth adds another three names:

1237 Drummer Daniel Trottman. 2/24. Aged 39.

2161 Drummer John Anderson. 2/24. Aged 23.

2153 Drummer John Holmes. 2/24. Aged 26.

'The Silver Wreath' has one more entry:

Thomas Harrington. Aged 26.

Robert Richards. Age unknown.

James Gurney. Aged 16.

46. Pat Rundgren, 'The "Little Drummer Boys" at Isandhlwana', https://www. battlefieldsroute.co.za

47. George Chadwick, 'The Anglo-Zulu War of 1879: Isandlwana and Rorke's Drift.' *MHJ* no. 4 (1979)

48. 'The Zulu War', *The English Lakes Visitor and Keswick Guardian*, 21 June 1879.

49. Percival Tatham Armitage was born in Oldham Lancashire in September 1859. At the time of writing his letter he was nineteen. He was appointed ensign in the 76th Regiment in 1878. He transferred to the 2nd Battalion, 24th Foot, on 26 March 1879 and served in South Africa from April 1879 until January 1880. Promoted to captain in November 1885, and saw service in the Burma campaign of 1887–89. He died near Brecon in September 1893, a week before his thirty-fourth birthday.

50. www.zuluwar.com. Letter dated 2-8-1879

51. Letter in *Sheffield Daily Telegraph*, 5 July 1879, dated from Rorke's Drift, 24 May

52. Emery, *The Red Soldier*, p. 114

53. Ibid, p. 113

9 The Ammunition Controversy

1. On 1 November 1878, Smith-Dorrien was posted to South Africa where he was employed as a Transport Officer and served with the British invasion force in that capacity for a detachment of Royal Artillery. As the Zulu impis

overwhelmed the British lines, destroying it in hand-to-hand fighting, Smith-Dorrien narrowly escaped on his transport pony over 20 miles of rough terrain with Zulu warriors in running pursuit, crossing the Buffalo River, 80 yards wide and with a strong current, by holding the tail of a loose horse. He was one of fewer than fifty British survivors from the battle and one of only five Imperial officers to escape it with his life. Because of his conduct in trying to help other soldiers escape from the battlefield, including a colonial commisariat officer named Hamer whose life he saved, he was recommended for the Victoria Cross, but it was not awarded. He took part in the rest of that war. His observations on the difficulty of opening ammunition boxes led to changes in British Army practice for the rest of the war.

2. C L Norris-Newman, *In Zululand with the British throughout the war of 1879*, pp. 43–4
3. H Hallam-Parr, *A Sketch of the Kafir and Zulu Wars*, pp. 211–2
4. Smith-Dorrien, *Memories*, p. 14
5. J. P. Mackinnon and S Shadbolt, *The South African Campaign, 1879*, p. 82
6. N. Holme, *The Silver Wreath*, p.46
7. Ibid, p. 47
8. Ibid, p. 48
9. Ibid, p. 46
10. J. Brickhill, *Later Annals of Natal*, p. 154
11. Ian Knight, *Isandhlwana and Rorke's Drift*, pp.84–5
12. F. Emery, *Red Soldier*, p. 87
13. Norris Newman, *In Zululand with the British*, pp 78–9.
14. Ibid, p. 83
15. Edmund Yorke, *Isandhlwana 1879*, p. 218
16. Major (Dr) Felix Machanik, *Firepower and Firearms in the Zulu War of 1879*
17. Ibid

10 The Heroism of Rorke's Drift

1. Frederick Hale, *The 'Battle Of Rorke's Drift' From a Swedish Missionary Perspective*, p. 4
2. Ibid, p. 5
3. 'Narrative of an Eye-Witness', *Sunderland Daily Echo and Shipping Gazette*, 6 March 1879, p. 3
4. 'An Eye-Witness Account of the Rorke's Drift Defence', *Adair's Maryport Advertiser*, 23 May 1879
5. 'Rorke's Drift Survivor Recalls Famous Defence', *Portsmouth Evening News*, 7 March 1933, p. 5

6. 'An Eye-Witness Account of the Rorke's Drift Defence', *Adair's Maryport Advertiser*, 23 May 1879; James Bancroft, *Rorke's Drift*, pp. 63-71
7. 'The Defence of Rorke's Drift and Thobal', *The Standard*, 16 April 1891, p. 3
8. 'Narrative of an Eye-Witness', *Sunderland Daily Echo and Shipping Gazette*, 6 March 1879, p. 3
9. Machanik, 'Firepower and Firearms in the Zulu War of 1879.' *Military History Journal*; 'The Fight at Rorke's Drift.' *Pall Mall Gazette*, 1 April 1879, pp. 11–2
10. *Chums* dated 11 March 1908, 'Kindly supplied by John Young'; 'The Massacre at Rorke's Drift', *The Burnley Advertiser*, 14 June 1879, p. 7
11. 'The Massacre at Rorke's Drift', *The Aberdeen Journal*, 12 June 1879, p.3.
12. Ibid
13. George Paton, *Historical Records of the 24th Regiment*, pp. 247–50; 'The Zulu War', *The People's Journal*, 15 March 1879; 'The Zulu War', *The Shipley and Saltaire Times*, 15 March 1879
14. 'Private Henry Hook Letter', 1879zuluwar.com
15. 'Soldiers' letters from the Zulu War', *Natalia* 8 (1978)
16. Ibid
17. Ibid
18. ibid
19. Alan Conway, Welsh Soldiers in the Zulu War.
20. Ibid
21. Ibid
22. 'The Defence of Rorke's Drift.' *Buckingham Advertiser*, 31 May 1879

11 British Defence after Isandlwana
1. Norris-Newman, *In Zululand with the British throughout the War of 1879*, p. 122
2. See P S Thompson, 'The Active Defence after Isandlwana', *MHJ* Vol. 5, No. 3, 1981

12 Gingindlovu and the Relief of Eshowe
1. Ken Gillings, 'Inyezane, Gingindlovu and the Relief of Eshowe', *MHJ* Vol. 4, No. 4, 1979
2. For the fortifications of Zululand, see J. P. C. Laband, 'British Fieldworks of the Zulu Campaign', *MHJ* Vol. 6, No. 1, 1983
3. 'The Zulu War', *Illustrated London News*, 26 April 1879, p. 398; 'The Zulu War', *Cardiff Times & South Wales Weekly*, 15 March 1879
4. Ken Gillings, 'Inyezane, Gingindlovu and the Relief of Eshowe'; 'The Zulu War', *Illustrated London News*, 26 April 1879, p. 398
5. Ibid
6. Ibid

7. Ian Knight, *Go to Your God*, p. 199
8. Ian Castle, 'Brave Men Indeed', Anglozuluwar.com
9. Ibid
10. 'The Zulu War', *Natal Mercury*, April 11 1879
11. Emery, *The Red Soldier*, p. 205
12. Ibid
13. Ken Gillings, 'Inyezane, Gingindlovu and the Relief of Eshowe'; 'The Zulu War', *Adair's Maryport Advertiser*, 23 May 1879

13 The Fight at Intombe River
1. R. Lock, *Blood on the Painted Mountain*, pp. 94–5, 100, 102
2. Ibid; Donald Morris, *The Washing of the Spears*, p. 471
3. Moriarty, David Barry (1837–79). Commissioned in 1857, Moriarty served in the Mediterranean, the Channel Islands, Ireland and India, where he fought in the Hazara campaign (1868). In 1870, he was promoted to captain and joined the 80th Regiment (Staffordshire Volunteers) in 1876, proceeding with it to South Africa, where he was stationed at Newcastle and then at Utrecht. During the Anglo-Zulu War, he was stationed at Derby under Brevet Colonel Henry Evelyn Wood's command on convoy duties. He was killed in hand-to-hand fighting during the Zulu attack at Intombe River.
4. Ibid, p.472
5. R Lock, *Blood on the Painted Mountain*, pp. 94–5, 100, 102
6. Ibid, p. 109
7. Donald Morris, *The Washing of the Spears*, p. 473
8. Ibid, p. 474; Ian Knight, *Great Zulu Battles 1838–1906*, pp. 133–4
9. R. Lock, *Blood on the Painted Mountain*, pp. 111, 207
10. Donald Morris, *The Washing of the Spears*, p. 475–6
11. Ibid, p. 478
12. R. Lock, *Blood on the Painted Mountain*, pp. 110

14 Hlobane Mountain: More Tragedy
1. Anglesey, *The History of the British Cavalry 1816–1919*, p. 187
2. 'Soldiers' Letter from the Zulu War', *Natalia* 8 (1978)
3. W. H. Tomasson, *With the Irregulars in the Transvaal and Zululand*, pp. 41–2
4. I. Castle, *Zulu War: Volunteers, Irregulars and Auxiliaries*, p. 33
5. Ian Knight, *Great Zulu Battles 1838–1906*, pp. 138–41
6. Ibid, pp. 142–4
7. W. H. Tomasson, *With the Irregulars in the Transvaal and Zululand*, p. 53
8. 'Officers Killed in the Zulu War', *The Illustrated London News*, 31 May 1879, p. 522

9. Ibid
10. Ibid
11. Ibid

15 Khambula: A Turning Point

1. R. Lock, *Blood on the Painted Mountain*, p. 189
2. Ibid, p. 190
3. Ibid, pp. 183–4, 190–4
4. R. Lock, *Blood on the Painted Mountain*, p. 196
5. Frances Colenso, p. 353
6. Knight, *Go to Your God*, p. 172
7. Ibid, p. 173
8. Ibid, p. 171
9. Ibid, p. 169
10. *The Friend of the Free State and Bloemfontein Gazette* for 1 May 1879; Schermbrücker wrote it on 30 March at Khambula.
11. Ibid
12. Ibid, 1 May 1879
13. Letter from A. Brett was undated but probably written on 31 March, from 'Camp Khambula'. It was printed in *The Portsmouth Times and Naval Gazette* for 10 May 1879.

16 The Prince Imperial Tragedy

1. Alf Wade, 'The Prince Imperial.' *Military History Journal* 3, No. 2, 1974
2. Ibid; Donald Morris, *The Washing of the Spears*, pp. 511–2
3. Alf Wade, 'The Prince Imperial.' *Military History Journal* 3, No. 2, 1974
4. 'The Late Prince Imperial', *The Illustrated London News*, 16 July 1879, p. 19
5. Alf Wade, 'The Prince Imperial', *Military History Journal* 3, No. 2, 1974
6. John Laband, 'He Fought Like a Lion,' *Journal of the Society for Army Historical Research* 76 (1998), pp. 194–201
7. Ibid; Donald Morris, *The Washing of the Spears*, p. 534
8. John Laband, 'He Fought Like a Lion,' *Journal of the Society for Army Historical Research* 76 (1998), pp. 194–201
9. John Laband, 'He Fought Like a Lion,' *Journal of the Society for Army Historical Research* 76 (1998), pp. 194–201
10. Donald Morris, *The Washing of the Spears*, p. 534; John Laband, 'He Fought like a Lion', *Journal of the Society for Army Historical Research* 76 (1998), pp. 194–201
11. Donald Morris, *The Washing of the Spears*, pp. 534–5; Alf Wade, 'The Prince Imperial', *Military History Journal* 3, No. 2, 1974

12. Alf Wade, 'The Prince Imperial', *Military History Journal* 3, No. 2, 1974
13. 'The Death of Prince Louis Napoleon', *The Witney Express*, 26 June 1879
14. Donald Morris, *The Washing of the Spears*, p. 539–40; John Laband, 'He Fought like a Lion', *Journal of the Society for Army Historical Research* 76 (1998), pp. 194–201
15. See 'The pilgrimage in 1880 by the Empress Eugenie to the site of the death of her son, the Prince Imperial of France', *Natalia* 30 (2000)
16. Alf Wade, 'The Prince Imperial', *Military History Journal* 3, No. 2, 1974

17 Ulundi: The Final Conquest

1. Frances Colenso, *History of the Zulu War and Its Origin*, p. 455
2. Ibid, p. 461
3. Frank Emery, 'Soldiers' Letters from the Zulu War', *Natalia* 8 (1978)
4. Horace Smith-Dorrien. *Memories of Forty-Eight Years Service*. Chapter 1b – The Zulu War
5. 'The Zulu War', *The English Lakes Visitor and Keswick Guardian*, 21 June 1879. Report dated 3 May 1879
6. James Gump, *The Dust Rose Like Smoke*, p. 99
7. 'The Zulu War', *The English Lakes Visitor and Keswick Guardian*, 21 June 1879; James Gump, *The Dust Rose Like Smoke*, pp. 105
8. Frances Colenso, *History of the Zulu War and Its Origin*, p. 440
9. 'The Zulu War', *Sheffield Daily Telegraph*, 28 August 1879
10. Keith Smith, 'The Irregular Progress of Empire: Lord Chelmsford and the Zulu War', *Orb and Sceptre: Studies on British Imperialism and its Legacies*
11. Frances Colenso, *History of the Zulu War and Its Origin*, p. 449
12. D. D. Hall, 'Squares in the Zulu War 1879'. *Military History Journal* 4, No.5, 1979
13. Ibid
14. Ibid
15. 'The Zulu War', *Keighley News*, 2 August 1879
16. 'The Zulu War', *The Illustrated London News*, 23 August 1979, p. 182
17. Ibid
18. James Gump, *The Dust Rose Like Smoke*, p. 99
19. Ibid, pp. 99–100
20. 'The Zulu War', *North Wales Express*, 19 September 1879
21. Ibid; 'The British Charge at Ulundi', *The Yorkshire Gazette*, 5 March 1892
22. Sonia Clake, *Zululand at War 1879*, p. 238
23. C. Dawnay, *Campaigns: Zulu 1879, Egypt 1882, Suakim 1885 – Being The Private Journal of Guy C. Dawnay*, p. 67

24. John Laband and Ian Knight, *The War Correspondents: The Anglo-Zulu War*, p. 138
25. Frank Emery, *The Red Soldier*, p. 233
26. Ibid, p. 237

18 Healers and Hospitals

1. Lt Col G. A. Kempthorne, 'Notes on the History of the Medical Staff Corps and Army Hospital Corps, 1854-1898', *British Medical Journal*, October 1928
2. Ibid
3. Ibid
4. *Quarterly Paper 1879*, 46, pp. 13–28
5. Mandy Goedhals, *Nuns, Guns and Nursing*, p. 1
6. See W. M. and Vincent Buss, *The Lure of the Stone: The Story of Henrietta Stockdale*
7. Mandy Goedhals, *Nuns, Guns and Nursing*, p. 3
8. Ibid, p. 7
9. *Quarterly Paper 1879*, 45, p. 20
10. *Quarterly Paper 1879*, 46 pp. 44–5
11. *Quarterly Paper 1879*, 45 p. 21
12. C. Searle, *The History of the Development of Nursing in South Africa 1652–1960*, p. 42
13. *Quarterly Paper 1879*, 46, pp. 13–28; G. B. A. Gerdener, *Geskiedenis van die NG Kerke in Natal, Vrystaat en Transvaal*, pp. 114–5
14. *Quarterly Paper 1879*, 45, p. 21; G. B. A. Gerdener, *Geskiedenis van die NG Kerke in Natal, Vrystaat en Transvaal*, pp. 117–8
15. G. B. A. Gerdener, *Geskiedenis van die NG Kerke in Natal, Vrystaat en Transvaal*, p. 117
16. Loots and Vermaak, *Pioneers of Professional Nursing in South Africa*, p. 67
17. Ibid, p. 70
18. *Quarterly Paper 1879*, 45, p. 21
19. Mandy Goedhals, *Nuns, Guns and Nursing*, p. 10
20. Ibid
21. Ibid
22. Ibid, pp. 10–11
23. *Quarterly Paper 1879*, 45, p. 22
24. *Quarterly Paper 1879*, 46
25. 'The Stafford House South African Aid Committee', *The Globe*, 10 June 1879
26. 'Embarked for Natal', *Burnley Express*, 14 June 1879

27. 'The Stafford House South African Aid Committee', *The Morning Post*, 22 August 1879
28. Katie Stossel and Brian Best, *Sister Janet: Nurse and Heroine of the Anglo-Zulu War 1879*, p. 87
29. 'The Stafford House South African Aid Committee', *The Morning Post*, 29 August 1879
30. Katie Stossel and Brian Best, *Sister Janet: Nurse and Heroine of the Anglo-Zulu War 1879*, p. 95, 97
31. Ibid, p. 99, 109
32. Ibid, p. 127
33. http://www.1879zuluwar.com/t1671-several-sisters-were-sent-to-the-zulu-war
34. Extract from: Lt Colonel R. J. C. Marter, 1st Kings Dragoon Guards Personal Diaries quoted in http://www.1879zuluwar.com/t1671-several-sisters-were-sent-to-the-zulu-war
35. 'Army Nurses for the Zulu War', *The Graphic*, 9 August 1979, p. 126
36. 'Several sisters were sent to the Zulu War.' *http://www.1879zuluwar.com*
37. Katie Stossel, Brian Best, *Sister Janet: Nurse and Heroine of the Anglo-Zulu War 1879*, pp. 92–3
38. http://www.1879zuluwar.com/t1671-several-sisters-were-sent-to-the-zulu-war.
39. https://www.netley-military-cemetery.co.uk

19 The Last Years of Cetshwayo

1. 'An Interview with Cetewayo', *The Alnwick Mercury*, 15 November 1879
2. W. R. Ludlow, *Zululand and Cetewayo*, p. 215
3. Ibid, pp. 215–6
4. Bolt, *Victorian Attitudes to Race*, pp. 83–139.
5. Guy, *The Destruction of the Zulu Kingdom*, p. 93
6. Ibid, p. 93
7. Ibid, pp. 133–135
8. 'The Historical Image of King Cetshwayo of Zululand', *Natalia* 13, p. 38
9. 'The Captive King Cetewayo', *Illustrated London News*, 29 November 1879, p. 512.
10. 'Politics and Society', *The Leeds Mercury*, 4 August. 1882
11. 'The Historical Image of King Cetshwayo of Zululand.' *Natalia* 13, p. 38
12. Lady Florence Caroline Dixie (née Douglas; 25 May 1855–7 November 1905), was a Scottish writer, war correspondent and feminist. Dixie was an enthusiastic writer of letters to newspapers on liberal and progressive issues, including support for Scottish and Irish Home Rule.
13. 'The Historical Image of King Cetshwayo of Zululand.' *Natalia* 13, p. 35–6

14. Dinuzulu kaCetshwayo (1868–18 October 1913 was king of the Zulu nation from 20 May 1884 until his death in 1913.
15. Ibid, pp. 38–9; Donald Morris, *The Washing of the Spears*, pp. 607–8
16. William Holman Hunt (1827–1910) was an English painter and one of the founders of the Pre-Raphaelite Brotherhood. His paintings were notable for their great attention to detail, vivid colour and elaborate symbolism.

BIBLIOGRAPHY

Books, Theses

Lloyd, Alan, *The Zulu War 1879* (London: Military Book Society, 1973)

Ashe, Major W. and Captain Wyatt-Edgell, E. V., *The Story of the Zulu Campaign* (Cape Town: N & S Press, 1989)

Bancroft, James, *The Zulu War, 1879: The Terrible Night at Rorke's Drift* (Tunbridge Wells: Spellmount, 1991)

Barthorp, Michael, *The Zulu War: Isandlwana to Ulundi* (Weidenfeld & Nicolson, 2002)

Beckett, Ian W., 'Chelmsford's Major Generals', *Soldiers of the Queen*, No. 84 (London: Bell & Sons, 1933)

Bengough, H. M., *Memories of a Soldiers Life* (London: Edward Arnold, 1913)

Bennett, Ian H. W., *Eyewitness in Zululand: the campaign reminiscences of Colonel W.A. Dunne, CB, South Africa, 1877–1881* (London: Greenhill, 1989)

Binns, C. T., *The Last Zulu King: the Life and Death of Cetshwayo* (London: Longmans, 1963)

Blaxland, Gregory, *The Buffs.* (London: Leo Cooper, 1972) (Famous Regiments Series).

Blood, Sir Bindon, *Four Score Years and Ten: Bindon Blood's Reminiscences* (London: G. Bell & Sons, 1933)

Bolt, Christine, *Victorian Attitudes to Race* (London & Toronto: Routledge and K. Paul, 1971)

Bourquin, S. (Comp.), 'The Zulu War of 1879 as reported' in *The Graphic* (Durban, 1965)

Brookes, Edgar H., and De Webb, Colin, *A History of Natal* (Pietermaritzburg: University of Natal Press, 1987)

Bryant, A., *A History of the Zulu and Neighbouring Tribes* (Cape Town: C. Struik, 1964)

Bulpin, T. V., *Shaka's Country* (Cape Town: Howard Timmins, 1952)

Callwell, C. E., *Small Wars* (London: War Office, 1896)

Castle, Ian, and Knight, Ian, *Fearful Hard Times: The Siege and Relief of Eshowe 1879* (London: Greenhill, 1994)

Chadwick, G. A., and Hobson, E. G. (eds): *The Zulu War and the Colony of Natal* (Pietermaritzburg: Qualitas, 1979)

Child, D. (ed.), *The Zulu War Journal of Colonel Henry Harford* (Pietermaritzburg: Shuter & Shooter, 1978)

Clarke, S., *The Invasion of Zululand 1879* (Johannesburg: Brenthurst Press, 1979)

Clarke, S., *Zululand at War 1879* (Johannesburg: Brenthurst Press, 1984)

Colenso. F. E. (ed), *History of the Zulu War and its origin, by F.E. Colenso assisted in those portions of the work which touch upon military matters by Lt-Col E. Durnford* (London: Chapman & Hall, 1880)

Durnford, E. C. L. (ed), *A soldier's life and work in South Africa, 1872 to 1879: a memoir of the late Col. A. W. Durnford, RE* (London: Sampson Low, Marson, Searle & Rivington, 1882)

David, Saul, *Zulu: The Heroism and Tragedy of the Zulu War of 1879* (London: Penguin Books, 2005)

Dawnay, Guy C., *Campaigns: Zulu 1879, Egypt 1882, Suakim 1885* (Cambridge: Ken Trotman, 1989 (reprinted))

De Kiewet, C. W., *The Imperial Factor in South Africa* (London: Frank Cass, 1965)

Driver, Luke, *Perceptions versus reality? Newspaper coverage on the Anglo-Zulu War of 1879*, degree of M.A. in Military History and Strategeic Studies (Maynooth University, Ireland, October 2010)

Drooglever, R. W. F., *A Figure of Controversy: Colonel Anthony Durnford in Natal* (Edition Pietermaritzburg: M. J. Daymond (ed.), 1994)

Edwards, T. J., *Regimental Badges*, 6th Rev. Ed. by A. L. Kipling (London, Charles Knight, 1974)

Emery, Frank, *The Red Soldiers: Letters from the Zulu War 1879* (London: Hodder and Stoughton, 1977)

Featherstone, D., *Captain Carey's Blunder: The Death of the Prince Imperial* (London: Leo Cooper, 1973)

Forsyth, D. R., *South African War Medal, 1877–79: the Medal Roll* (Johannesburg: D. R. Forsyth, 1976)

Frederick Hale, *Swedish Lutheran Missionaries on the Witwatersrand, 1902–1960*, D. Phil thesis (Pretoria: University of Pretoria, 2005)

Bibliography

French, Gerald, *Lord Chelmsford and the Zulu War* (London: Bodley Head, 1939)

Furneaux, Rupert, *The Zulu War: Isandlwana and Rorke's Drift* (London, Weidenfeld & Nicolson, 1963)

Gibson, J. Y., *Story of the Zulus* (London: Longmans, Green & Co., 1911)

Glover, Michael, *Rorke's Drift: A Victorian Epic* (London: Cooper, 1975)

Gon, Philip, *The Road to Isandlwana*. Johannesburg (AD Donker, 1979)

Gordon, L. L., *British Battles & Medals,* 4th Rev. Ed. by E. C. Joslin (London: Spink, 1971)

Greaves, Adrian, and Best, Brian (ed.), *The Curling Letters of the Zulu War* (Barnsley: Pen & Sword, 2001)

Greaves, Adrian, *Rorke's Drift* (London: Cassell, 2002)

Grenfell, Lord F. W., *Memoirs of Field-Marshal Lord Grenfell* (London: Hodder & Stoughton, 1925)

Gump, James, *The Dust Rose Like Smoke: The Subjugation of the Zulu and the Sioux* (Lincoln: University of Nebraska Press, 1996)

Guy, Jeff, *The Destruction of the Zulu Kingdom: The Civil War in Zululand, 1879–1884* (Pietermaritzburg: University of Natal Press, 1998)

Hart, Lt. Gen. H. G., *Hart's Army List 1879* (London: John Murray, 1879)

Holme, Norman, *The Noble 24th: Biographical Records of the 24th Regiment in the Zulu War and the South African Campaigns 1877–1879* (London: Savannah Publications, 2000)

Hurst, C. T., *Short History of the Volunteer Regiments of Natal and East Griqualand* (Durban: Knox, 1945)

Kirkwood, J. B., *The Regiments of Scotland* (Edinburgh: The Moray Press, 1949)

Knight, Ian, and Laband, John, *The Anglo-Zulu War* (Stroud: Sutton, 1996)

Knight, Ian., *Go to Your God Like a Soldier: The British Soldier Fighting for Empire, 1837–1902* (Stackpole Books, 1996)

Knight, Ian, *Brave Men's Blood: The Epic of the Zulu War* (Barnsley: Pen & Sword Books, 2006)

Knight, Ian, *British Fortifications in Zululand 1879* (Oxford: Osprey, 2005)

Knight, Ian, *Great Zulu Battles 1838–1906* (London: Arms and Armour Press, 1998)

Laband, John, and Thompson, P. S, *Field Guide to the War in Zululand and the Defence of Natal* (Pietermaritzburg: University of KwaZulu-Natal Press, 1983)

Laband, John, and Thompson, P. S., *The Buffalo Border 1879: The Anglo-Zulu War in Northern Natal* (Durban: University of Natal, 1983)

Laband, John, and Thompson, Paul, *Kingdom and Colony at War* (Pietermaritzburg: University of Natal Press, 1990)

Laband, John, and Thompson, P. S., *The Illustrated Guide to the Anglo-Zulu War* (Pietermaritzburg: University of Natal Press, 2000)

Laband, John, *Fight Us in the Open: The Anglo-Zulu War through Zulu Eyes* (Pietermaritzburg: Kwazulu Monuments Council, 1985)

Laband, John, *Historical Dictionary of the Zulu Wars* (Lanham: Scarecrow Press, 2009)

Laband, John, *Kingdom in Crisis: The Zulu Response to the British Invasion of 1879* (Barnsley: Pen and Sword Military, 2008)

Laband, John, *Lord Chelmsford's Zululand Campaign: 1878–1879* (Baldock: Army Records Society, 1997)

Laband, John, *The Battle of Ulundi* (Pietermaritzburg: Shuter & Shooter, 1988)

Laband, John, *The Rise and Fall of the Zulu Nation* (London: Arms and Armour, 1995)

Laband, Prof. John, & Knight, Ian, *The War Correspondents: The Anglo-Zulu War* (Johannesburg: Jonathan Ball, 1996)

Laband, John, and Knight, Ian, *The Anglo-Zulu War* (Stroud: Sutton Publishing Limited, 1996)

Lock, Ron, and Quantrill, Peter, *Zulu Victory: The Epic of Isandlwana and the Cover-Up* (London: Greenhill, 2002)

Lock, Ron, *Blood on the Painted Mountain: Zulu Victory and Defeat, Hlobane and Khambula* (London: Greenhill, 1995)

Lock, Ron, *Zulu Conquered: The March of the Red Soldiers 1828–1884* (London: Frontline Books, 2010)

Ludlow, Captain W. R., *Zululand and Cetewayo. Containing an Account of Zulu Customs, Manners, and Habits, after a Short Residence in their Kraals* (London: Simpkin, Marshall & Co., 1882)

Lugg, H. C., *A Natal Family looks back* (Durban: T. W.Griggs & Co., 1970)

Machin, Ingrid, *Antbears and Targets for Assegais* (Brevitas: Howick, 2002)

Mackinnon, J. P., and Shadbolt, S., *The South African Campaign of 1879* (London: Sampson Low, Marston, Searle & Rivington, 1880. Reprinted Portsmouth, 1973)

Martineau, John, *The life and correspondence of the Sir Bartle Frere* (London: John Murray, 1895)

Molyneux, Major-Gen. W. C. F., *Campaigning in South Africa and Egypt* (London: Macmillan, 1896)

Montague, Captain W. E., *Campaigning in South Africa: Reminiscences of an officer in 1879* (London: William Blackwood & Sons, 1880)

Moodie, D. C. F., *Moodie's Zulu War.* (Constantia: N & S Press, 1988. Originally published as part of History of the Battles and Adventures of the British, the Boers, and the Zulus, 1879)

Morris, Donald, *The Washing of the Spears* (London: Pimlico, 1965)

Norris-Newman, Charles, *In Zululand with the British throughout the War of 1879* (London: W. H. Allen, 1880)

Bibliography

Pearse, R. O., *Barrier of Spears: Drama of the Drakensberg* (Cape Town: Howard Timmins. 1973)

Preston, Adrian, *The South African Journal of Sir Garnet Wolseley 1879–1880* (Cape Town: A. A. Balkema, 1973)

Rider Haggard, Henry, *Cetywayo and his White Neighbours* (London: Trübner & Co., 1882)

Ritter, E. A.: *Shaka Zulu: The Rise of the Zulu Empire* (London: Longmans Green, 1955)

Schoeman, Chris, *Churchill's South Africa: Travels during the Anglo-Boer War* (Cape Town: Random House Struik, 2013)

Schoeman, Chris, *Die Negende Grensoorlog 1877–1878.* (The Ninth Frontier War 1877–1878) (M.A. thesis, University of Port Elizabeth, 1976)

Smith, Keith I., *The Commandants: The Leadership of the Natal Native Contingent in the Anglo-Zulu War* (Presented for the degree of Master of Arts of the University of Western Australia. October, 2005)

Snook, Lt Col Mike, *How Can Man Die Better: The Secrets of Isandlwana Revealed* (London: Greenhill Books, 2005)

Snook, Lt Col Mike, *Like Wolves on the Fold: The Defence of Rorke's Drift* (London: Greenhill, 2006)

Stossel, Katie & Best, Brian, *Sister Janet: Nurse and Heroine of the Anglo-Zulu War 1879* (Barnsley: Pen & Sword, 2006)

Sutherland, Douglas, *The Argyll & Sutherland Highlanders.* London: Leo Cooper, 1969

Swinson, A. *A Register of the Regiments and Corps of the British Army* (London: Archive Press, 1972)

Taylor, Stephen, *Shaka's Children: A History of the Zulu People* (London: Harper Collins, 1994)

Thompson, P. S., *The Natal Native Contingent in the Anglo-Zulu War* (Durban: University of Natal Research Fund, 1997)

Tylden, C., *The Armed Forces of South Africa* (Johannesburg: City of Johannesburg Africana Museum, 1954)

Vijn, Cornelius, *Cetshwayo's Dutchman: being the private journal of a white trader in Zululand during the British Invasion* (London: Longmans, Green, and Company, 1880. Reprinted London: Greenhill, 1988)

Wilmot, A., *History of the Zulu War* (London: Richardson & Best, 1880)

Wood, Evelyn, *From Midshipman to Field Marshal* (Methuen: London, 1906)

Young, John, *They Fell Like Stones: Battles and Casualties of the Zulu War* (London: Greenhill Books, 1992)

Journals
Military History Journal
Bourquin, S. B., 'Col. A. W. Durnford' *Military History Journal*, Vol. 6, No. 5, June 1985

Bourquin, S. B, 'The Zulu Military Organization and the Challenge of 1879', *Military History Journal*, Vol. 4, No. 4, January 1978

Chadwick, George, 'The Anglo-Zulu War of 1879: Isandlwana and Rorke's Drift.'*Military History Journal*, Vol. 4, No. 4, January 1979

Emery, Frank, 'The Anglo-Zulu War as Depicted in Soldiers' Letters' *Military History Journal*, Vol. 5 No. 5, June 1982

Gillings, Ken, 'Inyezane, Gingindlovu and the Relief of Eshowe', *Military History Journal*, Vol. 4, No. 4, January 1979

Gon, Dr Philip, 'The Last Frontier War', *Military History Journal*, Vol. 5 No. 6, December 1982

Hale, Frederick, 'The Defeat of History in the Film Zulu', *Military History Journal*, Vol. 10, No. 4, December 1996

Hall, D. D., 'Artillery in the Zulu War 1879', *Military History Journal*, Vol., 4 No. 4, 1978

Hall, D. D., 'Squares in the Zulu War 1879', *Military History Journal*, Vol. 4, No. 5, 1979

Jones, Huw M., 'Utrecht District and the Anglo-Zulu War', *Military History Journal*, Vol. 5 No. 1, June 1980

Kinsey, H. W., 'The Lonely Graves of Zululand', *Military History Journal*, Vol. 13, No. 3, 2005

Laband, John, 'British Fieldworks of the Zulu Campaign of 1879, with Special Reference to Fort Eshowe', *Military History Journal*, Vol. 6, No. 1, 1983

Machanick, Dr Felix, 'Firepower and Firearms in the Zulu War of 1879', *Military History Journal*, Vol. 4, No. 6, December 1979

Monick, S, 'Profile of an Army: The Colonial and Imperial Forces of the Zulu War of 1879', *Military History Journal*, Vol. 4, No. 5, June 1979

Scheurer, Ernst and K., 'History of the Swiss in Southern Africa', *Military History Journal*, Vol. 9, No. 3, June 1993

Thompson, P. S., 'The Active Defence after Isandlwana: British Raids across the Buffalo, March–May 1879', *Military History Journal*, Vol. 5, No. 3, June 1981

Natalia
'Saving the Queen's Colour', *Natalia* 8 (1978)

'An Empress in Zululand: The pilgrimage in 1880 by the Empress Eugenie to the site of the death of her son, the Prince Imperial of France', *Natalia* 30 (2000)

'Soldiers' Letters from the Zulu War: A Source of Historico-Geographical Value', *Natalia* 8 (1978)

Bibliography

'The War-readiness and Military Effectiveness of the Zulu Forces in the 1879 Anglo-Zulu War', *Natalia* 39 (2009)

Journal of the Society for Army Historical Research

Featherstone, David, 'Victorian Colonial Warfare: Africa, from the Campaigns against the Forces', *Journal for the Society of Army Historical Research*, Vol. 37, No. 1

Laband, John, 'He Fought like a Lion': An Assessment of Zulu Accounts of the Death of the Prince Imperial of France during the Anglo-Zulu War of 1879', *Journal of the Society for Army Historical Research*, Vol. 76 (1998)

Lieven, Michael, 'A Victorian Genre: Military Memoirs and the Anglo-Zulu War', *Journal of the Society for Army Historical Research*, Vol. 77 (1999)

Tylden, G, 'The Natal Native Contingent, Zulu War, 1879.' *Journal of the Society for Army Historical Research*, Vol. 43, No. 173, March 1965

Yorke, Edmund, 'Isandlwana 1879: Further Reflections on the Ammunition Controversy.' *Journal of the Society for Army Historical Research*, Vol. 72, No. 292, Winter 1994

Miscellaneous

Ballard, Charles C., 'The Role of Trade and Hunter-Traders in the Political Economy of Natal and Zululand', *African Economic History*, Vol. 10, 1981

Cope, A. T., 'The Zulu War in Zulu Perspective', *Theoria*, No. 56, May 1981

Goedhals, Mandy, 'Nuns, Guns and Nursing: an Anglican Sisterhood and Imperial Wars in South Africa 1879–1902', *Studia Historiae Ecclesiasticae*, Vol. 34, No. 1, July 2008

Guy, J. J., 'A Note on Firearms in the Zulu Kingdom with Special Reference to the Anglo-Zulu War, 1879', *The Journal of African History*, Vol. 12, No. 4, 1971

'Natal and Zululand 1824–1880', *African Economic History*, No. 10. 1981

Smith, Keith, 'The Irregular Progress of Empire: Lord Chelmsford and the Zulu War', *Orb and Sceptre: Studies on British Imperialism and its Legacies* (Melbourne: Monash University)

Newspapers, Magazines

Aberdeen Evening Express
Adair's Maryport Advertiser
Coventry Evening Telegraph
Gloucestershire Echo
Hamshire Telegraph and Post
Pall Mall Gazette
Sheffield Daily Telegraph
The Alnwick Mercury

The Cheltenham Looker-on
The Citizen
The Courier
The Daily Mail
The Devon and Exeter Gazette
The Echo
The English Lakes Visitor and Keswick Guardian
The Evening News
The Falkirk Herald and Lilithgow Journal
The Graphic
The Illustrated London News
The Leader
The Manchester Evening News
The Norfold News
The Northern Evening Mail
The Nottingsham Journal
The Sketch
The Sphere
The Standard
The Western Morning News
The Yorkshire Evening Post
Western Daily Press
Western Mail and South Wales News

Official Publications

Hansard, House of Lords Debates February 1879
British Parliamentary Papers:
C2318; C 2367; C 2374; C 2482; C 2584

Websites

www.anglozuluwar.com
www.1879zuluwar.com
www.battlefieldsroute.co.za › anglo-zulu-war
eshowe.com/zulu-war-battles
www.britishbattles.com/zulu-war

INDEX